AF688516

CENTER FOR JAPANESE STUDIES

BIBLIOGRAPHICAL SERIES

NUMBER 5

JAPANESE ECONOMICS:

A GUIDE TO JAPANESE REFERENCE AND RESEARCH MATERIALS

JAPANESE ECONOMICS:
A GUIDE TO JAPANESE REFERENCE AND RESEARCH MATERIALS

Charles F. Remer
and Saburo Kawai

GREENWOOD PRESS, PUBLISHERS
WESTPORT, CONNECTICUT

Library of Congress Cataloging in Publication Data

Remer, Charles Frederick, 1889-
Japanese economics.

Reprint of the ed. published by the University of Michigan Press, Ann Arbor, which was issued as no. 5 of Bibliographical series, University of Michigan Center for Japanese studies.
1. Japan--Economic conditions--Bibliography.
I. Kawai, Saburō, 1908- joint author. II. Title.
III. Series: Michigan. University. Center for Japanese Studies. Bibliographical series ; no. 5.
[Z7165.J3R4 1978] [HC462] 016.3309'52'04 78-5534
ISBN 0-313-20435-7

Copyright, 1956 by University of Michigan

Reprinted with the permission of Center for Japanese Studies at the University of Michigan

Reprinted in 1978 by Greenwood Press, Inc.
51 Riverside Avenue, Westport, CT. 06880

Printed in the United States of America

10 9 8 7 6 5 4 3 2 1

EDITOR'S FOREWORD ON THE BIBLIOGRAPHICAL SERIES

The Bibliographical Series of tne Center for Japanese Studies has for its main purpose the listing and evaluating of the major Japanese works pertaining to the humanities and social sciences, particularly as they deal with Japan and the areas immediately adjacent to Japan. It is assumed that Western materials pertaining to Japan are adequately covered in the bibliographies of Pagés, von Wenckstern, Nachod, Praesent-Haenisch, Pritchard, Gaskill, etc., and that Western specialists in the several fields will know how to get at the Western materials in their respective fields.

The bibliographies in the present series are intended to serve as an introduction to the native research materials in the several disciplines and hence as an aid to research for teachers and students. In each case an attempt has been made to describe or to evaluate each work that is listed, or at least to justify the inclusion of each item. The authors have also attempted to indicate the American libraries at which each item may be found. Scholars and librarians will perhaps find that the several bibliographies in this series will serve as useful guides to buying programs which they may wish to initiate.

The bibliographies are selective. Each item listed is believed to be of some value or interest to the scholarly user. In those cases in which it has been impossible to examine a book or article of known value, it still is included. A book or article is thus included if it is written by a competent scholar, if it is included in a bibliography which is itself competently compiled, if it appears to treat its subject matter in detail and with an approach to completeness, if it is frequently quoted, if it is well reviewed, or if it is referred to as being authoritative. Wherever possible, notes as to why an item seems to be of value have been given.

The scope of each bibliography is defined by the compiler or compilers in their introductions, but in general each of the bibliographies lists (a) important source materials, and (b) secondary sources dating from a fixed date in the recent past, as, for instance, the Meiji Restoration, 1900, 1910, etc.

Although the materials in most cases deal with the Japanese islands, each compiler has set the limits of the geographical area which his materials cover. In certain cases expansion into areas that are outside Japan appears to be justified by the fact that Japanese research has been the dominant research for these areas. Hence one or more of the bibliographies will cover Japanese materials on Formosa, Korea, Manchuria, and the Mandated Islands.

The format is uniform within each volume. In general the name of each author or compiler is given both in romanization and characters. The surnames are given first and the given names next, as the practice is in Japan. The names of corporate authors, such as government offices, are given in romanization and characters; they are then translated.

The title of each book or article is given in romanization and characters; it is then translated. The place of publication and the name of the publisher are given in romanization alone, but a separate listing within each bibliography gathers together the names of the publishers, with the characters used in writing their names.

1. Long ā, ō, and ū are indicated by macrons over the vowels.
2. Only the first letters of initial words and proper nouns are capitalized.
3. In the bibliographical data, the compilers have given both the edition and the printing of the work cited. Significant textual variations sometimes occur between different printings of the same edition of a given work.
4. When dealing with an item composed of one volume, complete pagination is given for that volume, including all separately paged sections. If any title is in more than one volume, only the total number of volumes is given, without paging.
5. In the event that the item cited happens to be part of a series or collection, the compilers have given in brackets introduced by an equals sign the title, characters, and translated title of that series or collection and the number of the volume concerned.
6. The location of each item in American libraries is shown by means of the symbols used in the Union List of Serials. The symbols for the major libraries concerned are as follows:

   CCC - Claremont Colleges
   CSt - Stanford General Library
   Cst-H - Hoover War Library
   CtY - Yale
   CU - University of California
   DLC - Library of Congress
   ICU - Chicago
   IEN - Northwestern
   NH - Harvard
   MiU - Michigan
   NN - New York Public Library
   NNC - Columbia
   WaU - University of Washington

7. Works such as encyclopedias, dictionaries, yearbooks, series, and collections are cited by title; the name of the editor or compiler, in romanization and characters, is usually given after the title.
8. In the case of articles found in journals, quotation marks surround the Japanese title, characters, and translated title.
9. Abbreviations are explained in lists, if necessary.

10. If any volume of a journal is continuously paged, number and month may be omitted. If it has both continuous volume pagination and separate pagination for each issue, only the volume, year, and the continuous volume pagination may be given. If more than one volume appears in any single year, and each is separately and continuously paged, the procedure has been to give the volume, inclusive months of the issues in the volume, year, and continuous volume pagination.
11. In the case of a single article comprising a chapter or a section of a book which is a compilation of articles by a number of authors, this fact is shown by inserting the word "in" between the title of the article and the compilation in which it is found. Following the "in," a complete citation of the book in question is given.
12. All descriptions, evaluation, criticisms, and comments pertaining to a volume or article follow the citations in separate, indented paragraphs. These may include brief biographies of the authors or compilers, but only one biography per author or compiler is given in each bibliography. Cross-references from one citation to another are used to call attention to comments, biographies, etc.
13. A list of the standard professional journals is given whenever found to be convenient.

The following remarks may interest the growing number of scholars who are concerned with the problem of publishing materials in the lesser known fields, in which the number of copies to be distributed is necessarily small and in which special problems, such as the one here faced of giving names and titles in characters, must be met. An electric typewriter was first used to type the materials in romanization. The characters were then written in, in spaces left for the purpose. The over-all dimensions of the typed area was 10 by 14 and 1/2 inches. This was reduced to the present size in photographing the pages. The photographs thus taken were then made the basis for reproduction by offset process. Except in the case of the introductory material, no attempt was made to justify the right-hand margins.

Joseph K. Yamagiwa

Note on Japanese Economics: a Guide to Japanese Reference and Research Materials,

by Charles F. Remer and Saburō Kawai

Since the inception of this bibliographical series, Far Eastern libraries in the United States have made substantial additions to their Japanese collections. Because of the wealth of these materials, it is no longer possible or necessary to indicate for each of the items listed in any bibliography the libraries which own it. The present series has therefore discontinued the practice of indicating these libraries.

The editor along with the authors of the present bibliography on Japanese economics regrets the fact that it has not been possible to indicate the collation of pages of works appearing as single volumes. Securing these collations would have meant a considerable delay in the publishing of this work. It is hoped that amends will be made when the entire Bibliographical Series of the Center for Japanese Studies is published as a unit.

J. K. Y.

Authors' Introduction

This work is intended to serve as a guide to the growing number of Western students concerned with the economics and economy of Japan. It is for those who desire to become acquainted at first hand with the writings of the Japanese economists and who wish to find their way among the official reports, unofficial monographs, research papers, statistical periodicals, academic and business journals, and the wealth of other printed materials that come from the presses of Japan.

Certain preliminary comments on the Japanese literature of economics seem necessary. The first of these is that the student should be prepared both for continuity and for discontinuity as he moves across the imaginary line that marks the great separation of Tokugawa from Meiji Japan. Unless he is prepared for both he may be taken unawares. The continuity of economic thought and method appears to have been broken during the early decades of the Meiji period by the introduction and acceptance of Western economics. In their theoretical speculations and in their methods of investigation the emerging economists of Japan renounced their antecessors and joined the general company of economic scientists. The debate over the policy of reflation during the 1930s was in general terms and the current work of the Japanese on national income is no different in essentials from such work in England, France, or the United States. From this point of view the tremendous interest of Japanese scholars of recent decades in the economics of the Tokugawa period is mere antiquarianism and there are many who so regard it. And yet there are doubts which arise from the contemplation of the continuities. No one can jump out of his own skin however swiftly he may move. To strike a proper balance, to take wisely into account the continuities and the discontinuities in the development of Japanese economics and of the Japanese economy is a difficult intellectual and spiritual feat, but it is one which every student must attempt. The difficulty, it may be added, exists for the Japanese as well as the Westerners. All this should be borne in mind not only for the period after 1868 but for the period since 1945 as well.

Another matter of preliminary general interest is that the Japanese literature on economics which is presented in the following chapters reflects need to assess the significance of change. This will help to explain the emphasis on economic history in the work of the Japanese. The economists of the Anglo-American tradition have developed concepts and methods which are most useful for analysis over short periods of time. If Marshall, who helped to fashion them, found these tools inadequate for longer periods it is easy to see that the Japanese economist, who has shown himself able to use them, might find them even less adequate than his British or American colleagues. It should, therefore, be no matter for surprise that the German economists of the historical school found a welcome among the Japanese. Here the Japanese found an economics that recognized the problem of those before whose eyes the transformation of traditional institutions was actually taking place. This is not to say that the German historical school solved the problem; that is beside the point. The Japanese interest in history, the observation of institutional change, and the desire to look into the future together with the stimulus from Germany built an impressive structure of scholarship which is a notable feature of the Japanese intellectual scene.

A third and final general observation has to do with the influence of Marxism on the economic thought of Japan. The annotations to the works listed in this guide show that Marxist influence has been great. The explanation of this fact has, in part, been indicated. It lies in that aspect of Marxism which deals with institutional change. If the German historical school recognized the institutional problem which the Japanese faced, so did the Marxist school. This is not to say that the Marxists solved the problem; that, again, is beside the point. But Marxism as method has exerted and still exerts an important influence in Japan.

To understand the Japanese interest in economic history and in the examination of institutional change, to observe the economic development of Japan over the past hundred years, and to bring into the picture the current interest in economic development leads to speculation on the future of economics in Japan. It is, for instance, conceivable that Japanese studies may play a part in creating an adequate economics of growth and development.

This guide to Japanese works in the various fields of economics has been compiled on the basis of materials available in the library of the University of Michigan and at the Michigan Center for Japanese Studies. The chief reliance was upon certain important Japanese bibliographies and reference works. Among them may be mentioned Takahashi Taizō, Taikei keizaigaku jiten (Systematic dictionary of economics) (entry number 15); Honjō Eijirō, Nihon keizaishi shimbunken (New bibliography of Japanese economic history) (entry number 287); and the Keizaigaku bunken taikan (Complete bibliography of works on economics) and other bibliographical works published by the Ōsaka Shōka Daigaku Keizai Kenkyūjo (Ōsaka Commercial College, Economics Research Institute) (entry numbers 10-13). There is frequent reference also to the Keizai hōritsu bunken mokuroku (Catalogue of literature on economics and law), published by the Kōbe Kōshō Shōgyō Kenkyūjo (Kōbe Commercial College, Business Research Institute) (entry number 4), the well known Shuppan nenkan (Publishers' annual), published by the Shuppan Nyūsusha; and the bibliographies of the Diet Library. For certain fields special bibliographies were available, such as the bibliography in the appendix to Nihon zaibatsu to sono kaitai (Japanese zaibatsu and their liquidation), published by the Mochikabukaisha Seiri Iinkai (Holding Company Liquidation Committee) (entry number 1123), and Masaki Chifuyu and Matsukawa Shichirō, Tōkei chōsa gaido bukku (A guide book for statistical investigation) (entry number 40), which lists government publications of a statistical sort.

The problem of selection from the extensive literature of economics in the Japanese language was the outstanding one. The selection was, in part, indicated by the inclusion of a work in one of the bibliographies mentioned above. In general, selection was made on the basis of the reputation of the author and his standing in his field, for the purpose of adequate coverage of the various fields, and to direct attention to significant works in the development of thought. Selection of statistical and similar publications has been for the purpose of presenting the chief statistical reports and periodicals of the various agencies of the Japanese Government and to direct attention to the smaller number of valuable private sources.

Limitations of time and space have prevented the inclusion of more than a highly selected few of the articles in journals and magazines. Historical and factual studies have been given some preference over purely theoretical works. This was done to meet the interest of the student who is not a specialist in economics and because adequate annotation of theoretical works would have required the services of a large panel of highly informed persons in the various fields.

It is recognized that this guide includes only a limited number of works on the war-time economy of Japan. This is due in part to the fact that publication was restricted. Some statistical information has become available since the war. There have been some post-war studies of the war-time finance. But the general assertion may be ventured that a satisfactory review of war-time publications in the field of economics calls for a special research effort.

Publishers in Japan frequently bring out works in economics---and in other fields---in extensive series. Individual works from certain of these series are listed in the following chapters but it seems desirable to draw attention to a number of well-known series in this introduction. A series usually presents a selection in itself of works in the various fields of economics. There is frequently an emphasis on theory and a series thus provides a review of the accepted theory of its time. The list which follows is believed to be representative but it makes no claim to being inclusive.

Gendai keizaigaku zenshū 現代經濟學全集 (Series on contemporary economics), Tōkyō, Nihon Hyōronsha, 1928, 31 v.

Gendai kin'yū keizai zenshū 現代金融經濟全集 (Series on contemporary finance and economics), Tōkyō, Kaizōsha, 1935, 35 v.

Keizaigaku zenshū 經濟學全集 (Complete series on economics), Tōkyō, Kaizōsha, 1928, 67 v.

Nihon keizai seisaku taikei 日本經濟政策大系 (Series on Japanese economic policy), Tōkyō, Chikura Shobō, 1937, 12 v.

Nihon tōsei keizai zenshū 日本統制經濟全集 (Series on controlled economy in Japan), Tōkyō, Kaizōsha, 1933, 10 v.

Shinkeizaigaku zenshū 新經濟學全集 (New series on economics), Tōkyō, Nihon Hyōronsha, 1939, 33 v.

Senji junsenji keizai kōza 戰時準戰時經濟講座 (Lectures on the war-time and quasi-war time economy), Tōkyō, Kaizōsha, 1937, 12 v.

The authors regret that it has not been possible to give the collation of pages of works appearing as single volumes.

Gratitude is expressed to Professor Joseph K. Yamagiwa, the general editor of the Bibliographical Series, for advice and assistance as well as to Professors Robert B. Hall, Robert E. Ward, and John W. Hall of the staff of the Michigan Center for Japanese Studies. The special assistance of Miss Kyōko Baba, Mr. James A. Kokoris, and Mr. Yuzuru Takeshita is hereby acknowledged.

Charles F. Remer
Saburō Kawai

TABLE OF CONTENTS

JAPANESE ECONOMICS

A GUIDE TO JAPANESE REFERENCE AND RESEARCH MATERIALS

Chapter I

Bibliographies

The bibliographies listed below are on economics in general and, in most cases, do not go beyond the field of economics. For bibliographical works that cover a number of social sciences generally the reader is referred to Robert E. Ward, A Guide to Japanese Reference and Research Materials in the Field of Political Science, pp. 1-24. Bibliographies on the various subdivisions of economics are not listed here but are to be found under the appropriate headings below, such as, for example, public finance and economic history. It should be mentioned also that lists of relevant works are to be found at the end of the text under various important headings in the dictionaries reported in Chapter II below. The lists which appear in the Ōsaka Shiritsu Daigaku Keizai Kenkyūsho's Keizaigaku shōjiten (Small dictionary of economics) (no. 21) are especially useful.

1. Achikku Myūzeamu アチック ミユーゼアム, Kaitei Nihon keizai koten sōran 改訂日本經濟古典綜覽 (Revised bibliography of Japanese classics in economics), Tōkyō, Achikku Myūzeamu, 1937.

2. Ganshōdō 巖松堂, Hōritsu keizai rondai shūran (seizoku) 法律經濟論題輯覽(正續) (Collection of titles on law and economics: main series and continuation), Tōkyō, Ganshōdō, 1908-10, 2 v.

3. "Keizai ronsō dai-ikkan yori dai-jikkan made: rondai sakuin 經濟論叢自第一巻至第十巻 論題索引 (Index of articles in Keizai ronsō from vol. 1 to vol. 10)," Keizai ronsō, v. 11, no. 1, 1920.
Similar indices for later volumes are to be found in v. 21, no. 5, 1925; v. 32, no. 2, 1931; and v. 41, no. 6, 1935.

4. Kōbe Kōshō Shōgyō Kenkyūjo 神戸高商商業研究所 (Business Research Institute of the Kōbe Commercial College), Keizai hōritsu bunken mokuroku 經濟法律文献目錄 (Catalogue of literature on economics and law), Ōsaka, Hōbunkan, 1927-32, 2 v.
An inclusive list of works on economics and law from 1910 to 1930. Not annotated.

5. "Kokumin keizai zasshi dai-ikkan yori dai-gojikkan made: sōmokuroku 國民經濟雜誌自第一巻至第五十巻総目錄 (Index of the titles of articles in Kokumin keizai zasshi from vol. 1 to vol. 50)," Kokumin keizai zasshi, v. 50, no. 6, 1931.
Includes the material which appeared in an earlier index for v. 1, no. 1 to v. 24, no. 2.

6. Kokushō Iwao 黒正巖 and Kikuta Tarō 菊田太郎, ed., Keizai chirigaku bunken sōran 經濟地理學文献総覽 (List of works on economics and geography), Tōkyō, Sōbunkaku, 1937.
Includes publications in the field before December 1935.

7. Mitsuhashi Takeo 三橋猛雄, ed., Keizai bunken nempyō 經濟文献年表 (Chronological list of literature on economics), in Ishii Kendō 石井研堂 and others, ed., Meiji bunka zenshū 明治文化全集 (Anthology of Meiji culture), Tōkyō, Nihon Hyōronsha, 1928-30, v. 9, 519-545.
Deals with materials of the Meiji period.

8. Niijima Shigeru 新島繁, ed., revised by Hirano Yoshitarō 平野義太郎, Shakai kagaku bunken kaidai: seiji, keizai hen 社會科學文献解題：政治經濟論 (Annotated bibliography of social science: volume on politics and economics), Tōkyō, Tōhō Shobō, 1949.

9. Ōkurashō Rizaikyoku 大蔵省理財局 (Finance Bureau of the Ministry of Finance), Chōsa geppō sōmokuroku 調査月報総目錄 (General index of monthly research bulletin), Tōkyō, Ōkurashō, 1936.

10. Ōsaka Shōka Daigaku Keizai Kenkyūjo 大阪商科大學經濟研究所 (Ōsaka Commercial College, Economic Research Institute), Keizaigaku bunken taikan 經濟文献大鑑 (Complete bibliography of works on economics), Ōsaka, Ōsaka Shōka Daigaku Keizai Kenkyūjo, 1934-39, 4 v.
All-inclusive bibliographical work in the fields of public finance (v. 1), money and finance (vols. 2, 3), and commerce and industry (vol. 4). Provides tables of contents of important entries.

11. Ōsaka Shōka Daigaku Keizai Kenkyūjo 大阪商科大學經濟研究所 (Ōsaka Commercial College, Economic Research Institute), Shakai keizai bunken nempō 社會經濟文献年報 (Annual report of social and economic literature), Ōsaka, Ōsaka Shōka Daigaku Keizai Kenkyūjo, 1938-43.

12. Ōsaka Shōka Daigaku 大阪商科大學 (Ōsaka Commercial College), Keizai shiryō sōran 經濟資料総覽 (General catalogue of materials on economics), Ōsaka, Ōsaka Shōka Daigaku, 1940, 505 + 125 pp.
Contains materials published from January 1928 to December 1937. Includes reports on research work, statistical magazines, and statistics. Appendix contains titles of yearbooks and magazines.

13. Ōsaka Shiritsu Daigaku Keizai Kenkyūjo 大阪市立大學經濟研究所 (Research Institute for Economics of Ōsaka Municipal University), Shakai kagaku bunken kaisetsu 社會科學文献解説 (Commentary on literature of social science), Ōsaka, Ōsaka Shiritsu Daigaku Keizai Kenkyūjo, 1946+, biennial.
Provides critical comment by the staff of the Institute on the significant publications of the period. Appendix presents a complete list covering all fields of economics.

14. Sakisaka Itsurō 向坂逸郎, ed., "Marukusu keizaigaku sankōsho マルクス經濟學参考書 (Reference books on Marxian economics)," in Marukusu keizaigaku (Marxian economics), Tōkyō, Nihon Hyōronsha, 1928.

15. Takahashi Taizō 高橋泰藏, ed., Taikei keizaigaku jiten 体系經濟學辞典 (Systematic dictionary of economics), Tōkyō, Tōyō Keizai Shimpōsha, enl. ed. 1950, "Sankō bunken 参考文献 (Literature for reference)," pp. 917-1226.

Selective bibliography. Provides certain group annotations.

16. Takimoto Seiichi•滝本誠一, Nihon keizai tensekikō 日本經濟典籍考 (Annotated bibliography of Japanese economic literature), Tōkyō, Nihon Hyōronsha, 1928.

Comments on Japanese works on economics before the Meiji Restoration.

17. Tōkyō Shōka Daigaku Hitotsubashi Shimbumbu 東京商科大學一橋新聞部 (Department of Journalism at Hitotsubashi, Tōkyō Commercial College), Keizaigaku kenkyū no shiori (A guide to the study of economics), Tōkyō, Shunjūsha, 1950, 4 v.

These volumes contain bibliographies at the end of each heading. Vol. 1, History of economic theory; vol. 2, Economic policy; vol. 3, Western economic history; vol. 4, Oriental economic history.

Chapter II

Dictionaries

A selected list of dictionaries of economics is presented under appropriate headings. The dictionary is a form of exposition much used in Japan. The statement under a particular title such as land rent or foreign exchange may run to several pages and it is usually followed by a brief bibliography.

1. Economics in General

18. Iwasaki Shoten Henshūbu 岩崎書店編集部 (Compilation Department of the Iwasaki Shoten), Gendai keizaigaku jiten 現代經濟學辞典 (Dictionary of modern economics), Tōkyō, Iwasaki Shoten, 1950.

19. Kaizōsha 改造社, Keizaigaku jiten 經濟學辞典 (Dictionary of economics)[=vols. 56, 57, and 58 of Keizaigaku zenshū 經濟學全集 (Anthology on economics)], Tōkyō, Kaizōsha, 1933.

20. Ōsaka Shōdai Keizai Kenkyūjo 大阪商大經濟研究所 (Institute for Economic Research of the Ōsaka Commercial College), Keizaigaku jiten 經濟學辞典 (Dictionary of economics), Tōkyō, Iwanami Shoten, 1930-36, 7 v.

One of the most exhaustive works in the field and generally regarded as one of the best.

21. Ōsaka Shiritsu Daigaku Keizai Kenkyūjo 大阪市立大學經濟研究所 (Research Institute for Economics, Ōsaka Municipal University), Keizaigaku shōjiten 經濟學小辞典 (Small dictionary of economics), Tōkyō, Iwanami Shoten, 1951.

A short but useful dictionary of high repute.

22. Takahashi Taizō 高橋泰藏, ed., Taikei keizaigaku jiten 体系經濟學辞典 (Systematic dictionary of economics), Tōkyō, Tōyō Keizai Shimpōsha, enl. ed. 1950, 1226+109 pp.

Items are not arranged in alphabetical order but in accordance with the editor's system of economics. Small but useful dictionary. Provides a valuable bibliography covering all fields of economics.

23. Tsuchiya Kiyoshi 土屋清, ed., Nihon keizai no kiso chishiki 日本經濟の基礎知識 (Fundamental knowledge on Japanese economics), Tōkyō, Jitsugyō no Nihonsha, 1949.

This work, edited by a number of the staff of the newspaper, Asahi, is not a conventional dictionary; it is rather a reference book on the Japanese economy which deals with important fields in the past and present. Each section is by one of seventy collaborators.

2. Economic History

24. Nihon Keizaishi Kenkyūjo 日本經濟史研究所 (Research Institute for Japanese Economic History), Nihon keizaishi jiten 日本經濟史辞典 (Dictionary of Japanese economic history), Tōkyō, Nihon Hyōronsha, 1940, 3 v.

An authoritative work by the institute headed by Professor Honjō. Illustrated. Covers not only the field of economic history but also the fields of political, legislative, and social history.

25. Okazaki Jirō 岡崎次郎, and others, ed., Nihon shihonshugi hattatsushi nempyō 日本資本主義發達史年表 (Chronological table of the development of Japanese capitalism), Tōkyō, Kawade Shobō, 1949.

A detailed chronological table which covers the period from the Meiji Restoration to the date of publication.

26. Taguchi Ukichi 田口卯吉, ed., Nihon shakai jii 日本社會事彙 (Glossary of things in Japanese society), Tōkyō, Keizaishisha, 1907, 3 v.

An illustrated general dictionary which emphasizes origins and development. It includes materials valuable for the study of economic history.

3. Agriculture

27. Ono Takeo 小野武夫, ed., Nihon nōminshi goi 日本農民史語彙 (Glossary for the history of Japanese farmers), Tōkyō, Kaizōsha, 1926.
This work explains terms used in the discussion of the problems of the farmer and provides examples of their use.

28. Ono Takeo 小野武夫, ed., Nōson mondai jiten 農村問題辞典 (Dictionary of agricultural problems), Tōkyō, Hibonkaku, 1934.

29. Satō Kanji 佐藤寛次, ed., Nōgyō daijiten 農業大辞典 (Encyclopedia of agriculture), Tōkyō, Nihon Hyōronsha, 1934, 2 v.

4. Manufacturing Industry

30. Dainihon Daijiten Kankōkai 大日本大辞典刊行會 (Association for the Publication of the Japanese Encyclopedia), Kōgyō daijiten 工業大辞典 (Great dictionary of manufacturing), Tōkyō, Shun'yōdō, 1930-34, 12 v.

31. Matsumoto Takeji 松元竹二, ed., Saishin kōgyō daijiten 最新工業大辞典 (Encyclopedia of manufacturing), Tōkyō, Hibonkaku, 1937-39, 18 v.

5. Commerce

32. Abe Ken'ichi 阿部賢一, ed., Saishin shōgyō keizai jiten 最新商業經濟辞典 (Newest dictionary of commerce and economics), Tōkyō, Dōbunkan, 1937.

33. Takagaki Torajirō 高垣寅次郎, ed., Shōgyō keizai jiten 商業經濟辞典 (Dictionary of commercial economics), Tōkyō, Nihon Hyōronsha, 1938, 1400 + 120 pp.

6. Labor

34. Chūo Rōdō Gakuen Daigaku Shakai Rōdō Mondai Chōsasho 中央勞働學園大學社會勞働問題調査所 (Research Institute for Labor Problems, Central Labor University), Shakai rōdō mondai jiten 社會勞動問題辞典 (Dictionary of social and labor problems), Tōkyō, Jitsugyō no Nihonsha, 1949.

35. Terumichi Gitō 暉峻義等, ed., Rōdō kagaku jiten 勞働科學辞典 (Dictionary of labor science), Tōkyō, Kawade Shobō, 1949.

7. Others

36. Hashizume Akio 橋爪明男, ed., Kin'yū daijiten 金融大辞典 (Dictionary of money and banking), Tōkyō, Nihon Hyōronsha, 1934, 3 v.
A compilation of laws and ordinances relating to this field appears in the appendix.

37. Sumida Shōichi 住田正一, ed., Kaiji daijisho 海事大辞書 (Dictionary of maritime affairs), Tōkyō, Kaibundō, 1925-26, 3 v.
This work covers the period both before and after the Meiji Restoration and deals with such fields as: legislation, history, foreign trade, ports and shipbuilding.

Chapter III

Statistical and Other Information on the Japanese Economy

1. Bibliographical Works

38. Gotō Teiji 後藤貞治, Hompō tōkei shiryō kaisetsu 本邦統計資料解説 (Commentary on Japanese statistical materials), Tōkyō, Sōbunkaku, 1936.
The first part gives the titles of statistical compilations classified by compiling agency. The second part provides a commentary on these materials.

39. Kaizōsha 改造社, Kahei kin'yū tōkei shiryō kaisetsu 貨幣金融統計資料解説 (Commentary on statistical materials)[=v. 34 of Gendai kin'yū zenshū 現代金融全集 (Series on contemporary financial economics)], Tōkyō, Kaizōsha, 1939, 80+223 pp.

40. Masaki Chifuyu 正木千冬 and Matsukawa Shichirō 松川七郎, Tōkei chōsa gaido bukku 統計調査ガイドブック (A guide book for statistical investigation), Tōkyō, Tōyō Keizai Shimpōsha, 1951.

A highly useful guide for the research worker through the maze of statistical publications currently issued by the Japanese government and semi-governmental agencies. There is an introduction on the development of statistical compilation in Japan. The chief agencies are listed and given brief descriptions. The main body of the work lists the publications in various fields, such as population, labor, manufacturing, forestry, agriculture, fishing, construction, transportation, foreign trade, domestic commerce, banking, finance, etc.

41. Naikaku Tōkeikyoku 内閣統計局 (Cabinet Bureau of Statistics), Tōkei shiryō kaidai 統計資料解題 (Annotated list of statistical materials), Tōkyō, Zenkoku Keizai Chōsa-kikan Rengōkai, 1936.

42. Okazaki Fuminori 岡崎文規, Tōkei kenkyū bunken 統計研究文献 (Bibliography of studies on statistics), Tōkyō, Yūhikaku, 1925.
A collection of statistical materials and literature relating to statistics after the early Meiji period. Annotated.

43. Sōrifu Tōkeikyoku 総理府統計局 (Statistics Bureau, Prime Minister's Office), Hompō genkō tōkei shiryō kaidai 本邦現行統計資料解題 (Annotated list of current statistical materials of Japan), Tōkyō, Sōrifu Tōkeikyoku, 1951.

A revised and enlarged edition of the publication of 1936 (no. 41). An all-inclusive list of governmental and non-governmental statistical sources including both occasional and periodical publications. Provides the titles of the chief statistical tables in these publications.

2. Annual, Biennial, Semi-annual, and Quarterly Publications

a. Governmental

(1) General

44. Naikaku Tōkeikyoku 内閣統計局 (Cabinet Bureau of Statistics), Nihon teikoku tōkei nenkan 日本帝國統計年鑑 (Statistical yearbook of the Japanese empire), Tōkyō, Tōkei Kyōkai, 1882-1941, annual.
All-inclusive statistical yearbook in the pre-war period which was followed by the Nihon tōkei nenkan (no. 46) after the war.

45. Naikaku Tōkeikyoku 内閣統計局 (Cabinet Bureau of Statistics), Nihon teikoku tōkei tekiyō 日本帝國統計摘要 (Abstract of the statistics of the Japanese empire), Tōkyō, Tōkei Kyōkai, 1887-1940, annual.
Summary edition of the more inclusive yearbook listed above.

46. Sōrifu Tōkeikyoku 総理府統計局 (Statistics Bureau of the Prime Minister's Office), Nihon tōkei nenkan 日本統計年鑑 (Japan statistical yearbook), Tōkyō Nihon Tōkei Kyōkai, 1949+, annual.
All-inclusive statistical yearbook. The first volume, the 1949 edition, is especially useful because it provides statistical figures for the war period.

47. Sōrifu Tōkeikyoku 総理府統計局 (Statistics Bureau of the Prime Minister's Office), Nihon tōkei nenkan tekiyō-ban 日本統計年鑑—摘要版 (Statistical abstract of Japan), Tōkyō, Nihon Tōkei Kyōkai, 1950+, annual.
Summary edition of the yearbook listed above.

(2) Public Finance

48. Naimushō Chihōkyoku 内務省地方局 (Local Government Bureau, Ministry of Domestic Affairs), Chihō zaisei gaiyō 地方財政概要 (Outline of local finance), Zenkoku Toshi Mondai Kaigi Jimukyoku, 1911+, annual.

49. Ōkura Daijin Kambō Bunshoka 大藏大臣官房文書課 (Archives Section, Secretariat of the Minister of Finance), Ōkurashō nempō 大藏省年報 (Annual report of the Finance Ministry), Tōkyō, Naikaku Insatsukyoku, 1875+, annual.

50. Ōkurashō Chōsabu 大藏省調査部 (Research Division of the Finance Ministry), Quarterly bulletin of financial statistics, Tōkyō, Zaimu Kyōkai, May, 1951+, quarterly.
This is prepared in English for overseas readers and consists of statistical information on general condition of public finance, movements in public finance, relation between public finance and the monetary situation, money and credit, balance of international payments, production, distribution, and price. Provides also the speech of the Minister of Finance in the Diet on the budget for the current year.

51. Ōkurashō Ginkōkyoku 大藏省銀行局 (Bureau of Banks, Finance Ministry), Ginkōkyoku nempō 銀行局年報 (Annual report of the Bureau of Banks), 1880+, annual.

52. Ōkurashō- Nihon Ginkō 大藏省・日本銀行 (The Finance Ministry and the Bank of Japan), Zaisei keizai tōkei nempō 財政經濟統計年報 (Statistical yearbook of finance and economy), Tōkyō, Ōkura Zaimu Kyōkai, 1948+, annual.
Provides highly detailed statistical figures in the field of public finance and banking as well as other important fields of the economy.

53. Ōkurashō Rizaikyoku 大藏省理財局 (Bureau of Finance, Finance Ministry), Kin'yū jikō sankōsho 金融事項参考書 (Reference book on matters relating to banking), Tōkyō, Naikaku Insatsukyoku, 1898+, annual.
Yearly compilation of statistics in the field of public finance and banking as well as other fields of the economy.

54. Ōkurashō Shuzeikyoku 大藏省主税局 (Tax Bureau, Finance Ministry), Shuzeikyoku tōkei nempōsho 主税局統計年報書 (Annual statistical report of the Tax Bureau), Tōkyō, Ōkurashō Shuzeikyoku, 1875+, annual.

See also entries 567, 568, 569, 570, 571, 572.

3) Agriculture, Fisheries, and Forestry

55. Nōrinshō Nōgyōkairyōkyoku Tōkeichōsabu 農林省農業改良局統計調査部 (Statistics and Research Division, Agricultural Improvement Bureau, Ministry of Agriculture and Forestry), Nōrinshō Tōkeihyō 農林省統計表 (Statistics of the Agriculture and Forestry Ministry), Tōkyō, Nōrinshō, 1886+, annual.
The most reliable source of materials relating to agriculture.

56. Nōrinshō Nōmukyoku 農林省農務局 (Bureau of Agricultural Affairs, Agriculture and Forestry Ministry), Sangyō kumiai yōran 産業組合要覽 (Handbook on industrial cooperatives), Tōkyō, Sangyō Kumiai Chūōkai, 1905+, annual.

57. Nōrinshō Nōmukyoku 農林省農務局 (Bureau of Agricultural Affairs, Agriculture and Forestry Ministry), Beikoku tōkei nempō 米穀統計年報 (Annual report of statistics on rice and other cereals), Tōkyō, Tōkei Kyōkai, 1925-, annual.
Includes statistics on production, foreign trade, consumption, and price of rice.

58. Nōrinshō Nōmukyoku 農林省農務局 (Bureau of Agricultural Affairs, Agriculture and Forestry Ministry), Kosaku nempō 小作年報 (Annual report on tenancy), Tōkyō, Nōrinshō Nōmukyoku, 1926+, annual.
Contains reports on such subjects as tenant disputes, mediation of disputes, tenants' union movement, and landlords' associations.

59. Nōrinshō Nōmukyoku 農林省農務局 (Bureau of Agricultural Affairs, Agriculture and Forestry Ministry), Jisakunō sōsetsu iji jigyō seiseki 自作農創設維持事業成績 (Effects of the policy of creating and maintaining peasant land ownership), Tōkyō, Nōrinshō Nōmukyoku, 1929+, annual.

60. Nōrinshō Nōseikyoku 農林省農政局 (Bureau of Agricultural Administration, Agriculture and Forestry Ministry), Hiryō yōran 肥料要覽 (Handbook on fertilizers), Tōkyō, Nōrinshō Nōseikyoku, 1928-41, 1948+, annual.

61. Nōrinshō Sanrinkyoku 農林省山林局 (Bureau of Forestry, Agriculture and Forestry Ministry), Sanrin tōkeisho 山林統計書 (Statistics on forestry), Tōkyō, Nōrinshō, 1908+, annual.

62. Nōrinshō Shokuryōchō 農林省食糧廳 (Board of Foodstuffs, Agriculture and Forestry Ministry), Shokuryō kanri tōkei nempō 食糧管理統計年報 (Annual statistical report on the administration of food stuffs), 1949+, annual.

63. Nōrinshō Suisankyoku 農林省水産局 (Bureau of Marine Products, Agriculture and Forestry Ministry), Suisan tōkei nenkan 水産統計年鑑 (Annual report of marine products statistics), Tōkyō, Nōrinshō, 1912+, annual.

64. Nōrinshō Tōkei Chōsabu 農林省統計調査部 (Division of Statistics and Research, Agriculture and Forestry Ministry), Nōka keizai chōsa 農家經濟調査 (Survey of the economy of the farmer), Tōkyō, Nōrinshō Tōkei Chōsabu, 1924+, annual.
General survey of the financial situation of the farmer. One of the most reliable sources of information concerning the economic life of the farmer. Available for a period of almost thirty years.

4) Commerce, Manufacturing, and Mining

65. Ōkurashō Zeikambu 大藏省税關部 (Bureau of Customs Duty, Finance Ministry), Nihon gaikoku bōeki nempō 日本外國貿易年報 (Annual returns of Japanese foreign trade), Tōkyō, Nihon Kanzei Kyōkai, 1901+, annual.
A detailed yearly report of the returns of Japanese foreign trade.

66. Shigenchō Kambō Tōkeika 資源廳官房統計課 (Statistics Section, Director's Secretariat, Board of Resources), Hompō kōgyō no sūsei 本邦鑛業の趨勢 (Conditions in the Japanese mining industry), Tōkyō, Kōsan Keizai Chōsakai, 1906-1941 and 1950+, annual.

67. Shigenchō Kambō Tōkeika 資源廳官房統計課 (Statistics Section, Director's Secretariat, Board of Resources), Sekiyu tōkei nenkan 石油統計年鑑 (Yearbook on petroleum), Tōkyō, Shigenchō Kambō Tōkeika, 1949+, annual.

68. Shōkōshō Chōsa Tōkeikyoku 商工省調査統計局 (Bureau of Research and Statistics, Commerce and Industry Ministry), Kaisha tōkeihyō 會社統計表 (Corporation statistics), 1925-46 (except 1943 and 1944), annual.

Report on all corporate enterprises. After 1947, data has been published in the Zaisei keizai tōkei geppō (See no. 128).

69. Tsūshō Sangyōshō 通商産業省, Tsūshō sangyōshō nempō 通商産業省年報 (Annual report of the Ministry of International Trade and Industry), Tōkyō, 1949+, annual.
A yearbook covering all matters under the jurisdiction of the Ministry.

70. Tsūshō Sangyōshō Daijin Kambō Chōsa Tōkeibu 通商産業省大臣官房調査統計部 (Research and Statistics Division, Minister's Secretariat, Ministry of International Trade and Industry), Kōgyō tōkeihyō 工業統計表 (Factory statistics), Tōkyō, Tōkei Kyōkai, 1911+, annual.

Report on all manufacturing enterprises. From 1911 to 1947, this work was called Kōjō tōkeihyō. Provides the most detailed data in this field.

(5) Population

71. Kōseishō Kambō Chōsa Tōkeibu 厚生省官房調査統計部 (Division of Research and Statistics, Minister's Secretariat, Welfare Ministry), Jinkō dōtai tōkei 人口動態統計 (Vital statistics), Tōkyō, Tōkei Kyōkai, 1902+, annual.

This report was previously compiled by the Naikaku Tōkei Kyoku 内閣統計局 (Statistical Bureau of the Cabinet). The responsibility for this work was transferred to the Kōseishō 厚生省 (Welfare Ministry) in 1947.

72. Sōrifu Tōkeikyoku 総理府統計局 (Statistics Bureau of the Prime Minister's Office), Kokusei chōsa hōkoku 國勢調査報告 (Report on the national population census), v. d.

This report is published in a number of volumes within about two years of the date of each census. The first legally based national census was taken in 1920 and it has been carried out at five year intervals since then, the latest census having been taken in 1955.

(6) Labor

73. Chūō Rōdō Iinkai Jimkyoku 中央勞働委員會事務局 (Secretariat of the Central Labor Relations Committee), Rōdō iinkai nempō 勞働委員會年報 (Annual report of the Labor Relations Board), Tōkyō, Chūō Rōdō Gakuen, 1947+, annual.

74. Naimushō Shakaikyoku 内務省社會局 (Ministry of Domestic Affairs, Bureau of Social Affairs), Kōjō kantoku nempō 工場監督年報 (Annual report on factory supervision), 1916+, annual.

Presents a general survey of the carrying out of legislation in this field.

75. Rōdōshō Rōdōkijunkyoku 勞働省勞働基準局 (Labor Standards Bureau, Labor Ministry), Kantoku nempō 監督年報 (Annual report on labor supervision), Tōkyō, Rōdōshō Rōdōkijunkyoku, 1948+, annual.

The post-war successor of the yearbook listed above.

76. Rōdōshō Shokugyō Anteikyoku 勞働省職業安定局 (Employment Stabilization Bureau, Labor Ministry), Rōdō shijō nempō 勞働市場年報 (Annual report on the labor market), Tōkyō, Rōdōshō Shokugyō Anteikyoku, 1948+, annual.

77. Rōdōshō Tōkei Chōsabu 勞働省統計調査部 (Statistics and Research Division, Labor Ministry), Rōdō tōkei chōsa nempō 勞働統計調査年報 (Annual report on labor statistics and research), Tōkyō, Rōdōshō Tōkei Chōsabu, 1951+, annual.

A general and inclusive report on labor statistics.

(7) Transportation

78. Teishinshō Kansenkyoku 遞信省管船局 (Ship Administration Bureau, Communications Ministry), Kaiun gaikyō 海運概況 (General survey of marine transportation), Tōkyō, Nihon Kaiji Gakkai, 1919+, annual.

79. Tetsudō Daijin Kambō Bunshoka 鐵道大臣官房文書課 (The Archives Section, Secretariat of the Transportation Minister), Tetsudōshō nempō 鐵道省年報 (Annual report of the Transportation Ministry), Tōkyō, Tetsudōshō, 1886-1948, annual.

80. Un'yushō Kambō 運輸省官房 (Minister's Secretariat, Transportation Ministry), Un'yu yōran 運輸要覽 (Handbook on transportation), Tōkyō, Un'yushō, 1948+, annual.

General report of the administration of the Ministry. Includes statistics of both land and marine transportation.

b. Non-governmental

(1) General

81. Asahi Shimbunsha 朝日新聞社 (The Asahi Press), Asahi keizai nenshi 朝日經濟年誌 (Asahi economic annual), The Asahi Press, 1928+, annual.

The yearbook of an important newspaper which provides a general view of economic conditions during the year. Some statistical tables are presented.

82. Daiyamondosha ダイヤモンド社, Keizai tōkei nenkan 經濟統計年鑑 (Yearbook of economic statistics), Daiyamondosha, 1935+, annual.

83. Mitsubishi Keizai Kenkyūsho 三菱經濟研究所 (Mitsubishi Institute for Economic Research), Nihon sangyō keizai sōran 日本產業經濟総覽 (General survey of Japanese industry and economy), Tōkyō, Mitsubishi Keizai Kenkyūsho, 1949+.

A new series by a well-known institute for economic research. Analytical as well as factual.

84. Nihon Ginkō 日本銀行 (The Bank of Japan), Quarterly review, Tōkyō, the Bank of Japan, May 1948 - March 1950, quarterly.

Succeeded in April, 1950 by a monthly review (see no. 133). Presents a general financial and economic survey in English with one or two articles in addition to the statistical tables.

85. Nihon Ginkō Tōkeikyoku 日本銀行統計局 (Statistics Bureau of the Bank of Japan), Hompō keizai tōkei 本邦經濟統計 (Economic statistics of Japan), Tōkyō, Nihon Ginkō, 1919+, annual.

86. Ōsaka Mainichi Shimbunsha 大阪毎日新聞社 (The Ōsaka Mainichi Newspaper), Naigai keizai nenkan 内外經濟年鑑 (Domestic and foreign economic yearbook), Ōsaka, Mainichi Shimbunsha, annual.

87. Tōkyō Shōkō Kaigisho 東京商工會議所 (Tōkyō Chamber of Commerce), Tōkyō shōkō kaigisho tōkei nempō 東京商工會議所統計年報 (Statistical yearbook of the Tōkyō Chamber of Commerce), Tōkyō, Tōkyō Shōkōkaigisho, 1901+, annual.

88. Tōyō Keizai Shimpōsha 東洋經濟新報社 (Oriental Economist), Nihon keizai nempō 日本經濟年報 (Yearbook on the Japanese economy), Tōkyō, Tōyō Keizai Shimpōsha, 1930+, quarterly.

Provides statistics and comment on many fields of economics. Highly regarded.

89. Yano Tsuneta 矢野恒太 and Shirasaki Kyōji 白崎享二, Nihon kokusei zukai 日本國勢圖會 (Graphic illustration of conditions in Japan), Tōkyō, Kokuseisha, 1927+, annual.

Consists of graphic illustrations of statistical figures and comments thereon. Covers all fields of economics. One of the best known compilations of economic statistics.

90. Zenkoku Keizai Chōsa Kikan Rengōkai 全國經濟調査機關聯合會 (National Federation of Economic Research Organizations), Nihon keizai nenshi 日本經濟年誌 (Yearbook of the Japanese economy), Tōkyō, Senshinsha, 1931+, annual.

Appropriate organizations, governmental and private, have contributed the various sections of this yearbook.

(2) Specific

91. Chūō Rōdō Gakuen 中央勞働學園 (Central Labor College), Rōdō nenkan 勞働年鑑 (Yearbook of labor), Tōkyō, Chūō Rōdō Gakuen, 1949+, annual.

92. Kyōchōkai 協調會 (Reconciliation Association), Rōdō nenkan 勞働年鑑 (Yearbook on labor), Tōkyō, Kyōchōkai, 1933-41, annual.

93. Nihon Chūō Sanshikai 日本中央蠶絲會 (The Japanese Central Silk Reeling Association), Sanshi nenkan 蠶絲年鑑 (Yearbook on silk reeling), Tōkyō, Nihon Chūō Sanshikai, 1932+, annual.

94. Nihon Keizaishi Kenkyūjo 日本經濟史研究所 (Research Institute for Japanese Economic History), Keizaishi nenkan 經濟史年鑑 (Yearbook of economic history), Tōkyō, Nihon Hyōronsha, 1933+, annual.

This is a special annual number of the journal, Keizaishi kenkyū (Study of economic history) (no. 176).

95. Nihon Keizai Shimbunsha 日本經濟新聞社 (The Japan Economist Newspaper), Kaisha nenkan 會社年鑑 (Corporations annual), Nihon Keizai Shimbunsha, 1949+, annual.

A list of about a thousand important banks and corporations in Japan giving detailed information on persons, activities, etc.

96. Nihon Kokuyū Tetsudō Kōsha 日本國有鐵道公社 (The Public Corporation of the National Railways of Japan), Tetsudō tōkei nempō 鐵道統計年報 (Statistical yearbook of railways), Tōkyō, Nihon Kokuyū Tetsudō Kōsha, 1948+, annual.

From 1912 to 1948 this information was published by the Railways Ministry of the Government under the same title.

97. Nihon Kokuyū Tetsudō Kōsha 日本國有鐵道公社 (The Public Corporation of the National Railways of Japan), Un'yu seiseki tōkei nempō 運輸成績統計年報 (Annual report on statistics of transportation), Tōkyō, Nihon Kokuyū Tetsudō Kōsha, 1948+, annual.

Before 1948 this information was published by the Railways Ministry under the same title.

98. Ōhara Shakai Mondai Kenkyūjo 大原社會問題研究所 (Ōhara Research Institute for Social Problems), Nihon rōdō nenkan 日本勞働年鑑 (Japanese yearbook on labor), Tōkyō, Dōjinsha, 1920-41, 1949+, annual.

Regarded as the best yearbook in the labor field. Among the chapters are those on labor conditions, labor movements, labor policy, social work. There is a review of legal development and a bibliography.

99. Ōhara Shakai Mondai Kenkyūjo 大原社會問題研究所 (Ōhara Research Institute for Social Problems), Nihon shakai jigyō nenkan 日本社會事業年鑑 (Yearbook of social work in Japan), Tōkyō, Dōjinsha, 1920-27, annual.

This yearbook was cimbined in 1927 with Nihon rōdō nenkan (Japanese yearbook on labor) (no. 98). It dealt with such subjects as social policy, social education, and public health with attention to legislation and bibliographical information.

100. Sangyō Kumiai Chūōkai 產業組合中央會 (Central Organization of Industrial Cooperatives), Sangyō kumiai nenkan 產業組合年鑑 (Yearbook on industrial cooperatives), Tōkyō, Sangyō Kumiai Chūōkai, 1929+, annual.

101. Teikoku Nōkai 帝國農會 (Agricultural Association of the Empire), Nōgyō nenkan 農業年鑑 (Agricultural yearbook), Tōkyō, Teikoku Nōkai, 1931+, annual.

A general survey of agriculture is followed by information on production and marketing, agricultural economics, rural life and social problems, and administrative and legal matters.

102. Teikoku Nōkai 帝國農會 (Agricultural Association of the Empire), Kome seisanhi chōsa shiryō 米生產費調查資料 (Materials for research on the cost of production of rice), Tōkyō, Teikoku Nōkai, 1926+, annual.

103. Tōkyō Kabushiki Torihikisho 東京株式取引所 (Tōkyō Stock Exchange), Tōkyō kabushiki torihikisho tōkei nempō 東京株式取引所統計年報 (Statistical yearbook of the Tōkyō Stock Exchange), Tōkyō Kabushiki Torihikisho, 1934+, annual.

104. Tōkyō Shisei Chōsakai 東京市政調查會 (The Tōkyō Research Institute on Metropolitan Administration), Nihon toshi nenkan 日本都市年鑑 (Yearbook on Japanese cities), 1931-43, 1948+, annual.

105. Tōyō Keizai Shimpōsha 東洋經濟新報社, (Oriental Economist), Tōyō Keizai ginkō nenkan 東洋經濟銀行年鑑 (Tōyō Keizai's yearbook on banks), Tōkyō, Tōyō Keizai Shimpōsha, 1923-27, annual.

Combined in 1927 with Tōyō Keizai kabushiki nenkan (no. 106).

106. Tōyō Keizai Shimpōsha 東洋經濟新報社 (Oriental Economist), Tōyō Keizai kabushiki nenkan 東洋經濟株式年鑑 (Tōyō Keizai's yearbook on stocks), Tōkyō, Tōyō Keizai Shimpōsha, 1922+, annual.

107. Tōyō Keizai Shimpōsha 東洋經濟新報社 (Oriental Economist), Kaisha shikihō 會社四季報 (Quarterly report on corporations), Tōkyō, Tōyō Keizai Shimpōsha, 1936+, quarterly.

(3) Monthly and Weekly Publications

(A) Governmental

108. Chingin bukka tōkei geppō 賃金物價統計月報 (Monthly report on wages and prices), comp. by Naikaku Tōkeikyoku (Cabinet Bureau of Statistics), Tōkyō, Tōkyō Tōkei Kyōkai, 1925+, monthly until the period of World War II.

109. Jinkō dōtai tōkei sokuhō 人口動態統計速報 (Preliminary report on vital statistics), Tōkyō, Kōseishō Tōkei Chōsabu, July, 1946.

Beginning in 1947 converted into an annual report by the Kōseishō Tōkei Chōsabu 厚生省統計調查部 (Division of Statistics and Research, Ministry of Welfare).

110. Jūyō seisan geppō 重要生產月報 (Monthly production report of key industries), Tōkyō, Shōkōshō Chōsaka, 1938+, monthly.

Pre-war report on monthly production of important industries by the Shōkōshō 商工省 (Ministry of Commerce and Industry).

111. Kokumin shotoku tōkei shiryō chōsa geppō 國民所得統計資料調查月報 (Monthly bulletin of materials for the survey of national income), comp. by Keizai Antei Hombu Kokumin Shotoku Chosashitsu 經濟安定本部國民所得調查室 (Research Chamber on National Income, Economic Stabilization Board), Tōkyō, Keizai Antei Hombu, June 1949+, monthly.

Report on national income estimates and materials relating to the field.

112. Kōsei tōkei geppō 厚生統計月報 (Monthly bulletin of welfare statistics), Tōkyō, Kōseishō Tōkei Chōsabu, April, 1947+, monthly.

Statistical information on activities under the jurisdiction of the Kōseishō (Ministry of Welfare), such as social insurance.

113. Nihon gaikoku bōeki geppō 日本外國貿易月報 (Monthly report on Japanese foreign trade), comp. by the Ōkurashō Kanzeibu (Customs Division of the Ministry of Finance), Tōkyō, Nihon Kanzei Kyōkai, 1930-40, 1950+, monthly.

114. Nihon keizai shihyō 日本經濟指標 (Japanese economic indicators), comp. and publ. by Keizai Shingichō 經濟審議廳 (Economic Counsel Board), Tōkyō, 1950+, monthly.

A brief presentation of statistical information selected to indicate the economic situation in Japan.

115. Nōgyō keizai chōsa geppō 農業經濟調查月報 (Monthly report of agricultural economic research), Tōkyō, Nōrin Tōkei Kyōkai, 1921+, monthly.

116. Nōrin tōkei geppō 農林統計月報 (Monthly report of statistics on agriculture and forestry), comp. by Nōrinshō Nōgyō Kairyōkyoku Tōkei Chōsabu 農林省農業改良局統計調查部 (Statistics and Research Division, Bureau of Agricultural Improvement, Ministry of Agriculture and Forestry), Tōkyō, Nōrin Tōkei Kyōkai, July 1939- December 1950, monthly.

A general statistical report on agriculture, forestry, and fishing.

117. Nōrin tōkei shiryō 農林統計資料 (Statistical data on agriculture and forestry), Tōkyō, Nōrinshō Tōkei Chōsabu, January, 1949+, irregular.

This publication is the successor to the Nōrin tōkei geppō (Monthly report of statistics on agriculture and forestry) (no. 116).

118. Nōson bukka chingin geppō 農村物價賃金月報 (Monthly report on prices and wages in the agricultural village), Tōkyō, Nōrin Tōkei Kyōkai, April, 1950+, monthly.

119. Rōdō tōkei chōsa geppō 勞働統計調査月報 (Monthly bulletin of labor statistics and research), comp. and publ. by Rōdōshō Tōkei Chōsabu (Division of Statistics and Research, Ministry of Labor), Tōkyō, January 1949+, monthly.

Statistics in its field.

120. Sekitan tōkei geppō 石炭統計月報 (Monthly report on coal), comp. by Shigenchō Tōkeika (Statistics Section of the Board of Resources), Tōkyō, Kōsan Keizai Chōsakai, April, 1949+, monthly.

121. Sekiyu tōkei geppō 石油統計月報 (Monthly report on petroleum), comp. by Shigenchō Tōkeika (Statistics Section of the Board of Resources), Tōkyō, Sekiyu Keizai Kenkyūkai, October 1947+, monthly.

122. Shokugyō antei kōhō 職業安定公報 (Report on employment stabilization), comp. and publ. by Rōdōshō Shokugyō Anteikyoku (Employment Stabilization Bureau, Ministry of Labor), Tōkyō, 1950+, monthly.

In the pre-war period similar information was provided in Shokugyō shōkai nempō (Annual report of the employment agency) by Chūō Shokugyō Shōkai Jimukyoku (Secretariat of the Central Employment Agency).

123. Shokuryō kanri geppō 食糧管理月報 (Monthly report on food administration), comp. and publ. by Shokuryōchō (Board of Food), Tōkyō, January 1949+, monthly.

124. Tekkō tōkei geppō 鉄鋼統計月報 (Monthly report on iron and steel), comp. by Shingenchō Tōkeika (Statistics Section of the Board of Resources), Tōkyō, Kōsan Keizai Chōsakai, 1948+, monthly.

125. Tōkei geppō 統計月報 (Monthly statistical bulletin), comp. by Sōrifu Tōkeikyoku (Statistics Bureau of the Prime Minister's Office), Tōkyō, Tōkei Kyōkai, August 1947+, monthly.

Reports statistical information in fields for which this office has responsibility. Statistical series are presented on consumer's prices, retail prices, labor force and other matters of general economic importance.

126. Tsūsan tōkei geppō 通産統計月報 (Monthly report on international trade and commerce), comp. by Tsūshōsangyōshō Chōsatōkeibu (Research and Statistics Division of the Ministry of International Trade and Industry), Tōkyō, Nikkan Kōgyō Shimbunsha, February 1948+, monthly.

There is brief comment on the figures.

127. Un'yu tōkei geppō 運輸統計月報 (Monthly report on transportation statistics), comp. and publ. by Un'yu Daijin Kambō Kikakuka (Planning Section, Secretariat of the Minister of Transportation), Tōkyō, October 1949+, monthly.

128. Zaisei keizai tōkei geppō 財政經濟統計月報 (Monthly bulletin of financial and economic statistics), comp. by Ōkurashō (Ministry of Finance) and Nihon Ginkō (Bank of Japan), Tōkyō, Zaimu Kyōkai, 1948+, monthly.

General report on the monthly statistical figures in this field.

129. Zaisei kin'yū tōkei geppō 財政金融統計月報 (Monthly statistical bulletin of public finance and banking), comp. by Ōkurashō Kambō Chōsaka 大藏省官房調査課 (Research Section, Minister's Secretariat, Ministry of Finance), Tōkyō, Ōkura Zaimu Kyōkai, August 1949+, monthly.

Once in each quarter the journal provides monthly statistical figures in the fields of money, banking, public finance and other important areas. For the other months the bulletin contains comments on statistical information on special subjects.

(B) Non-governmental

1. General

130. Chōsa oyobi shiryō ihō 調査及資料彙報 (Collection of research and source materials), comp. and publ. by Zenkoku Keizai Chōsakikan Rengōkai (National Federation of Economic Research Institutes), Tōkyō, September 1920+, monthly.

131. Keizai jōsei 經濟情勢 (The economic situation), comp. and publ. by Mitsubishi Keizai Kenkyūsho (Mitsubishi Institute for Economic Research), 1932+, monthly.

Monthly review of business conditions.

132. Keizai shiryō 經濟資料 (Economic data), Tōkyō, Keidanren Nissankyō Jimukyoku, 1947+, semi-monthly.

Collection of materials and information on economic conditions by the Keidanren Nissankyō Jimukyoku (Executive Offices of the Federation of Business Associations and of the Council of Japanese Industries).

133. Monthly Review, Tōkyō, The Bank of Japan, April, 1950+, monthly.

A brief general economic survey is followed by tables of statistics. There is an occasional short article. Prepared in the English language for overseas use.

134. Naigai chōsa shiryō 内外調査資料 (Domestic and foreign research materials), Tōkyō, Chōsa Shiryō Kyōkai, May 1929+, monthly.
Valuable source of materials of the period before the second World War.

135. Zaisei keizai jihō 財政經濟時報 (Report on finance and economic conditions), Tōkyō, Zaisei Keizai Jihōsha, January 1914+, monthly.

2. Specific

136. Chūō rōdō chōsa geppō 中央勞働調査月報 (Monthly bulletin on labor research), comp. and publ. by Chūō Rōdō Gakuen (Central Labor University), Tōkyō, 1946+, monthly.

137. Kin'yū tōkei geppō 金融統計月報 (Monthly bulletin of banking statistics), comp. and publ. by Nihon Ginkō Tōkeikyoku (Statistics Bureau of the Bank of Japan), Tōkyō, 1947+, monthly.
Contains all important statistical figures in the field of money and banking. Generally regarded as the best bulletin in the field.

138. Kōsai shasai tōkei geppō 公債社債統計月報 (Monthly statistical bulletin of public loans and bonds), comp. and publ. by Nihon Kōgyō Ginkō Chōsabu 日本興業銀行調査部 (Research Division of the Hypothec Bank of Japan), Tōkyō, 1942+, monthly.

139. Kouri bukka geppō 小賣物價月報 (Monthly bulletin of retail prices), comp. and publ. by Nihon Shōkō Kaigisho (Japan Chamber of Commerce), Tōkyō, 1929+, monthly.

140. Rōdō shiryō geppō 勞働資料月報 (Monthly report on material relating to labor), comp. and publ. by Ōhara Shakai Mondai Kenkyūsho (Ōhara Research Institute for Social Problems), Tōkyō, monthly.
A survey of the current labor situation with statistical and other information.

141. Tōkyō Kabushiki Torihikisho tōkei geppō 東京株式取引所統計月報 (Monthly statistics of the Tōkyō Stock Exchange), comp. and publ. by Tōkyō Kabushiki Torihikisho Chōsaka 東京株式取引所調査課 (Research Section of the Tōkyō Stock Exchange), Tōkyō, January 1886+, monthly.

142. Tōkyō kouri bukka geppō 東京小賣物價月報 (Monthly bulletin of retail prices in Tōkyō), comp. and publ. by Tōkyō Shōkō Kaigisho (Tōkyō Chamber of Commerce), Tōkyō, January, 1927+, monthly.

143. Tōkyō oroshiuri bukka geppō 東京卸賣物價月報 (Monthly bulletin of wholesale prices in Tōkyō), comp. and publ. by Tōkyō Shōkō Kaigisho (Tōkyō Chamber of Commerce), Tōkyō, August 1926+, monthly.

144. Zenkoku chingin tōkei geppō 全國賃金統計月報 (Monthly statistical report of wages), comp. and publ. by Tōkyō Shōkō Kaigisho (Tōkyō Chamber of Commerce), Tōkyō, 1929+, monthly.

145. Zenkoku oroshi kouri bukka geppō 全國卸小賣物價月報 (Monthly report of wholesale and retail prices), comp. and publ. by Nihon Shōkō Kaigisho (Japan Chamber of Commerce), Tōkyō, 1929+, monthly.

(4) The Colonial Economy

(A) Korea

146. Chōsen bōeki geppō 朝鮮貿易月報 (Monthly return of foreign trade of Korea), comp. and publ. by Chōsen Sōtokufu (Office of the Governor-general of Korea), Keijō, 1910+, monthly.

147. Chōsen Ginkō tōkei geppyō 朝鮮銀行統計月表 (Monthly statistical bulletin of the Bank of Chōsen), comp. and publ. by Chōsen Ginkō Chōsakyoku (Bureau of Research, Bank of Chōsen), Keijō, 1915+, monthly.

148. Chōsen kin'yū jijō gaikan 朝鮮金融事情概觀 (General report on the financial situation in Korea), comp. and publ. by Chōsen Shokusan Ginkō Chōsaka (Research Section, Korean Industrial Bank), Keijō, annual.

149. Chōsen kin'yū jikō sankōsho 朝鮮金融事項參考書 (Reference book on banking in Korea), comp. and publ. by Chōsen Sōtokufu Zaimukyoku (Bureau of Finance, Office of the Governor-general of Korea), Keijō, 1923+, annual.

150. Chōsen nōmu ihō 朝鮮農務彙報 (Report on Korean agricultural affairs), comp. and publ. by Chōsen Sōtokufu (Office of the Governor-general of Korea), Keijō, 1924+, monthly.

151. Chōsen Sōtokufu shisei nempō 朝鮮総督府施政年報 (Annual report of the administration of the Office of the Governor-general of Chōsen), comp. and publ. by Chōsen Sōtokufu Sōmuka 朝鮮総督府総務課 (General Affairs Section, Office of the Governor-general of Korea), Keijō, 1911+, annual.

152. Chōsen Sōtokufu tōkei nempō 朝鮮総督府統計年報 (Statistical yearbook of the Office of the Governor-general of Chōsen), comp. and publ. by Chōsen Sōtokufu (Office of the Governor-general of Korea), Keijō, 1911+, annual.

(B) Formosa (Taiwan)

153. Taiwan bōeki geppyō 台灣貿易月表 (Monthly return of the trade of Taiwan), comp. and publ. by Taiwan Sōtokufu (Office of the Governor-general of Formosa), Taihoku, 1901+, monthly.

154. Taiwan bōeki nempō 台灣貿易年報 (Annual return of the trade of Taiwan), comp. and publ. by Taiwan Sōtokufu (Office of the Governor-general of Formosa), Taihoku, 1897+, annual.

155. Taiwan kin'yū jikō sankōsho 台灣金融事項参考書 (erence book on banking in Formosa), comp. and publ. by Taiwan Ginkō (Bank of Taiwan), annual.

156. Taiwan Sōtokufu Tetsudōbu nempō 台灣総督府鉄道部年報 (Annual report on railways), comp. by Taiwan Sōtokufu Kōtsūkyoku 台灣総督府交通局 (Bureau of Transportation, Office of the Governor-general of Formosa), Taihoku, Taiwan Sōtokufu Kōtsūkyoku Tetsudōbu, December 1900+, annual.

After 1924, the title was changed and this annual was issued as Taiwan Sōtokufu tetsudō nempō. A monthly report on the railways was issued by the same office beginning with 1915.

157. Taiwan Sōtokufu tōkeisho 台灣総督府統計書 (Statistical yearbook of the Office of the Governor-general of Taiwan), comp. and publ. by Taiwan Sōtokufu Chōsaka (Research Section of the Office of the Governor-general of Formosa), Taihoku, 1897+, annual.

(C) Others

158. Kantōchō tōkeisho 関東廳統計書 (Statistical yearbook of Kwantung province), comp. and publ. by Kantōchō Bunshoka (Archives Section, Board of Kwantung Province), 1907+, annual.

159. Kantōshū bōeki tōkei 関東州貿易統計 (Returns of foreign trade of Kwantung province), comp. and publ. by Kantōchō (Board of Kwantung Province), 1929+, irregular.

160. Karafutochō tōkeisho 樺太廳統計書 (Statistical yearbook of Sakhalin), comp. and publ. by Karafutochō Bunshoka 樺太廳文書課 (Archives Section, Board of Sakhalin), Toyohara, 1909+, annual.

161. Nan'yōchō 南洋廳 (Board of South Sea Islands), Nan'yōchō tōkei nenkan 南洋廳統計年鑑 (Statistical yearbook of the Board of South Sea Islands), Tōkyō, Nan'yōchō Tōkyō Jimusho, 1933+, annual.

Chapter IV

Journals and Magazines

A selected list of periodicals, useful to students of economics, is here given. The periodicals include academic journals in the general field of economics, general reviews of business and business conditions and a small number of more specialized publications. Comment on the omissions from this list will serve to make its nature clear. Academic journals are numerous in Japan and the number has increased in recent years as the number of universities has grown. Only the best known academic journals have been included. Some general business periodicals may have been omitted but their number is small. Japanese corporations and business organizations publish many magazines of local and limited circulation. There has been no effort to cover this field. The technological periodicals of Japan are numerous and many of these include economic and business information. In general such periodicals have been omitted. The result is a list which is short but general.

162. Chōsa geppō 調査月報 (Monthly research bulletin), comp. by Ōkurashō Kambō Chōsaka 大蔵省官房調査課 (Research Section, Minister's Secretariat, Ministry of Finance), Tōkyō, Ōkurashō Rizaikyoku Chōsaka, 1911+, monthly.

Contains articles on general economics.

163. Daiyamondo ダイヤモンド (Diamond), Tōkyō, Daiyamondosha, May 1913+, weekly.

A journal with a general circulation which presents brief articles on the business situation and current affairs.

164. Ekonomisuto エコノミスト (Economist), Ōsaka, Mainichi Press, March 1923+, weekly.
Comments on current affairs from the point of view of business and economics.

165. Ginkō ronsō 銀行論叢 (Banks and banking), Ōsaka, Ginkō Mondai Kenkyūkai, July 1923+, monthly.

166. Ginkō tsūshinroku 銀行通信録 (Collection of information on banking), comp. and publ. by Tōkyō Ginkō Shūkaisho (Tōkyō Bankers' Club), Tōkyō, 1885+, monthly.

167. Hitotsubashi ronsō 一橋論叢 (The Hitotsubashi review), Tōkyō, Nihon Hyōronsha, 1939+, monthly.
The periodical in which those who are associated with the Tōkyō Shōka Daigaku (Tōkyō University of Commerce) publish the results of study and research.

168. Jitsugyō no Nihon 實業之日本 (Japanese business), Tōkyō, Jitsugyō no Nihonsha, June 1897+, semi-monthly.
An old and well-known journal in the field of business.

169. Kaikei 會計 (Accounting), comp. by Nihon Kaikei Gakkai 日本會計學會 (Japanese Society of Accounting), Tōkyō, Maruyama Shoten, April 1917+, monthly.

170. Keizaigaku ronshū 經濟學論集 (Articles on economics), comp. by Tōkyō Daigaku Keizai Gakubu (Department of Economics of Tōkyō University), Tōkyō, Yūhikaku, April 1931+, monthly.

171. Keizaigaku zasshi 經濟學雜誌 (Journal of Economics), comp. by Ōsaka Shōdai Keizai Kenkyūsho (Economic Research Institute of Ōsaka Commercial University), Tōkyō, Nihon Hyōronsha, 1929+; Ōsaka, Ōsaka Shōka Daigaku Keizai Kenkyūsho, April 1937+, monthly.

172. Keizai hyōron 經濟評論 (Economic review), Tōkyō, Nihon Hyōronsha, 1946+, monthly.
A journal which contains both theoretical and factual studies in economics.

173. Keizai kenkyū 經濟研究 (Studies in economics), Tōkyō, Iwanami Shoten, 1950+, quarterly.
Contains theoretical articles on economics.

174. Keizai Rengō 經濟連合 (Economic Federation), comp. by Keizai Rengō Kumiai 經濟連合組合 (Federation of Economic Associations), Tōkyō, Keizaidantai Rengōkai, 1950+, monthly.

175. Keizai ronsō 經濟論叢 (The economic review), comp. by Kyōto Daigaku Keizai Gakubu 京都大學經濟學部 (College of Economics of Kyōto University), Tōkyō, Yūhikaku, July 1915+, monthly.
The organ of the Kyōto Daigaku Keizai Gakubu which has an English version.

176. Keizaishi kenkyū 經濟史研究 (Studies in economic history), comp. by Keizaishi Kenkyūjo 經濟史研究所 (Research Institute for Economic History), Kyōto, Nihon Keizaishi Kenkyūsho, November 1929+, monthly.
One of the best in the field.

177. Kenkyū nempō keizaigaku 研究年報經濟學 (Reports of economic studies), comp. by faculty members of Tōhoku Daigaku 東北大學 (Tōhoku University), Tōkyō, Iwanami Shoten, December 1934+, semi-annual.
A journal which contains academic studies in economics.

178. Kokumin keizai zasshi 國民經濟雜誌 (Journal of national economy), comp. by Kōbe Shōgyō Daigaku 神戸商業大學 (Kōbe Commercial College), Ōsaka, Ōsaka Hōbunkan, June 1906+, monthly.

179. Mita Gakkai zasshi 三田學會雜誌 (Journal of the Mita Association), comp. by Keiō Daigaku Keizai Gakubu 慶應大學經濟學部 (College of Economics of Keiō University), Tōkyō, Keiō Shuppansha, 1909+, monthly.

180. Nihon Tōkei Gakkai hō 日本統計學會報 (Report of Japan Statistics Society), Tōkyō, Nihon Tōkei Gakkai, 1932+, annual.
The organ of the Nihon Tōkei Gakkai (Japan Statistics Society) which emphasizes theoretical articles.

181. Nissankyō geppō 日產協月報 (Nissankyō monthly bulletin), Tōkyō, Nihon Sangyō Kyōgikai, 1951+, monthly.
The organ of Nihon Sangyō Kyōgikai (Japan Industrial Council), a national association of business men.

182. Nōgyō keizai kenkyū 農業經濟研究 (Studies in agricultural economics), Tōkyō, Iwanami Shoten, 1925+, quarterly.
The organ of the Nōgyō Keizai Gakkai (Agricultural Economics Society), the outstanding association in this field.

183. Riron keizaigaku 理論經濟學 (Theoretical economics), Tōkyō, Tōyō Keizai Shimpōsha, 1950+, quarterly.
A collection of theoretical articles on economics.

184. Shakai keizaishigaku 社會經濟史學 (Social economic history), comp. and publ. by Shakai Keizaishi Gakkai (Society of Social and Economic History), Tōkyō, May 1931+, monthly.

185. Shōkō Kaigisho geppō 商工會議所月報 (Monthly report of Chamber of Commerce), comp. and publ. by Nihon Shōkō Kaigisho (Japan Chamber of Commerce), Tōkyō, October 1929+, monthly.

186. Shōkō keizai 商工經濟 (Economics of trade and industry), comp. and publ. by Tōkyō Shōkō Kaigisho (Tōkyō Chamber of Commerce), Tōkyō, June 1936+, monthly.

187. Tōyō keizai shimpō 東洋經濟新報 (Oriental economist), Tōkyō, Tōyō Keizai Shimpōsha, October, 1895+, weekly.

An old and well-known journal which presents a review of current business and economic conditions and carries a valuable statistical supplement. Attention is given to the stock market and to the reports of corporations. A version in the English language has been published since 1934.

188. Waseda Daigaku seiji keizaigaku zasshi 早稲田大學政治經濟學雜誌 (Waseda journal of political science and economics), comp. and publ. by Waseda Daigaku Seiji Keizai Gakkai (Society of Political Science and Economics of Waseda University), Tōkyō, 1925+, bi-monthly.

Chapter V

Economic Theory

Japanese interest in the theoretical aspects of economic activity goes back at least to the beginning of Tokugawa times. In the earlier Tokugawa Period economic thought was, in general, dominated by Confucian ideas and was devoted to the support and maintenance of the feudal system. During the later Tokugawa Period a number of economists undertook analysis which implied some measure of reform of the system which was current at the time. Men of this sort made some contribution to the Meiji Restoration of 1868. Thinking along lines that made for reform was prevented from further development and systematization by the great influx of western ideas which followed the Restoration. On account of this discontinuity in the development of economic thought, the study of the Tokugawa Period at the present time is an exercise in history rather than an examination of economic theory.

The Meiji Restoration makes a clear division in the development of economic theory in Japan. After a period of enlightenment based in part upon extensive translations of western writings, the western concepts may be said to have become naturalized in Japan and to have become incorporated in Japanese thought by the end of the nineteenth century. Most of the studies of economic theory during this century have been in line with and in quick response to the developments in the West. At the same time, as is shown in the chapter on economic history, efforts have been made to interpret the actual development of the economy in Japan from before the Restoration to the present day.

Before the Meiji Restoration, that is, during the Tokugawa Period, the problems of public finance, money, prices, domestic trade, and population occupied the attention of economists and government officials. During the latter half of this period importance was attached to the additional problems of foreign trade and peasant uprisings.

During the early Tokugawa Period (1600-1680) the power of the Shogunate was being built up and the writings of the economists reveal no fear for the future of the feudal system. The leading men of this period were Nakae Tōju (1608-1648), Yamazaki Ansai (1618-1682), Kumazawa Banzan (1619-1690), Yamaga Sokō (1622-1685), Miyazaki Antei (1623-1697), and Kaibara Ekken (1630-1714). They were all Confucianists and advocated the maintenance of the feudal system of civil status, public and private thrift, and ideas which in the West are associated with the Physiocrats. Even in this early period the development of a money economy created difficulties for the natural, or rice economy. The solution of these difficulties was sought in a "back to the farm" idea which, it was thought, would minimize the contact of the samurai with the money economy.

The early years were followed by the most flourishing period of the Shogunate. Prosperity tended to increase the need for public revenue. The samurai tended to look with fear upon the profits of the merchants which, as they saw it, meant the accumulation of money in the merchants' hands. These and other consequences of the spread of a money economy led to the frequent adoption of a policy of monetary debasement. This policy, through a sort of inflationary effect, led to further debasement. Such developments promoted a vigorous discussion of monetary and general economic questions. Among those who wrote on these matters were: Arai Hakuseki (1657-1725), Ogyū Sorai (1666-1728), Muro Kyūsō (1658-1734), Dazai Shundai (1680-1744), and Ishida Baigan (1685-1744). Arai Hakuseki was highly influential because he was a trusted advisor of the Shogun of this time.

The general physiocratic ideas prevailed during this period as they had in the preceding period. Certain economists, however, such as Ishida Baigan and Dazai Shundai, recognized the importance of the development of domestic trade. Ishida argued, for instance, that the profit earned by the merchant was essentially the same as the samurai's income from feudal sources. Dazai went so far as to advocate that the governments of the feudal lords undertake trade to meet their financial needs and to enable the samurai class to avoid the economic control of the merchants.

Such opinions were held by small groups. The prevailing idea still was that the existing contradictions could be resolved by the return to the old natural economy. This idea was expressed by Arai and Ogyū.

After the second period, the political power of the Shogunate government began to decline and in spite of the tremendous efforts of the government expressed in the well-known political and economic reforms of Matsudaira Sadanobu (around the 1790s) and of Mizuno Tadakuni (around 1840), the Tokugawa government came to its end by 1867.

This period presented various types of economist; among them were the old feudalists like Matsudaira Sadanobu (1758-1829), the advocates of foreign trade like Honda Toshiaki (1744-1812) and Satō Nobuhiro (1769-1850), the promoters of the government's undertaking of industry and domestic trade like Kaiho Seiryō (1755-1821), and the promoters of agriculture such as Ninomiya Sontoku (1787-1856) and Ōkura Eijō (1768-1844). Also, many accounts appeared dealing with agricultural distress and peasant uprisings, for example, those of Motoori Norinaga (1730-1801) and Andō Shōeki.

Satō Nobuhiro may be looked upon as one of the most interesting figures of the period. He was a distinguished economist who wrote on foreign trade. His interest extended to political economy in general and to the field of social reform. The ideas of Satō and Honda on foreign trade and overseas expansion are sometimes referred to as mercantilistic by contemporary economists.

After the Meiji Restoration western economic thought soon made its entrance into Japan. The first to be introduced was the liberal thought of the British classical school. During the first decade of the Meiji Period liberal thought was influential as a reaction against the feudal economic system. Those who introduced liberal economic thought were: Fukuzawa Yukichi (1835-1901), Katō Hiroyuki (1836-1916) (later converted to protectionism), Kanda Kōhei (1830-1898) and Taguchi Ukichi (1855-1905). The works of J. S. Mill, Fawcett and Wayland were translated.

Toward the end of the first decade, there was a counter reaction against laissez-faire economics. Men such as Ōshima Sadamasu (1845-1914), Wakayama Giichi (1840-1891), and Inukai Takeshi (1855-1932) represented the influence of the earlier German historical school and advocated the protective system. Books by Boyles, Carey, List, and Roscher were translated.

These differences led to severe controversy between Taguchi and Inukai during the last decade of the nineteenth century.

In the earlier Meiji Period, there were certain economists who opposed Westernization. A representative one was Sada Kaiseki who argued that Japan should depend on her own domestic industry.

With the turn of the century, the later German historical school came to influence economic theory in Japan. This period was represented by Kanai Nobu, Tajima Kinji, Fukuda Tokuzō, and later by Yamazaki Kakujirō. The works of these men were not mere translations as was usual during the earlier period; they presented well-organized systems of their own.

Fukuda is generally regarded as one of the most important figures of the period. He studied economics in Germany under Professors Brentano and Buecher, and taught for many years in the Tōkyō Shōka Daigaku (Tōkyō University of Commerce). He was influential not only in the field of economic theory but also in the field of economic history and social policy.

The marginal utility school was introduced into Japan before World War I by Koizumi Shinzō's translation of Jevon's work, and this school exercised a strong influence through the Shōwa period.

The development of Japanese economy brought into existence an array of problems in the field of social relations. This was especially true after World War I. As a result, socialist economics, which had been introduced earlier, came to hold great power over many economists at this time. The most important of these economists was Kawakami Hajime. He had started his career as a non-socialist economist but by the end of the second decade of this century he had begun to alter his theoretical point of view and to adopt a Marxist position. He exercised a tremendous influence upon the socialist economists of his time and of later years. His works, Keizaigaku taikō (Principles of economics) (No. 196) and Bimbō monogatari (Stories of poverty) (Nos. 978, 979), are among the best known in the Japanese literature of economics.

Throughout the Taishō Period and the early Shōwa Period the Japanese economists who were interested in theory gave first attention to the debate between the Marxists and those who opposed them. Those who supported the Marxist side included Kawakami Hajime, Kushida Tamizō and Inomata Tsunao. The opposition to the Marxist viewpoint was led by Koizumi Shinzō, Fukuda Tokuzō, Hijikata Seibi and Takada Yasuma. A special heading is provided below for the writings concerned with this debate.

The members of the historical school, which has been referred above, established in 1900 the Shakaiseisaku Gakkai 社會政策學會 (Society for Social Policy). The importance and influence of this Society declined with the acceptance and spread of socialist economics, but there was some revival of interest during the war as the result of the translation and discussion of the works of some German economists.

While it is true that the English classical school was introduced in the early Meiji Period by the men who have been mentioned above, it is to be observed that first attention was given to the later classical economists. The earlier writers, Adam Smith, Malthus, and Ricardo, were not really studied until after the introduction of socialist economics during the later Taishō Period, that is, after the First World War.

The increasing suppression of socialist economics by the governmental authorities which became severe after the first decade of Shōwa, that is, about 1935, tended to give a more important place to analysis based on marginal concepts and to the so-called marginal utility school.

The neo-classical school has exercised a considerable influence upon the Japanese study of economic theory. This influence was increased by the translation of Marshall's Principles of economics during the Taishō Period. Works by Pigou and others were translated during the first decade of Shōwa (1925-35). The translation of Keynes' General theory was published around the year 1940. It carried some early influence but it was not until after World War II that the aggregative method came to be generally understood and employed. The developments which have here been indicated in outline should not be permitted to obscure the fact that the relation between Marxist and non-Marxist economics has been an outstanding feature of the post-war period.

The classification of works on economic theory which is employed below gives great importance to schools of thought in the West. The reasons for this have been indicated. The development of Japanese thought has not, it is believed, brought into existence schools which are of general significance outside of Japan; nor has it created any general approach to economics which is distinctively Japanese. It must not be supposed, however, that Japanese economists have failed to give vigorous attention to theoretical problems.

1. History of Economic Theory

189. Hatano Kanae 波多野鼎, Kachi gakusetsushi 價値學說史 (History of value theories), Tōkyō, Ganshōdō, 1928-30; rev. ed., 1937-38, 3 v.
General treatise on the history of value theories. Deals with the value theory of the classical school in volume 1, of the Austrian school in volume 2, and of the eclectic school in volume 3.

190. Hori Tsuneo 堀經夫, Keizaigakushi yōron 經濟學史要論 (Summary of the history of economics), Tōkyō, Kōbundō, 1931-33, 3 v.
The author, a professor in the Ōsaka Commercial University, is noted for his study of classical economics.

191. Kawakami Hajime 河上肇, "Shihonshugi keizaigaku no shiteki hatten 資本主義經濟學の史的發展 (Historical development of capitalist economics)," in Keizaigaku taikō (General principles of economics), Tōkyō, Kaizōsha, 1928.
This work was included in the author's more general work on the principles of economics (No. 196). It provided a history of theory from the Marxist point of view. The author was a professor of economics in Kyōto University.

192. Koizumi Shinzō 小泉信三, Kindai keizai shichō gaikan 近代經濟思潮概觀 (Outline of modern economic thought), Tōkyō, Kōgakusha, 1949.
The author, former president of Keiō University, is one of the best interpreters of Western economics in Japan and noted for his criticism of Marxian economics. The book covers all important schools of economics from Adam Smith to contemporary economists.

193. Maide Chōgorō 舞出長五郎, Keizaigakushi gaiyō (jōkan) 經濟學史概要(上卷) (Outline of the history of economic science, volume 1), Tōkyō, Iwanami Shoten, 1937.
The author is professor of economics in Tokyo University and one-time Dean of the College of Economics. The work is divided into two parts: predecessors of the classical school and the classical school.

194. Takahashi Seiichirō 高橋誠一郎, Keizaigakushi (jōkan) 經濟學史(上卷) (History of economics, volume 1), Tōkyō, Nihon Hyōronsha, 1939.
The author is professor of economics in Keiō University. The work deals with the origin and the development of classical economic theories.

195. Yamada Yūzō 山田雄三, Keizaigaku no shiteki hatten 經濟學の史的發展 (Historical development of the science of economics), Tōkyō, Tōyō Keizai Shimpōsha, 1947.
The author is professor of economics in the Hitotsubashi University and a leading figure among the students of national income in Japan.

2. General Works

196. Kawakami Hajime 河上肇, Keizaigaku taikō 經濟學大綱 (Principles of economics), Tōkyō, Kaizōsha, 1928.

A representative example of the interpretation of Marxist economics in Japan.

197. Kishimoto Seijirō 岸本誠二郎, Keizaigaku genri 經濟學原理 (Principles of economics), Tōkyō, Nihon Hyōronsha, 1948.

198. Koizumi Shinzō 小泉信三, Keizai genron 經濟原論 (Principles of economics), Tōkyō, Nihon Hyōronsha, 1948.

199. Nakayama Ichirō 中山伊知郎, Keizaigaku ippan riron 經濟學一般理論 (General principles of economics), Tōkyō, Nihon Hyōronsha, 1941; reprinted 1948.
General textbook on economics written from the viewpoint of general equilibrium theory.

200. Ōuchi Hyōe 大内兵衛, Keizaigaku 經濟學 (Economics), Tōkyō, Hōsei Daigaku Shuppankyoku, 1950, 4 v.

201. Takada Yasuma 高田保馬, Keizaigaku shinkō 經濟學新講 (New lectures on economics), Tōkyō, Iwanami Shoten, 1929-32, 5 v.

202. Takada Yasuma 高田保馬, Keizaigaku genri 經濟學原理 (Principles of economics), Tōkyō, Nihon Hyōronsha, 1947.

3. Japanese Studies along the Lines of Western Economic Thought

a. Classical School

203. Hori Tsuneo 堀經夫, Rikādo no kachiron oyobi sono hihanshi リカアドの價値論及其批判史 (The value theory of Ricardo and the history of its criticism), Tōkyō, Iwanami Shoten, 1929.

204. Koizumi Shinzō 小泉信三, Adamu Sumisu, Marusasu, Rikarudo アダム スミス・マルサス・リカルド (Adam Smith, Malthus, Ricardo), Tōkyō, Iwanami Shoten, 1934.
The book presents research on the classical school, with particular emphasis on the men named.

205. Nakayama Ichirō 中山伊知郎, Sumisu kokufuron スミス國富論 (Smith's Wealth of nations), Tōkyō, Iwanami Shoten, 1936; ed. 6, 1948.

206. Ōkōchi Kazuo 大河内一男, Sumisu to Risuto スミスとリスト (Smith and List), Tōkyō, Nihon Hyōronsha, 1934.

207. Suenaga Shigeki 末永茂喜, Kotenha keizaigaku kenkyū 古典派經濟學研究 (Studies of classical economics), Tōkyō, Hakujitsu Shoin, 1948.

b. Historical School

208. Itagaki Yoichi 板垣與一, Seiji keizaigaku no hōhō 政治經濟學の方法 (Method of political economy), Tōkyō, Nihon Hyōronsha, 1942.

209. Kishimoto Seijirō 岸本誠二郎, Rekishigakuha 歴史學派 (Historical school), Tōkyō, Nihon Hyōronsha, 1940.

210. Okazaki Jirō 岡崎次郎, Zombaruto kinsei shihonshugi no rekishiteki kiso ゾムバルト近世資本主義の歴史的基礎 (Historical background of Sombart's modern capitalism), Tōkyō, Natsume Shoten, 1948.

211. Takashima Zen'ya 高島善哉, Keizaishakaigaku no kompon mondai 經濟社會學の根本問題 (Fundamental problems of economic sociology), Tōkyō, Nihon Hyōronsha, 1941.

See also entry 206.

c. Socialist School

212. Inomata Tsunao 猪俣津南雄, Kin no keizaigaku 金の經濟學 (Economics of gold), Tōkyō, Chūō Kōronsha, 1932.

213. Kawakami Hajime 河上肇, Shihonron nyūmon 資本論入門 (Introduction to "Das Kapital"), Tōkyō, Sekai Hyōronsha, 1946-49, 5 v.

214. Kushida Tamizō 櫛田民藏, Kushida Tamizō zenshū 櫛田民藏全集 (Complete works of Kushida Tamizō), Tōkyō, Kaizōsha, 1935, 5 v.
Contents: vol. 1, Agricultural problems; vol. 2, Value and money; vol. 3, Historical materialism; vol. 4, Social problems; vol. 5, Military taxation and war economy.

215. Sakoma Shinjirō 迫間真治郎, Shakaishugi keikaku keizairon 社會主義計劃經濟論 (Planned economy under socialism), Tōkyō, Kawade Shobō, 1947.

216. Uno Kōzō 宇野弘藏, Shihonron no kenkyū 資本論の研究 (Study of "Das Kapital"), Tōkyō, Iwanami Shoten, 1949.
The author is professor at Tōkyō University. The book contains six separate articles of pure theoretical study on Karl Marx, Hilferding, and Rosa Luxemburg.

See also entries 196, 246, 249, 250, 252.

d. Austrian School

217. Araki Kōtarō 荒木光太郎 Ōsutoriya-ha keizaigaku 墺太利派經濟學 (Austrian school of economics) [=vols. 14 and 17 of Shakai keizai taikei (Socail and economic system)], Tōkyō, Nihon Hyōronsha, 1928.

218. Takahashi Taizō 高橋泰藏, Kaheiteki keizai riron no shintenkai 貨幣的經濟理論の新展開 (New developments in monetary economic theory), Tōkyō, Ginza Shuppansha, 1948.

219. Yamada Yūzō 山田雄三, Keikaku no keizai riron 計画の經濟理論(Economic theory of planning), Tōkyō, Iwanami Shoten, 1942.

e. Cambridge School

220. Kitō Nisaburō 鬼頭仁三郎, Keinzu kenkyū ケインズ研究(A study of Keynes), Tōkyō, Tōyō Keizai Shimpōsha, 1948.

221. Koizumi Akira 小泉明, Keinzu ippan riron ケインズ一般理論(General theory of Keynes), Tōkyō, Shunjūsha, 1948.

222. Nakayama Ichirō 中山伊知郎, Hatten katei no kinkō bunseki 發展過程の均衡分析 (Analysis of dynamic equilibrium), Tōkyō, Iwanami Shoten, 1939.
Contains chapters such as: development of theories of employment and unemployment, critical study of natural interest, and analysis of dynamic equilibrium.

223. Nakayama Ichirō 中山伊知郎, Kōsei keizaigaku 厚生經濟學 (Economics of welfare), Tōkyō, Risōsha, 1947.
This is an introduction to Pigou's Economics of welfare.

224. Satō Toyosaburō 佐藤豊三郎, Keizaigaku no atarashii tsukamikata: kokumin keizai no shakaiteki kōzō 經濟學の新しいつかみ方—國民經濟の社會的構造 (New approach to economics: social structure of national economy), Tōkyō, Tōyō Keizai Shimpōsha, 1949.

225. Sugimoto Eiichi 杉本榮一, Riron keizaigaku no kihon mondai 理論經濟學の基本問題 (Fundamental problems of theoretical economics), Tōkyō, Nihon Hyōronsha, 1939.
Consists of 2 chapters: dynamic development of an economy and quantitative approach to economic principles.

226. Suzuki Ryōichi 鈴木諒一, Māsharu keizaigaku kenkyū マーシャル經濟學研究(A study of Marshallian economics), Tōkyō, Natsume Shoten, 1948.

227. Takada Yasuma 高田保馬, Shin-rishiron kenkyū 新利子論研究 (A new study of the rate of interest), Tōkyō, Iwanami Shoten, 1940.
Critical analysis of Keynes' interest theory.

228. Takahashi Masao 高橋正雄, Keinzu kaheiron kenkyū ケインズ貨幣論研究(A study of the monetary theory of Keynes), Tōkyō, Junshindō, 1948.
Criticism of Keynesian monetary theory from the Marxist point of view.

229. Takahashi Taizō 高橋泰藏, Keizai hatten to koyō mondai--- Sumisu, Marusasu, Keinzu 經濟發展と雇傭問題—スミス・マルサス・ケインズ (Economic development and the employment problem: Smith, Malthus, Keynes), Tōkyō, Fuji Shuppansha, 1948.
Analysis of Keynesian employment theory looking for its theoretical origin in the works of Malthus and Adam Smith.

230. Yamada Yūzō 山田雄三, Pigū kōsei keizaigaku ピグー厚生經濟學 (Pigou's Economics of welfare), Tōkyō, Shunjūsha, 1948.

f. Mathematical School

231. Hayakawa Miyoji 早川三代治, Junri keizaigaku joron 純理經濟學序論(Introduction to pure theoretical economics), Tōkyō, Iwanami Shoten, 1930.

232. Nakayama Ichirō 中山伊知郎, Sūri keizaigaku hōhōron 數理經濟學方法論 (Treatise on the method of mathematical economics), Tōkyō, Kaizōsha, 1932.

233. Nakayama Ichirō 中山伊知郎, Sūri keizaigaku kenkyū 數理經濟學研究(Study of mathematical economics), Tōkyō, Nihon Hyōronsha, 1937.
A general introduction to mathematical economics.

234. Nakayama Ichirō 中山伊知郎 and Hisatake Masao 久武雅夫, Keizai no sūri --- keizai seitai no sūgaku riron 經濟の數理—經濟靜態の數學理論(Mathematics of economy: the mathematical theory of static economics), Tōkyō, Kangaekata Kenkyūsha, 1938.

235. Shinohara Miyohei 篠原三代平, Chingin to koyō 賃金と雇傭 (Wages and employment), Tōkyō, Jitsugyō no Nihonsha, 1949.

g. Econometrics

236. Yamada Isamu 山田勇, Keiryō keizaigaku no kihon mondai 計量經濟學の基本問題 (Fundamental problems of econometrics), Tōkyō, Chūbunkan Shoten, 1949.
The author undertakes in this book to make a theoretical and statistical analysis of the economic structure.

237. Yamada Isamu 山田勇, Keizai no keiryō 經濟の計量 (Measurement of economy), Tōkyō, Jitsugyō no Nihonsha, 1949.
Contain three chapters and a supplementary chapter: (1) Recent development of econometrics; (2) Economic analysis of economic models; (3) International comparison of productive power with emphasis on national income; Supplementary chapter: Economic theory and statistical technique.

See also entry 363.

h. Business Cycle Theory

238. Takada Yasuma 高田保馬, Keiki hendōron 景氣變動論 (Business cycle theory) [= Vol. 13 of Gendai keizaigaku zenshū (Series on contemporary economics)], Tōkyō, Nihon Hyōronsha, 1928.

239. Toyozaki Minoru 豊崎稔, Keizai hendōron 經濟変動論 (On the fluctuation of the economy), Ōsaka, Sōgensha, 1949.

240. Nambu Seiichirō 南部誠一郎, Hikawa Tōru 氷川透, and Taniguchi Yoshihiko 谷口吉彦, Kyōkō gakusetsu 恐慌學說 (The theory of crises), Tōkyō, Kaizōsha, 1932.
Deals with the business cycle theory of the classical school.

241. Shinjō Hiroshi 新庄博, Kin'yū riron no shinkeikō 金融理論の新傾向 (New trends in banking theory), Kyōtō, Kōbundō, 1927.

242. Toyozaki Minoru 豊崎稔, Kaheiteki keiki riron 貨幣的景氣理論 (Monetary theory of business cycles), Kyōto, Kōbundō, 1937.
This one and the preceding work are studies of business cycles based on monetary theory.

243. Tamura Ichirō 田村市郎, Waga kuni no keiki junkan to keiki shisū 我國の景氣循環と景氣指數 (Business cycles and business indices of Japan), Tōkyō, Bungadō, 1930.
Statistical study of Japanese business cycles.

244. Takashima Saichirō 高島佐一郎, Shin'yō tōsei to keiki hendō 信用統制と景氣変動 (Credit control and business cycles), Tōkyō, Dōbunkan, 1930.

245. Toyozaki Minoru 豊崎稔, Keikiron dokusen shihonsei no shihon chikuseki to keiki hendō 景氣論—獨占資本制の資本蓄積と変動 (On business cycles: capital accumulation and business cycles under the monopolistic capitalist system), Tōkyō, Kaizōsha, 1935.
This and the preceding work deal with the business cycle under a controlled economy.

246. Kuruma Kōzō 久留間鮫造, Marukusu kyōkōron kenkyū マルクス恐慌論研究 (Study of Marx' theory of crises), Tōkyō, Hokuryūkan, 1949.

247. Suzuki Takeo 鈴木武雄, Shijō riron 市場理論 (Theory of the market), Tōkyō, Kawade Shobō, 1948.

248. Toyoda Shirō 豊田四郎, Nihon shihonshugi kōzō no riron 日本資本主義構造の理論 (Theory of the structure of Japanese capitalism), Tōkyō, Shichō Shorin, 1947.
This and the two preceding works deal with the Marxian theory of production and crisis.

i. The Debate over Value Theory

A vigorous debate took place during the 1920s and early 1930s and after the second World War over value theory between the followers of Marx and those who maintained the so-called subjective theory of value. An extensive list of contributions to this debate is provided in Asobe Kyūzō's Kachi ronsōshi (no. 250).

Representative works on the Marxist side are:

249. Asobe Kyūzō 遊部久藏, Kachi to kakaku 價値と價格 (Value and price), Tōkyō, Aoki Shoten, 1948.

250. Asobe Kyūzō 遊部久藏, Kachi ronsōshi 價値論争史 (History of the debate over value theory), Tōkyō, Aoki Shoten, 1949.

251. Kushida Tamizō 櫛田民藏, Kachi oyobi kahei 價値及貨幣 (Value and money), Tōkyō, Kaizōsha, 1935; repr. 1947.
The author was a leading Marxist theorist in the 1920s and early 1930s. This book, one volume of his complete work (no. 214), contains nine articles on the theory of value and four on monetary theory.

252. Uno Kōzō 宇野弘藏, Kachiron 價値論 (On value), Tōkyō, Kawade Shobō, 1947.

Representative works on the subjective theory of value are:

253. Fukuda Tokuzō 福田徳三, Shakai seisaku to kaikyū tōsō 社會政策と階級闘爭 (Social policy and class struggle), Tōkyō, Ōkura Shoten, 1922.

254. Hijikata Seibi 土方成美, Marukusu kachiron no haigeki マルクス價値論の排撃 (Rejection of the Marxian value theory), Tōkyō, Nihon Hyōronsha, 1927.

255. Koizumi Shinzō 小泉信三, Kachiron to shakaishugi 價値論と社會主義 (Value theory and socialism), Tōkyō, Kaizōsha, 1924; enl. ed., 1928.

256. Takada Yasuma 高田保馬, Rōdō kachisetsu no gimmi 勞働價値說の吟味 (Examination of the labor theory of value), Tōkyō, Nihon Hyōronsha, 1931.

257. Takada Yasuma 高田保馬, Marukusu keizaigaku rompyō マルクス經濟學論評 (Criticism of Marxist economics), Tōkyō, Kaizōsha, 1934.

4. Japanese Economic Thought

a. Before the Meiji Restoration

258. Hani Gorō 羽仁五郎, Satō Nobuhiro ni kansuru kisoteki kenkyū 佐藤信淵に關する基礎的研究 (Fundamental research on Satō Nobuhiro), Tōkyō, Iwanami Shoten, 1929.
An account of a political economist (1769-1850) of the late Tokugawa period. The author is a well-known historian.

259. Honjō Eijirō 本庄榮治郎, Kinsei no keizai shisō 近世の經濟思想 (Economic thoughts in the modern age [the Tokugawa period]), Tōkyō, Nihon Hyōronsha, 1931-38, 2 v.
Studies of the economic thought of certain individual writers, such as Arai Hakuseki, Ogyū Sorai, Motoori Norinaga, Nakai Chikuzan, Honda Toshiaki, and Sada Kaiseki, are presented in the first volume together with the names of other economists arranged to show the source and development of ideas.
The second volume is concerned chiefly with particular topics dealt with during the period. Among the subjects presented are: economic thought in the late Tokugawa period, the foreign policy of the period, the argument over the opening of the country which developed during the closing days of the Tokugawa period and the transactions tax of the same period.

260. Honjō Eijirō 本庄榮治郎, Nihon keizai shisōshi kenkyū 日本經濟思想史研究 (Studies on the development of Japanese economic thought), Tōkyō, Nihon Hyōronsha, 1942-47, 2 v.
In volume one the author deals with the economic thought expressed on various occasions by the public officials of the Shogunate Government or of the local government of feudal lords and with the author's interpretations and evaluations of the economic thought of ten famous economists of this period.

261. Honjō Eijirō 本庄榮治郎, Nihon keizai shisōshi 日本經濟思想史 (History of Japanese economic thought), Tōkyō, Ryūginsha, 1948.

262. Izu Kimio 伊豆公夫, Arai Hakuseki 新井白石, Tōkyō, Hakuyōsha, 1938.
Biography of a well-known political economist (1657-1725) of the middle Tokugawa period. The work deals with Arai as a man and as a scholar. The second part includes an account of "Hakuseki and political econnomy."

263. Kinsei shakai keizai gakusetsu taikei 近世社會經濟學說大系 (Series on social and economic theories in the modern period), Tōkyō, Seibundō, 1935-37, 18 v.
Collection of works of leading economists during the Tokugawa and early Meiji periods. Includes such economists as Kumazawa Banzan, Yamaga Sokō, Kaibara Ekken, Asami Keisai, Arai Hakuseki, Ogyū Sorai, Dazai Shundai, Motoori Norinaga, Nakai Chikuzan, Honda Toshiaki, Yamakata Banchō, Kaiho Seiryō, Satō Nobuhiro, Ninomiya Sontoku, Takashima Shūhan, Sakuma Shōzan, Sakamoto Ryūma, Yuri Kōsei, Kanda Kōhei, and Fukuzawa Yukichi. Provides an introduction of each person, written by a leading contemporary economist or social scientist.

264. Nagata Hiroshi 永田廣志, Nihon hōkensei ideorogii 日本封建制イデオロギー (Ideology of the Japanese feudal system), Tōkyō, Hakuyōsha, 1938.
The author is a well-known writer on historical materialism. In this work he undertakes a theoretical analysis of what he calls the ideology of feudal Japan. There are chapters on the history of ideology in the West and the East, on Buddhism in the feudal period and on the history of ideology in Tokugawa Japan.

265. Nakamura Kōya 中村孝也, Genroku Kyōho jidai ni okeru keizai shisō no kenkyū 元祿享保時代に於ける經濟思想の研究 (Study of economic thought in the periods of Genroku and Kyōho), Tōkyō, Kokumin Bunka Kenkyūkai, 1922; rev. and enl. 1927, 1103+48 pp.
The economic thought of the time, that is, at the end of the seventeenth and the beginning of the eighteenth century, is presented and evaluated under the following heads: production, exchange, distribution, consumption, and public finance.

266. Nomura Kanetarō 野村兼太郎, Ogyū Sorai 荻生徂徠, Tōkyō, Sanseidō, 1934.
Biography of a well-known political economist (1666-1728) in the middle Tokugawa period who was also a leading figure among the Confucianists of the time. The general account of his life and thought contains chapters on his attitude toward the money economy and toward social reform.

267. Nomura Kanetarō 野村兼太郎, Nihon keizai gakusetsushi shiryō (Tokugawa jidai) 日本經濟學說史資料(德川時代) (Materials relating to the history of Japanese economic theory: the Tokugawa period), Tōkyō, Keiō Gijuku, 1935.
Excerpts from the works of forty-one leading economists throughout the Tokugawa period to show significant features of their thinking.

268. Nomura Kanetarō 野村兼太郎, Gaikan Nihon keizai shisōshi 概觀日本經濟思想史 (Outline of the history of Japanese economic thought), Tōkyō, Keiō Shuppansha, 1939; rev. 1949.
Deals with the economic thought of the Tokugawa period under four subdivisions and of the early Meiji period under three. The prevailing ideas of each subdivision are presented rather than those of individual economists. A work of the same nature was published by the author under the title, Tokugawa jidai no shakai keizai shisō gairon (Outline of social economic thought in the Tokugawa period), Tōkyō, Nihon Hyōronsha, 1934, 276 pp.

269. Nomura Kanetarō 野村兼太郎, Tokugawa jidai no keizai shisō 德川時代の經濟思想 (Economic thought in the Tokugawa period), Tōkyō, Nihon Hyōronsha, 1939.
The first part deals with the general nature of the economics of the period and with changes during the period in the theoretical approach to agriculture, commerce, and the economy in general. The second part examines the economic thought of individual economists including Kumazawa Banzan, Yamaga Sokō, Kaibara Ekken, Arai Hakuseki, Ogyū Sorai, Dazai Shundai, Motoori Norinaga, Honda Toshiaki, Hirata Atsutane, Satō Nobuhiro.

270. Ono Takeo 小野武夫, Satō Nobuhiro 佐藤信渊, Tōkyō, Sanseidō, 1934.
Satō was a well-known agricultural economist (1769-1850) in the later Tokugawa period. The author is an expert on the agricultural problems of the middle ages and the Tokugawa period.

271. Sasai Shintarō 佐々井信太郎, Ninomiya Sontoku kenkyū 二宮尊德研究 (Study of Ninomiya Sontoku), Tōkyō, Iwanami Shoten, 1927.
Biographical study of a man (1787-1856) noted for financial reform in the government of his feudal lord and for the promotion of agricultural production. He is known throughout Japan for his influence on the moral life of the people through his principles of thrift and hard work.

272. Takimoto Seiichi 滝本誠一, Nihon keizai gakusetsu no yōryō 日本經濟學說の要領 (Summary of Japanese economic theories), Tōkyō, Yoshikawa Kōbunkan, 1908.
Consists of three chapters which deal with the explanation of economic thought of the Tokugawa period, the influence of Chinese theories, and the interrelation of economic theory and economic or political institutions.

273. Takimoto Seiichi 滝本誠一, ed., Nihon keizai taiten 日本經濟大典 (Collection of Japanese economic literature), Tōkyō, Yoshikawa Kōbundō, 1928-1930, 54 v.
A supremely valuable collection of economic literature from the Fujiwara to the Tokugawa periods. Supplementary to the author's earlier work, Nihon keizai sōsho (Japanese economic series), 1914-17 and 1923, 39 v. Most of the volumes present Tokugawa literature, two being pre-Tokugawa. The works selected deal with every field of economics including relevant legislation and institutions.

274. Takimoto Seiichi 滝本誠一, Nihon keizaigakushi 日本經濟學史 (History of Japanese economic theories), Tōkyō, Shunjūsha, 1929.
The twelve chapters of this work deal with economic thought on particular topics or of particular individuals during the Tokugawa period. Among the subjects are: the meaning of economics in the Tokugawa period, the "Honsaroku" of Honda Sado-no-kami, talks on economics by Kaiho Seiryō, Satō Nobuhiro's system of government monopoly, thoughts on social policy, the significance of thrift in the feudal period, the theory of population.

275. Takimoto Seiichi 滝本誠一, Nihon keizai shisōshi 日本經濟思想史 (History of Japanese economic thought), Tōkyō, Nihon Hyōronsha, 1929.
Introduction to the economic thought of leading economists during the Tokugawa period based on their representative publications.

b. After the Meiji Restoration

276. Fukuzawa Yukichi 福澤諭吉, Fuku-ō jiden 福翁自傳 (Autobiography of Fukuzawa), Tōkyō, Iwanami Shoten, 1946.
Fukuzawa Yukichi (1834-1901) was an influential figure in the history of Japanese economic thought during the early Meiji Period. He contributed to the modernization of Japan by introducing modern Western thought and knowledge not only in the economic but in other fields as well.

277. Hori Tsuneo 堀經夫, Meiji keizaigakushi 明治經濟學史 (History of economic theory in the Meiji period), Tōkyō, Kōbundō, 1935.
Deals with the history of Japanese economic theory and policy during the first thirty years of the Meiji Period.

278. Ishikawa Kammei 石河幹明, Fukuzawa Yukichi-den 福沢諭吉傳 (Biography of Fukuzawa Yukichi), Tōkyō, Iwanami Shoten, 1932, 4 v.
An exhaustive biography of Fukuzawa Yukichi which contains some information valuable for the study of the history of Japanese economic thought, especially during the early Meiji Period.

279. Kada Tetsuji 加田哲二, Meiji shoki shakai shisō no kenkyū 明治初期社會思想の研究 (Study of social thought in the early Meiji period), Tōkyō, Shunjūsha, 1933.
A general presentation of the subject is followed by an account of the nine leading theorists of the period and by the treatment of a number of special topics.

280. Kada Tetsuji 加田哲二, Meiji shoki shakai keizai shisōshi 明治初期社會經濟思想史 (History of social and economic thought in the early Meiji period), Tōkyō, Iwanami Shoten, 1937.
A well organized study of the development of social thought during the early Meiji Period. A list of works relating to this subject is provided.

281. Kada Tetsuji 加田哲二, Keizaigakusha no hanashi 經濟學者の話 (The stories of economists), Tōkyō, Zaisei Keizai Jihōsha, 1939.
A section on Western economists is followed by one on Japanese economists, including Kumazawa Banzan, Arai Hakuseki, Ōgyū Sorai, Dazai Shundai, Satō Nobuhiro, Fukuzawa Yukichi, Taguchi Ukichi, Nakae Chōmin, Sada Kaiseki, Tarui Tokichi, Ōshima Sadamasu, Fukuda Tokuzō.

282. Kawakami Hajime 河上肇, Jijoden 自敍傳 (Autobiography of Kawakami Hajime), Tōkyō, Sekai Hyōronsha, 1947-48, 3 v.
The autobiography of a well-known Marxist who taught economics at Kyōto University. He is regarded as one of the best interpreters of Marxism and his work Keizaigaku taikō (no. 196) is an outstanding illustration of Marxist thought in Japan. He was known for his political activities as a member of the Communist party during the later years of his life.

283. Nagata Hiroshi 永田廣志, Nihon yuibutsuronshi 日本唯物論史 (History of Japanese materialism), Tōkyō, Hakuyōsha, 1936.

284. Shiojima Jinkichi 塩島仁吉, Teiken Taguchi-sensei-den 鼎軒田口先生傳 (Life of Dr. Taguchi Ukichi), Tōkyō, 1912.
Promoter (1855-1905) of the laissez-faire economic system in the early Meiji Period. Noted for his Nihon keizairon and for his controversy with Inukai Takeshi who advocated protectionism.

285. Takahashi Seiichirō 高橋誠一郎, Fukuzawa Yukichi: hito to gakusetsu 福沢諭吉：人と學説 (Fukuzawa Yukichi: his personality and theories), Tōkyō, Jitsugyō no Nihonsha, 1947.
A biographical work on Fukuzawa Yukichi based on close observation by a contemporary economist trained at Keiō University, an institution established by Fukuzawa himself.

Chapter VI

Economic History

The study of the economic history of Japan has produced a rich literature, more extensive, perhaps, than for any other fields of study under the general heading of economics. The number of scholars working in this field has been large at all times. This emphasis calls for a word of explanation.

Japanese history has presented native scholars with great and fundamental institutional changes which have occurred in a relatively short period of time. In part these changes have been in economic institutions. There has been a strong impulse to study the earlier institutions as a basis for the examination of change and in search for the source of change. The economic history of the Tokugawa Period, for example, has been a field of extensive research.

The change in economic institutions has reflected contradictions and difficulties which have attracted scholars. These have been associated with the level of industrialization in relation to raw materials, the place of the internal market in relation to the distribution of income, the relation between agriculture and manufacturing during the process of development, and other matters which need not be enumerated.

The institutional changes have also been political and social. It is easy to understand that the economic factors in general institutional change have called for examination and that the results of this study produced controversy and difference of opinion.

The coverage of this chapter is limited to the history of the general economy of Japan, as a whole and by periods. The history of specific fields, as for example agriculture, is to be found under the appropriate headings. The works of Japanese economists on the economic history of Western countries is entirely omitted, although it must be recognized that Japanese study of this history has exerted a general influence.

The present chapter is divided into the following nine sections: 1. Bibliographies; 2. General Economic History; 3. Ancient Times; 4. The Middle Period; 5. The Tokugawa Period; 6. The Recent Period, since the Meiji Restoration; 7. Colonial Economic Development; 8. The Post-war Economic Situation; 9. Biographies of Leaders in Japanese Economic Development.

The division of Japanese economic history into its several periods or subdivisions presents difficulties to the compiler of a bibliography. For example, many economic historians refer to the Tokugawa Period under Kinsei, a term usually translated as "Modern." Others refer to the Tokugawa Period as feudal with the implication that it is not modern. The solution offered is to present the Tokugawa as a separate period. When in the title of a work this presents difficulties, the original title is given in translation and this followed by the appropriate period as shown in the preceding paragraph. It may be useful to note that Ancient Times end with the Fujiwara Period (about the 12th Century) and that the Middle Period ends with the Toyotomi Period (16th Century).

The scientific study of the economic history of Japan is generally considered to have begun early in this century. In 1900, Fukuda Tokuzō wrote in the German language his work Social and economic development of Japan, one of the earliest economic histories and one which indicates the influence of German thought. This was translated into Japanese under the title, Nihon keizaishiron (On the economic history of Japan) (No. 297). Two years later, Uchida Ginzō, another of the leading figures in the early study of Japanese economic history, published his Nihon keizaishi (Japanese economic history). These two works are pioneer efforts in scientific research in their field.

Important works have followed these early essays. The most remarkable among them is probably Takegoshi Yosaburō's Nihon keizaishi (Japanese economic history) (No. 314) published in 1920. During the same year Takimoto Seiichi published his work with the same title, but with more limited scope. During the late years of the first decade of the century and the early years of the second many writings in this field appeared. Among the active economic historians of these years were: Honjō Eijirō, Ono Takeo, Sano Manabu, Tsuchiya Takeo, and Takahashi Kamekichi.

Emphasis during these years seems to have been put upon the study and analysis of the Tokugawa Period. Takahashi may be named as an exception. Many of the writers dealt with what was called the " pre-capitalistic age, " a term used to refer in a general way to history before the end of the Tokugawa Period. Among the publications were Honjō's Nihon shakaishi (Japanese social history) (No. 298) and his Nihon zaiseishi (History of Japanese public finance) (No. 537), Sano's Nihon shakaishi joron (Introduction to Japanese social history) (No. 313) and his Nihon keizaishi gairon (Outline of Japanese economic history) (No. 312), and Tsuchiya's Hōken shakai hōkai katei no kenkyū (Study of the progression of the collapse in feudal society) (No. 348).

After about the middle of the 1920s studies of the development of Japanese capitalism began to appear. These studies were no doubt stimulated by the succession of financial crises in Japan during the 1920s and they reveal also the increasing influence of a movement related to these economic difficulties to which the term proletarian was attached. Takahashi Kamekichi was a leading figure during the earlier period of the study of Japanese capitalistic development. His analysis of the development of Japanese capitalism may be said to be of a social democratic sort. From his viewpoint Japanese imperialism was essentially different from the imperialism of the advanced countries of the West, for the Western countries depended upon great colonial areas for raw materials and markets for their manufactures while Japan was suffering from population pressure and had to look to her colonies for a solution of the population problem which Takahashi looked upon as the chief cause of the poverty of the Japanese laboring class.

Takahashi's analysis was strongly attacked by those in the Marxist camp; among them, the chief figures were Noro Eitarō and Inomata Tsunao. These attacks were followed by controversy and cleavage among the Marxists. In the earlier stage of this controversy Noro was on one side and Inomata on the other. This controversy is known to the Japanese as Nihon shihon shugi ronsō (Controversy over Japanese capitalism) or Hōken ronsō (Controversy over feudalism). It extended a powerful influence over almost all of the leading Marxist economists of Japan and it has been carried, with some change of focus, into the post-war period. The controversy brought about significant and important contributions to the study of Japanese economic history, although it was limited in its essentials to Marxist theory and the implications of such theory. It stimulated much valuable research in historical materials and theoretical analysis of the true state of the Japanese economy. Aspects of this controversy are referred to elsewhere in this chapter.

The economic historians who were not Marxists were more or less influenced by the controversy among the Marxists but at the same time they continued to work along their own lines. Takahashi published many valuable studies in this field during the 1930s. Honjō of Kyōto Imperial University and his followers, Nakamura Yoshiji, Sugano Kazutarō, Miyamoto Mataji, Kuroha Hyōjirō, and others put their emphasis on the study of the economy of the Tokugawa Period.

1. Bibliographies

286. Honjō Eijirō 本庄榮治郎, Kaihan Nihon keizaishi bunken 改版日本經濟史文献 (Bibliography of Japanese economic history, revised edition), Tōkyō, Nihon Hyōronsha, 1933, 703+195 pp.

287. Honjō Eijirō 本庄榮治郎, Nihon keizaishi shimbunken 日本經濟史新文献 (New bibliography of Japanese economic history), Tōkyō, Nihon Hyōronsha, 1942.

The two volumes cited above are the most extensive annotated bibliographies in the field. No. 286 covers publications to the end of 1931. It includes an earlier bibliography dated 1921, one dated 1927, and other bibliographical works by the author. No. 287 covers publications from 1932 to 1940. Item 286 contains Chapter 1, General view; Chapter 2, Materials: history, local history, history by specific fields, legislation, biography, ancient documents and historical materials, series, collections of articles; Chapter 3, Separate works: general economic history, population and food, rural, urban, and local economic history, mining and extractive industries other than agriculture, agriculture, silk, land system, manufacturing, commerce, foreign trade, organization of enterprises and industrial associations, transportation, money, banking and finance, business groups, prices and wages, statistics, public finance, social organization, social classes and social problems, economic thought, colonial expansion and emigration, Okinawa, Formosa, Sakhalin, and Korea. Appendices: (1) bibliography of the literature of local history, (2) literature written by Westerners, (3) index. Item 287 has a similar table of contents.

288. Horie Yasuzō 堀江保藏, Nihon keizaishi 日本經濟史 (Japanese economic history) (No. 305), appendix, "Sankō bunken 参考文献 (Reference books)."
Short but useful bibliography with brief annotations.

289. Irimajiri Kōshū 入交好脩, Meiji ishinshi kenkyū no hatten---sono kenkyūshi to bunken kaidai 明治維新史研究の發展 その研究史と文獻解題 (Development of the study of the history of the Meiji Restoration: the history of this study and an annotated bibliography), Tōkyō, Dōbunkan, 1951.

290. Itani Zen'ichi 猪谷善一, Meiji Ishin keizaishi 明治維新經濟史 (Economic history of the Meiji Restoration) (No. 355), "Meiji Ishin keizaishi bunken 明治維新經濟史文献 (Catalogue of works on the economic history of the Meiji Restoration."

291. Mochikabukaisha Seiri Iinkai 持株會社整理委員會 (Holding Company Liquidation Committee), Nihon zaibatsu to sono kaitai 日本財閥とその解体 (The Japanese zaibatsu and their liquidation) (No. 1123), v. 2, appendix, "'Nihon zaibatsu to sono kaitai' ni kansuru bunken mokuroku「日本財閥とその解体」に関する文献目錄 (List of titles pertaining to the Japanese zaibatsu and their liquidation)."
An extensive list of the literature reviewed by the committee charged with the post-war liquidation of zaibatsu, not annotated but well classified. The chief headings are: (1) the development of Japanese zaibatsu with such sub-heads as the development of Japanese capitalism and the origin of zaibatsu, (2) the liquidation of zaibatsu with a sub-head on the ordinances, (3) zaibatsu in important industries, with ten sub-heads and biographical materials.

292. Nihon Keizaishi Kenkyūjo 日本經濟史研究所 (Research Institute for Japanese Economic History), Nihon keizaishigaku no shosempai 日本經濟史學の諸先輩 (Earlier writers in the field of Japanese economic history) [=Keizaishi kenkyū, v. 21, no. 1], Tōkyō, Nihon Hyōronsha, 1939.
Deals with the lives and works of the pioneers in the study of Japanese economic history, such as Yokoyama Yoshikiyo, Suganuma Teifū, Yokoi Tokifuyu, Endō Yoshiki, Yoshida Tōgo, Uchida Ginzō, Toda Kaiichi, Fukuda Tokuzō, Miura Shūkō, Takimoto Seiichi.

293. Shakai Keizaishi Gakkai 社會經濟史學會 (Social Economic History Society), Shakai keizaishigaku no hattatsu 社會經濟史學の發達 (Development of the science of social economic history), Tōkyō, Iwanami Shoten, 1941, 2v.

294. Takahashi Kamekichi 高橋亀吉, Saikin no Nihon keizaishi 最近の日本經濟史 (Recent Japanese economic history), Tōkyō, Heibonsha, 1930, appendix, "Saikin Nihon keizaishi sankō shomoku 最近日本經濟史参考書目 (List of reference books on recent Japanese economic history)."

295. Tsuchiya Takao 土屋喬雄, Gendai Nihon keizaishi kōwa 現代日本經濟史講話 (Lectures on contemporary Japanese economic history), Tōkyō, Koishikawa Shobō, 1948 (No. 369), appendix, "Kenkyū no shiori 研究の栞 (Guide to research)."
List of representative works with a brief general introduction.

296. Uchida Ginzō 内田銀藏, ed., Nihon keizaishi sankōsho 日本經濟史参考書 (List of reference works on Japanese economic history), in the appendices to the Kokumin keizai zasshi (No. 178), v. 7, no. 3 - v. 11, no. 6; also in v. 1 of the author's Nihon keizaishi no kenkyū (No. 319).

2. General Economic History

297. Sakanishi Yoshizō 坂西由藏, trans., Fukuda Tōkuzō's 福田徳三 Nihon keizaishiron 日本經濟史論 (On Japanese economic history), Tōkyō, Hōbunkan, 1907.
Practically the first work on the subject. Written in German while the author was a student in Germany.

298. Honjō Eijirō 本庄榮治郎, Nihon shakaishi 日本社會史 (Social history of Japan), Tōkyō, Kaizōsha, 1924, 270 pp.; revised and enlarged, 1937.
The author of this work and of a number of others listed below is well known in Japan and abroad. He was for many years Professor of Economics in Kyōto University. He has many followers and has exerted a wide influence. The earliest of his published works is dated 1924 and the latest 1948. In general he presents a balanced and factual account of Japanese economic history with some emphasis on its social aspects.

299. Honjō Eijirō 本庄榮治郎, Nihon shakai keizaishi 日本社會經濟史 (Social economic history of Japan), Tōkyō, Kaizōsha, 1928.
This work deals with the whole period from what the author calls the Age of the Clans to the end of the Tokugawa Period, but the account of the Tokugawa Period fills more than half of its pages. The chief subjects are political and social organization, economic life, financial affairs, social classes and social problems.

300. Honjō Eijirō 本庄榮治郎, Kaihan Nihon keizaishi 改版日本經濟史 (Revised outline of Japanese economic history), Tōkyō, Nihon Hyōronsha, 1932.
This work shows a somewhat altered emphasis from that of the earlier social history. The subjects dealt with in the twelve chapters include natural resources, population, mining, forestry, agriculture and the land system, industry and commerce, money and banking, and a general chapter on the development of the Japanese economy.

301. Honjō Eijirō 本庄榮治郎, Nihon keizaishi 日本經濟史 (Japanese economic history), Tōkyō, Chijin Shokan, 1940.

302. Honjō Eijirō 本庄榮治郎, Nihon keizaishi sōron 日本經濟史總論 (Summary of Japanese economic history), Tōkyō, Ryūginsha, 1947.

303. Honjō Eijirō 本庄榮治郎, Nihon shakai keizaishi gaisetsu 日本社會經濟史概說 (Outline of Japanese social and economic history), Tōkyō, Nihon Hyōronsha, 1948.

304. Honjō Eijirō 本庄榮治郎 and Kokushō Iwao 黑正巖, Nihon keizaishi 日本經濟史 (Japanese economic history), Tōkyō, Nihon Hyōronsha, 1929.
The introductory chapter deals with the concept of Japanese economic history, the theory of stages, and other matters of methodology.

305. Horie Yasuzō 堀江保藏, Nihon keizaishi 日本經濟史 (History of Japanese economy), Tōkyō, Tōyō Shokan, 1949.
The author is Professor of Economics at Kyōto University. This is a brief but inclusive account of Japanese economic history from the beginning to about 1930. The introduction states that the period since the Restoration is too simply presented and reference is made to the author's Nihon shihonshugi no seiritsu (Formation of Japanese capitalism) (No. 354) for his presentation of the post-Restoration period.

306. Kokushō Iwao 黑正巖, Nihon keizaishi 日本經濟史 (Japanese economic history) [=vols. 1 and 3-6 of the Shin keizaigaku zenshū (New series on economics)], Tōkyō, Nihon Hyōronsha, 1939-40, 5 v.

307. Miura Shūkō 三浦周行, Kokushijō no shakai mondai 國史上の社會問題 (Social problems in the national history), Tōkyō, Taitōkaku, 1920; repr. Tōkyō, Sōgensha, 1938.
Short but well-known early work on social problems which covers the period from ancient times.

308. Miyamoto Mataji 宮本又次, Nihon keizaishi kōwa 日本經濟史講話 (Lectures on Japanese economic history), Tōkyō, Daiyamondosha, 1947.

309. Nakamura Yoshiji 中村吉治, Nihon keizaishi gaisetsu 日本經濟史概說 (Outline of Japanese economic history), Tōkyō, Nihon Hyōronsha, 1949.

310. Nakamura Yoshiji 中村吉治, Nihon shakaishi gaisetsu 日本社會史概說 (Outline of Japanese social history), Tōkyō, Usui Shobō, 1947.

311. "Nihon keizaishi kenkyū 日本經濟史研究 (Studies in Japanese economic history)," Shakai kagaku 社會科學 (Social Science), v. 2, no. 7, 1925.
A collection of articles by a number of well known economic historians such as Honjō Eijirō, Tsuchiya Takao, and Takahashi Kamekichi. It includes an essay by Fukumoto Kazuo who presents a communist viewpoint.

312. Sano Manabu 佐野學, Nihon keizaishi gairon 日本經濟史概論 (Outline of the Japanese economic history), Tōkyō, Taibunsha, 1923.
Emphasis is put on the social organization and labor relations of each period of the economic history of Japan.

313. Sano Manabu 佐野學, Nihon shakaishi joron 日本社會史序論 (Introduction to Japanese social history), Tōkyō, Dōjinsha Shoten, 1922; Tōkyō, Kibōkaku, 1930.
Two divisions of this work are devoted to what the author calls the controlled class and the controlling class. A third division presents studies of the history of social life.

314. Takegoshi Yosaburō 竹越與三郎, Nihon keizaishi 日本經濟史 (Japanese economic history), Tōkyō, Nihon Keizaishi Hensankai, 1920, 8v.; ed. 5, 1934-35, 12 v.
A huge work, some 5,600 pages, by a well known journalist, member of the Diet, and, later, of the Privy Council. Has many features of a general history. Four of its eight chapters are devoted to an account of the Tokugawa Period.

315. Takigawa Masajirō 瀧川政次郎, Nihon shakaishi 日本社會史 (Social history of Japan), Tōkyō, Tōkō Shoin, 1929, 391 pp.; rev. ed., 1935.
This work by a well known legal historian emphasizes the land system, public finance, and other institutional features.

316. Takimoto Seiichi 瀧本誠一, Keizaishi kenkyū 經濟史研究 (Studies in economic history), Tōkyō, Keimeisha, 1930.
A collection of articles dealing with economic history and economic theory.

317. Takimoto Seiichi 瀧本誠一 and Toyoda Jin 豊田仁, trans., Nihon hōsei keizaishi 日本法制經濟史 (Japanese legal and economic history), Tōkyō, Fukuda Shobō, 1935.
Translation of the Dai Nihonshi shokkashi (History of Japanese food and money), compiled by the Mito Clan during the Tokugawa Period, originally written in Chinese. Deals with the economic history of Japan to the Tokugawa Period.

318. Tsuchiya Takao 土屋喬雄, Nihon keizaishi gaiyō 日本經濟史概要 (Outline of Japanese economic history), Tōkyō, Iwanami Shoten, 1934; Zoku Nihon keizaishi gaiyō 續日本經濟史概要 (Outline of Japanese economic history: continued), Tōkyō, Iwanami Shoten, 1939, 369 pp.
The two volumes constitute a valuable and authoritative work on the whole history of the Japanese economy. They were published in the well-known Iwanami series which covers all fields of science. The author is Professor of Economics in Tōkyō University and one of the distinguished scholars in his field. The Meiji Restoration is the dividing point between the two volumes. Three chapters in the second volume deal with the reforms, the transplanting of new institutions and the encouragement of new industries, and the economic situation to 1887. The following three chapters present economic development before and after the Sino-Japanese, the Russo-Japanese, and the first World War. The second volume thus provides a general view of the economic development of modern Japan.

319. Uchida Ginzō 内田銀藏, Nihon keizaishi no kenkyū 日本經濟史の研究 (Study of Japanese economic history), Tōkyō, Dōbunkan, 1924, 2 v.
Collection of essays in this field by the author who was a pioneer. Includes many valuable studies of particular topics.

320. Uchida Ginzō 内田銀藏, Nihon keizaishi gaiyō 日本經濟史概要 (Outline of Japanese economic history), Tōkyō, Sōgensha, 1939.
Formerly included in the same author's Nihon keizaishi no kenkyū (above). One of the classical works in this field.

3. Ancient Times

321. Hosokawa Kiichi 細川亀一, Nihon genshi kyōsantai no kenkyū 日本原始共產体の研究 (Study of primitive communistic bodies in Japan), Tōkyō, Hakuyōsha, 1931.
Deals with: (1) theoretical controversy as to the existence of primitive communistic societies in Japan, (2) social relations in ancient Japan and the Buddhist view of the world, (3) military system of Japanese primitive communistic society, (4) the process of the foundation of Japan as a state.

322. Kokushō Iwao 黒正巖, Nōgyō kyōsansei shiron 農業共產制史論 (On the history of agricultural communistic systems), Tōkyō, Iwanami Shoten, 1925.

323. Nishimura Shinji 西村真次, Nihon kodai keizai (kōkanhen) 日本古代經濟(交換篇) (Japanese economy in ancient times: exchange), Tōkyō, Tōkyōdō, 1933-39, 5 v.
Detailed description of exchange, markets, commerce, money, and foreign trade, from ancient times to the Heian Period.

324. Nomura Kanetarō 野村兼太郎, Nihon keizaishi josetsu (kodai, chūsei) 日本經濟史序說(古代・中世) (Introduction to Japanese economic history: ancient and middle ages), Tōkyō, Yūhikaku, 1948.
The author is a well-known Professor of Economics at Keiō University. The present work is the first volume of a series which, according to his plan, will cover the whole economic history of Japan.

325. Sawada Goichi 澤田吾一, Nara jidai minsei keizai no sūteki kenkyū 奈良時代民政經濟の數的研究 (Statistical study of the economy of the civil administration of the Nara period), Tōkyō, Fuzambō, 1927.
This volume is noted for its richness in facts and data.

326. Takigawa Masajirō 瀧川政治郎, Nihon dorei keizaishi 日本奴隸經濟史 (History of slave economy in Japan), Tōkyō, Tōkō Shoin, 1930.

327. Tōma Seidai 藤間生大, Nihon kodai kokka 日本古代國家 (Ancient Japan), Tōkyō, Itō Shoten, 1946.

328. Tōma Seidai 藤間生大, Seijiteki shakai no seiritsu 政治的社會の成立 (Establishment of political society), Tōkyō, Nihon Hyōronsha, 1949.

329. Tsuda Sōkichi 津田左右吉, Nihon jōdaishi kenkyū 日本上代史研究 (Study of the ancient history of Japan), Tōkyō, Iwanami Shoten, 1930.

330. Tsuda Sōkichi 津田左右吉, Jōdai Nihon no shakai oyobi shisō 上代日本の社會及び思想 (Ancient Japanese society and its thought), Tōkyō, Iwanami Shoten, 1933.

331. Watanabe Yoshimichi 渡辺義通, Kodai shakai no kōzō 古代社會の構造 (Structure of ancient society), Tōkyō, Itō Shoten, 1948.

4. The Middle Period

332. Endō Motoo 遠藤元男, Nihon hōkensei seiritsushi 日本封建制成立史 (History of the formation of feudalism in Japan), Tōkyō, Mikasa Shobō, 1939.

333. Miyamoto Mataji 宮本又次, Nihon hōken shugi no saishuppatsu 日本封建主義の再出發 (Rearrangement of Japanese feudalism), Tōkyō, Ōyashimasha Shoten, 1948.
Deals with the problems of economic institutions in the age of civil war and in the Azuchi-Momoyama Period (late 16th Century). Author is a professor in Kyūshū University.

334. Nakamura Yoshiji 中村吉治, Chūsei shakai no kenkyū 中世社會の研究 (Studies of medieval society), Tōkyō, Kawade Shobō, 1939.
Collection of articles dealing with the social and agricultural problems in the early and late Middle Period.

335. Nakamura Yoshiji 中村吉治, Nihon hōkensei saihenseishi 日本封建制再編成史 (History of reorganization of Japanese feudalism), Tōkyō, Mikasa Shobō, 1939.

336. Nakamura Yoshiji 中村吉治, Buke to shakai 武家と社會 (Warriors and society), Tōkyō, Baifūkan, 1949.

337. Shiba Kentarō 柴謙太郎, Chūsei no keizai 中世の經濟 (Economy in the Middle Ages)[in Iwanami Kōza: Nihon-rekishi (Iwanami studies in Japanese history)], Tōkyō, Iwanami Shoten, 1934.
This work deals with the general features of the economy of the Middle Age.

5. The Tokugawa Period

338. Honjō Eijirō 本庄榮治郎, Keizaishi kenkyū 經濟史研究 (Study of economic history), Tōkyō, Kōbundō, 1920.

A collection of articles important because the author is an authority on the period. The articles deal with the theory of stages, with population, with certain industries, salt, weaving, and with characteristic economic features of Tokugawa times.

339. Honjō Eijirō 本庄榮治郎, Zōtei kaihan keizai shikō 増訂改版經濟史考 (Revised and enlarged edition: Research on economic history), Kyōto, Naigai Shuppan Kabushiki Kaisha, 1925.
An additional collection of essays on the Tokugawa Period, including a number on economic thought. Two of the essays deal with Adam Smith and one is on the economic history of Ōsaka.

340. Honjō Eijirō 本庄榮治郎, Kinsei hōken shakai no kenkyū 近世封建社會の研究 (Study of feudal society in the modern age [Tokugawa period], Tōkyō, Kaizōsha, 1928; rev. and enl. ed., 1930.

341. Honjō Eijirō 本庄榮治郎, Bakumatsu no shinseisaku 幕末の新政策 (New policies in the last days of the Tokugawa shogunate), Tōkyō, Yūhikaku, 1935, 344 pp.; rev. ed., 1940.
The emphasis in this work is upon economic policies during the late Tokugawa Period. The revision in 1940 added three articles relating to the foreign trade of the period.

342. Honjō Eijirō 本庄榮治郎, Tsuchiya Takao 土屋喬雄, Nakamura Naokatsu 中村直勝, and Kokushō Iwao 黒正巖, ed., Kinsei shakai keizai sōsho 近世社會經濟叢書 (Collection of writings on social and economic affairs in the modern period [the Tokugawa period]), Tōkyō, Kaizōsha, 1926-27, 12 v.
Valuable collection of materials relating to social conditions, the economic situation, and economic thought of the period.

343. Kokushō Iwao 黒正巖, Hōken shakai no tōsei to tōsō 封建社會の統制と闘爭 (Control and struggle in feudal society), Tōkyō, Kaizōsha, 1928.
The author is Professor of Economics at Kyōto University and a specialist in economic geography. This is a collection of his articles. One part deals with economic controls in the Tokugawa Period and a second with peasant rebellions.

344. Nihon Keizaishi Kenkyūjo 日本經濟史研究所 (Research Institute for Japanese Economic History), Bakumatsu keizaishi kenkyū 幕末經濟史研究 (Study of the economic history of the last days of the Tokugawa shogunate), Tōkyō, Yūhikaku, 1935.
A collection of articles written by Honjō and other economic historians. Covers economic policies, public finance, taxation, and foreign trade of a number of feudal areas.

345. Nomura Kanetarō 野村兼太郎, Nihon keizaishi (Tokugawa jidai) 日本經濟史（德川時代）(Japanese economic history --- Tokugawa period), Tōkyō, Tōyō Keizai Shimpōsha, 1947.

346. Takahashi Kamekichi 高橋亀吉, Tokugawa hōken keizai no kenkyū 德川封建經濟の研究 (Study of the feudal economy in the Tokugawa period), Tōkyō, Senshinsha, 1932.
Chapters 1 and 2 deal with the general features. Chapter 3 deals with governmental controls of kerosene. Chapter 4 deals with the development of silk reeling. Chapter 5 deals with the development of cotton cultivation and the cotton weaving industry. Chapter 6 deals with the development of cane sugar cultivation and the sugar refining industry.

347. Takimoto Seiichi 瀧本誠一, Nihon keizaishi: Tokugawa hōken seido no keizaiteki setsumei 日本經濟史—德川封建制度の經濟的說明 (Japanese economic history: economic analysis of the Tokugawa feudal system), Tōkyō, Maruzen, 1930, 464+153+36 pp.

Psychological analysis is emphasized. Such subjects are dealt with as the land system, the financial system, industry and trade as well as the peasant rebellions and the economic thought of the period.

348. Tsuchiya Takao 土屋喬雄, Hōken shakai hōkai katei no kenkyū 封建社會崩壞過程の研究 (Study of the progression of collapse in feudal society), Kyōto, Kōbundō, 1927.

Deals with the financial and industrial situation of several selected feudal fiefs in the later Tokugawa Period.

349. Tsuchiya Takao 土屋喬雄, Kinsei Nihon hōken shakai no shiteki kenkyū 近世日本封建社會の史的研究 (Historical study of the Japanese feudalistic society in the modern age [the Tokugawa period]), Tōkyō, Kagakushugi Kōgyōsha, 1949.

350. Tsuchiya Takao 土屋喬雄, Kinsei Nihon keizai hattenshi kōwa 近世日本經濟發展史講話 (Lectures on the development of the Japanese economy in the modern age [the Tokugawa period]), Tōkyō, Shakaishugi Kōgyōsha, 1942.

351. Tsuchiya Takao 土屋喬雄, ed., Hōken shakai no kōzo bunseki 封建社會の構造分析 (Analysis of the structure of feudal society), Tōkyō, Keiso Shobō, 1951.

A recent collection of articles concerned with the feudal structure in the Tokugawa Period. Includes Imai Rintarō, "Establishment of Tokugawa feudal society"; Naramoto Tatsuya, "Feudal society and commercial capital"; Abe Makoto, "Political system"; Harada Tomohiko, "Development of cities"; Yamaguchi Kazuo, "Development of modern production during the Tokugawa period"; Kajinishi Mitsuhaya, "Family industry linked with the putting-out system and manufacture"; Irimajiri Kōshū, "Structure of agriculture under the Tokugawa feudal system"; Tsuchiya Takao, "Differentiation of the peasant class"; Hattori Shisō, "Tokugawa feudalism and absolutism"; Komatsu Yoshitaka, "Establishment of the feudal system in England."

352. Uchida Ginzō 内田銀藏, Kinsei no Nihon 近世の日本 (Japan in modern history), Tōkyō, Fuzambō, 1919.

This work by a pioneer in the study of Japanese economic history deals with the whole Tokugawa Period and includes many references to sources.

6. The Recent Period

a. General Works

353. Honjō Eijirō 本庄榮治郎, ed., Meiji Ishin keizaishi kenkyū 明治維新經濟史研究 (Studies in economic history during the period of the Meiji Restoration), Tōkyō, Kaizōsha, 1930.

Collection of articles by Honjō, Sugano, Yoshikawa, Horie, Kuroha, and Kokushō. With a chronological table of economic history during the period of the Meiji Restoration.

354. Horie Yasuzō 堀江保藏, Nihon shihonshugi no seiritsu 日本資本主義の成立 (Formation of Japanese capitalism), Tōkyō, Daidō Shoin, 1938, 240 pp.; repr., Tōkyō, Yūhikaku, 1948.

Includes three chapters: Outline of the economy during the Tokugawa period; economic significance of the Meiji Restoration; establishment of the capitalist economy.

355. Itani Zen'ichi 猪谷善一, Meiji Ishin keizaishi 明治維新經濟史 (Economic history of the Meiji Restoration), Tōkyō, Kaizōsha, 1928.

Deals with the economic and social situation before and after the Meiji Restoration. With a bibliography of the literature relating to the economic history of this period and a chronological table.

356. Kajinishi Mitsuhaya 楫西光速, Ōshima Kiyoshi 大島清, Katō Toshihiko 加藤俊彦, and Ōuchi Tsutomu 大内力, Nihon ni okeru shihonshugi no hattatsu 日本に於ける資本主義の發達 (The development of capitalism in Japan), Tōkyō, Daigaku Shuppambu, 1951, 2 v.

Economic history covering the whole period from the Meiji Restoration to the present. The introductory chapter deals with the preparatory period for capitalistic development -- from the Meiji Restoration to the Russo-Japanese War. Chapter 2 deals with the development of Japanese capitalism until the Manchurian affair, 1931. Chapter 3 deals with the collapse of the Japanese economy during the war period, and Chapter 4 deals with the post-war reconstruction of the Japanese economy.

357. Keiō Gijuku Keizaishi Gakkai 慶應義塾經濟史學會 (Society of the Economic History of the Keiō Gijuku University), Meiji shoki keizaishi kenkyū 明治初期經濟史研究 (Study of the economic history of the earlier Meiji Period), Tōkyō, Ganshōdō, 1937, 2 v.

Collection of fourteen articles based on research in several specific fields of economic history during the earlier Meiji period, such as agricultural technology, cotton raising, military industries, chemical industry, public finance, establishment of the Bank of Japan, and foreign trade.

358. Minobe Ryōkichi 美濃部亮吉, Nihon no keizai 日本の經濟 (The Japanese economy), Tōkyō, Mainichi Shimbun, 1951.

Originally written in English in preparation for lectures at a university in America. The author explores the influence of the following three characteristics of the Japanese economy: economic backwardness, poor natural resources, and feudal remains.

359. Minobe Ryōkichi 美濃部亮吉 and Naitō Masaru 内藤勝, Nihon keizai zusetsu 1949-nen-han 日本經濟圖說 1949年版 (Japanese economy with graphic illustrations: 1949 edition), Tōkyō, Mainichi Shimbun, 1949.

An explanation of the collapse of the Japanese economy during World War II and of the severe inflation in the post-war period which, according to authors, was the inevitable result of the suppressed inflation during the war. There is great dependence on graphic illustrations.

360. Mitsubishi Keizai Kenkyūsho 三菱經濟研究所 (Mitsubishi Institute for Economic Research), Nihon no sangyō to bōeki no hatten 日本の產業と貿易の發展 (Development of Japanese industry and foreign trade), Tōkyō, Mitsubishi Keizai Kenkyūsho, 1935.

An extensive and valuable reference work on Japanese industry and foreign trade in the first half of the 1930s by one of the representative unofficial research institutions. Contains six sections dealing with the recent development of industry, basic industries, important manufacturing industries, banking insurance, chemical, ceramic and foodstuff industries, and development of foreign trade.

361. Nihon Ginkō Chōsakyoku 日本銀行調查局 (The Research Bureau of the Bank of Japan), Shōwa gonen ikō ni okeru waga kuni jūyō sangyō no sūsei 昭和五年以降に於ける我が國重要產業の趨勢 (Trends of our important industries after 1930), Tōkyō, Nihon Ginkō Chōsakyoku, 1947.

362. Ōkuma Shigenobu 大隈重信, ed., Kaikoku gojūnenshi 開國五十年史 (Fifty years history of Japan after her opening), Tōkyō, Kaikoku Gojūnenshi Hakkōsho, 1907-8, 2 v.

This compilation, undertaken to influence world opinion, appeared in the English language. It includes many articles on economic matters, among them: Imperial Public Finance, by Matsukata Masayoshi; Marine Transportation, by Kondō Rempei; Marine Industry, by Hayashida Tamotsu; Textile Industry, by Kawashima Jimbei; Banking Act, by Shibusawa Eiichi; Foreign Trade, by Masuda Takashi; History of Formosa, by Gotō Shimpei; and Development of Cities, by Ozaki Yukio.

363. Suzuki Ryōichi 鈴木諒一, Nihon keizai no keiryōteki bunseki — kokumin shotoku to koyō no mondai 日本經濟の計量的分析 — 國民所得と雇傭の問題 (Quantitative analysis of Japanese economy: the problem of national income and employment), Tōkyō, Jitsugyō no Nihonsha, 1948.

364. Takahashi Kamekichi 高橋亀吉, Meiji Taishō sangyō hattatsushi 明治大正產業發達史 (Development of industries in the Meiji and Taishō periods), Tōkyō, Kaizōsha, 1929.

History of industrial development from the period of the Meiji Restoration to the late 1920s with emphasis upon the process of the industrial revolution and upon the readjustments associated with it. The appendices include a chronological table and a list of reference works.

365. Takahashi Kamekichi 高橋亀吉, Nihon shihonshugi hattatsushi 日本資本主義發達史 (History of the development of capitalism in Japan), Tōkyō, Nihon Hyōronsha, 1928; rev. and enl. ed., 1939.

Deals with the development of the Japanese economy during the period from the Meiji Restoration to the later part of the 1920s. Contains chapters on collapse of the feudal system at the end of Tokugawa period, capitalistic revolution in the Meiji Restoration, development of the capitalist system in earlier Japan, development of the industrial revolution, maturity of the capitalist system, development of financial capital, the capitalist development of the Japanese economy and the intensified class struggle. Takahashi has published several volumes relating to this field.

In the early 1920s, he was a leading figure in the analysis of Japanese capitalist development after the Meiji Restoration. His view was severely attacked by writers influenced by Marxism such as Noro Eitarō, Sano Manabu, Ōmori Gitarō, and Inomata Tsunao. These attacks were focussed on Takahashi's interpretation of the current stage of Japanese capitalism.

366. Tsuchiya Takao 土屋喬雄, Ishin keizaishi 維新經濟史 (Economic history of the Meiji Restoration), Tōkyō, Chūō Kōronsha, 1942; repr., Tōkyō, Seikatsusha, 1947.

The book is by one of the leading economic historians in Japan and deals with the general view of the pre-Restoration period, economic factors in the Restoration, the main economic reforms during the Restoration period, the transplantation of Western systems, the governmental encouragement of modern industry, foreign trade policy, colonial policy, and the reorganization of the financial system.

367. Tsuchiya Takao 土屋喬雄, Sangyōshi 產業史 (History of industry), Tōkyō, Tōyō Keizai Shimpōsha, 1944.

History of Japanese industry after the Meiji Restoration up to about 1940.

368. Tsuchiya Takao 土屋喬雄, Nihon shakai keizaishi no shomondai 日本社會經濟史の諸問題 (Some problems in Japanese social and economic history), Tōkyō, Nankōsha, 1937; repr., Tōkyō, Heibonsha, 1947.

In the first section, the author deals with general problems under the following headings: the characteristics of Japanese economic history; development of the study of Japanese social economic history after the Meiji period; civil status in the Tokugawa period and the rise of classes.

In the second section, the author deals with specific problems under the following headings: essential features of the warriors of the late Tokugawa period as a class; social-historic significance of the anti-foreign movement in the late Tokugawa period, etc.

369. Tsuchiya Takao 土屋喬雄, Gendai Nihon keizaishi kōwa 現代日本經濟史講話 (Lectures on the economic history of contemporary Japan), Tōkyō, Koishikawa Shobō, 1948.

See also entries 370, 371, 409, 411, 425, 433, 581, 583, 584, 1104, 1109.

b. The Rōnō-Kōza Controversy

A long and important controversy involving economic historians, economists, and social scientists has suggested the manner of presenting the works listed in this section. A word of explanation of this controversy will make the bibliographical material more useful and provide some account of a significant aspect of Japanese thought.

The controversy began in the late 1920s among scholars influenced by Marxian thought who may be divided, broadly speaking, into two groups: the Kōza-ha (the Kōza School) and the Rōnō-ha (the Rōnō School). The Kōza School took its name from a famous publication, Nihon shihonshugi hattatsushi kōza (Lectures on the development of Japanese capitalism), edited by Noro Eitarō, Yamada Moritarō, Ōtsuka Kinnosuke, and Hirano Yoshitarō (See No. 370). The other school was given its name because many articles written by its adherents were published in the periodical Rōnō (Laborers and Farmers).

The controversy concerned a number of crucial points in the Marxian analysis of Japanese economic development. The argument on both sides showed minor changes with the passage of time. It is to be observed also that the arguments of the same school differed according to the person presenting them. These variations make a satisfactory summary difficult. Nevertheless, the main cleavages, the leading figures on both sides, and the chief articles are presented below.

The origin of the controversy was related to the politics and strategy of the Japanese Communist Party of the time. The Kōza School is generally regarded as having been close to the official viewpoint and theory of the Communist Party. In its first stage, the controversy ran in terms of the nature of the Meiji Restoration and its influence on the contemporary economic situation in Japan. These were and are matters important to the Japanese Communist Party for the determination of its strategic doctrines.

Noro Eitarō, the early leader of the Kōza School, represented one side, and Inomata Tsunao, who has been one of the leaders of the Rōnō School throughout the controversy, represented the other. Noro's argument emphasized the feudal power of the landlords over their tenants. This feudal power, it was maintained, was of great influence on the political leadership of Japan during and after the Meiji Restoration. Even at so late a date as the 1920s Noro regarded Japan as under the predominant influence of feudal landlords. It may be seen from this why the term feudal has often been applied to this controversy.

Inomata, on the other hand, took the position that most of the feudal institutions of Japan had lost their force. This was the result of the many institutional reforms which began with the Meiji Restoration and the result also of the industrial development of Japan. He regarded the landlord class as having lost much of the basis of its influence and as having become less powerful politically.

Among the followers of Noro were Terajima Kazuo, Hattori Shisō, Yamada Moritarō, and Hirano Yoshitarō. These men banded themselves together and in 1932 they edited and published the well known Nihon shihonshugi hattatsushi kōza, to which we have already referred. The followers of Inomata included Sakisaka Itsurō and Tsuchiya Takao. In general the Rōnō School is regarded as having been less well organized than the Kōza School.

The important works of the early stage of this controversy were the following:

370. Noro Eitarō 野呂榮太郎, Yamada Moritarō 山田盛田郎, Ōtsuka Kinnosuke 大塚金之助 and Hirano Yoshitarō 平野義太郎, ed., Nihon shihonshugi hattatsushi kōza 日本資本主義發達史講座 (Lectures on the development of capitalism in Japan), Tōkyō, Kaizōsha, 1932, 25 v.
These lectures deal with general as well as early phases of the controversy. The work is in four parts. Part I, on the history of the Meiji Restoration, presents 13 articles by such men as Hani Gorō, Hattori Shisō, and Hirano Yoshitarō. Part II, the development of capitalism, contains 20 articles. Among the writers are Yamada Moritarō, Yamada Katsujirō, Hirano Yoshitarō, and Ōtsuka Kinnosuke. Part III carries the title, the actual state of imperialistic Japan. Part IV consists of three bibliographic works and a commentary on historical materials.

371. Noro Eitarō 野呂榮太郎, Nihon shihonshugi hattatsushi 日本資本主義發達史 (Development of capitalism in Japan), Tōkyō, Tettō Shoin, 1930.
A collection of five articles by the author previously published in periodicals and including lectures delivered during the late twenties. The title of the collection is that of the first title. The second, critique of imperialism, was derived against Takahashi's ideas. The third, historical conditions of Japanese capitalist development, deals with the effect of the Meiji Restoration on class relations upon the peasant and on the development of capitalist production. The fourth article, on the characteristics of landownership in Japan, opposed the doctrines of Inomata Tsunao. The final article, on the contradictions of Japanese capitalism in its present stage, deals with fluctuations and depression.

372. Noro Eitarō 野呂榮太郎, "Shihonshugi-teki gōrika to musan kaikyū 資本主義的合理化と無產階級 (Capitalistic promotion of efficiency and the proletariat)," Shisō (Thoughts), July, 1930.

373. Noro Eitarō 野呂榮太郎, "Nihon shihonshugi gendankai no mujun to kyōkō 日本資本主義現代の矛盾と恐慌 (Contradictions and crisis of Japanese capitalism at its present stage)," Kaizō (Reform), March, 1931.

374. Noro Eitarō 野呂榮太郎, "Botsuraku e no tenkōki ni tatsu rironka 没落への轉向期に立つ理論家 (Theorists at the turning point toward their downfall)," Chūō kōron (Central review), May, 1931.

375. Hattori Shisō 服部之総, Meiji ishinshi 明治維新史 (History of the Meiji Restoration), Tōkyō, Taihōkaku Shobō, 1930.

376. Terajima Kazuo 寺島一夫, "Daisanki sekai kyōkō to sono Nihon ni okeru tokushitsu 第三期世界恐慌とその日本に於ける特質 (The world crisis in its third stage and its characteristic features in Japan)," Puroretaria kagaku (Proletarian science), March, 1931.

377. Terajima Kazuo 寺島一夫, "Nihon shihonshugi gendankairon no kompon mondai 日本資本主義現段階論の根本問題 (Fundamental problems in the controversy over the present stage of Japanese capitalism)," Puroretaria kagaku (Proletarian science), Dec., 1931.

378. Inomata Tsunao 猪俣津南雄, "Gendai Nihon burujowajii no seijiteki chii 現代日本ブルジョアジーの政治的地位 (Political position of the contemporary Japanese bourgeoisie)," Taiyō, Nov., 1927.

379. Inomata Tsunao 猪俣津南雄, Gendai Nihon kenkyū 現代日本研究 (Study of contemporary Japan), Tōkyō, Kaizōsha, 1929.

380. Inomata Tsunao 猪俣津南雄, Botsuraku shihonshugi no daisanki 没落資本主義の第三期 (The third stage of declining capitalism), Tōkyō, Taishūkōronsha, 1930.

See also entries 1103, 1104.

The debates referred to above were related to feudalism and land ownership in Japan and they brought about a close examination of Japanese agriculture and especially those features which were said to be feudal. Much attention was given to the relation between landlord and tenant. High land rents and the payment of land rent in kind were observed. Theories touching land rent were much discussed.

The debate on these agricultural problems goes back to the earlier period of controversy between Noro and Inomata. The most important contribution to this debate was now made by Kushida Tamizō who published an article on the nature of land rental in Japan in 1931. In this and in succeeding articles Kushida made clear his opposition to the viewpoint of Noro and other members of the Kōza School who regarded the existing high rentals as essentially feudal and the labor of the tenant as of the same nature as the forced labor of feudal times. Kushida, on the contrary, argued that rental in kind was actually calculated on the basis of its money value. He saw high rentals as the result of a high demand for and a low supply of land. He rejected the idea of the excessive influence of feudalism in Japanese tenancy after the reform of the land tax early in the Meiji Period. In his view the existing land rental was not a feudal phenomenon but that of a transition from pre-capitalism to capitalism. In support of his argument he maintained that agricultural products had, in considerable part, been brought under the influence of the market, that farm life had been drawn into the money economy, and that tenants' unions had, in some measure, been organized. The main points which Kushida made are still maintained by the Rōnō School. Kushida's views were further developed by Sakisaka, Tsuchiya, and Ōuchi Hyōe.

The Kōza School, represented by Noro and later by Yamada, Hirano, and Yamada Katsujirō, undertook to attack the views of Kushida on theoretical as well as empirical grounds. They marshalled the factual evidence against Kushida's ideas for the purpose of showing that the relation between landlord and tenant had always been dominated by non-economic and feudal forces.

The important literature of this stage of the controversy includes the following:

381. Kushida Tamizō 櫛田民藏, "Waga kuni kosakuryō no tokushitsu ni tsuite 我國小作料の特質に就いて (On the characteristic features of farm rent in Japan)," Ōhara Shakai Mondai Kenkyūjo zasshi (Journal of the Ōhara Research Institute for Social Problems), 8. 1, June, 1931, 63-103.

382. Kushida Tamizō 櫛田民藏, "Kawakami-hakase ni kotau---awasete Noro-shi e 河上博士に答ふ―併せて野呂氏へ (A reply to Dr. Kawakami---and to Mr. Noro)," Chūō kōron (Central review), 46. 11, Nov., 1931, 36-42.

383. Kushida Tamizō 櫛田民藏, "Kosakuryō no jidai hanchū ni tsuite 小作料の地代範疇について (On the category of farm rent)," Ōhara Shakai Mondai Kenkyūjo zasshi (Journal of the Ōhara Research Institute for Social Problems), July, 1933.

384. Kushida Tamizō 櫛田民藏, "Katoki ni okeru gembutsunō jidai no igi 過渡期における現物納地代の意義 (Significance of rent in kind in the transitional period)," Kaizō (Reform), 17. 3, March, 1935, 50-60.

385. Kushida Tamizō 櫛田民藏, "Nihon nōgyō ni okeru shihonshugi no hatten 日本農業における資本主義の發展 (Development of capitalism in Japanese agriculture)," Chūō kōron (Central review), 50. 2, Feb., 1935, 47-59.

386. Kushida Tamizō 櫛田民藏, "Saikinji ni okeru tochi shoyū no ikō 最近時における土地所有の移行 (Changes in landownership in recent times)," Kaizō (Reform), 17. 2, Feb., 1935, 82-107.

387. Kushida Tamizō 櫛田民藏, "Kome seisanhi ni tsuite 米生産費について (On the cost of rice production)," Ōhara Shakai Mondai Kenkyūjo zasshi (Journal of the Ōhara Research Institute for Social Problems), Oct. and Nov., 1934; Jan., 1935.

388. Kushida Tamizō 櫛田民蔵, Nōgyō mondai 農業問題 (Agricultural problems) [=v. 3 of Kushida Tamizō zenshū (Complete works of Kushida Tamizō) (No. 214)], Tōkyō, Kaizōsha, 1935.

389. Ōuchi Hyōe 大内兵衛, "Kushida-shi no nōgyō riron 櫛田氏の農業理論 (Agricultural theory of Mr. Kushida)," Ōhara Shakai Mondai Kenkyūjo zasshi (Journal of the Ōhara Research Institute for Social Problems), Sept., 1935.

390. Tsuchiya Takao 土屋喬雄, "Ishin zengo no Nihon ni okeru chin rōdō 維新前後の日本農業における賃労働 (Hired labor in Japanese agriculture before and after the Meiji Restoration)," Kaizō (Reform), 16. 13, Dec., 1934, 50-70.

391. Inomata Tsunao 猪俣津南雄, "Tochimondai to hōken no isei 土地問題と封建の遺制 (Land problems and remains of feudalism)," Kaizō (Reform), 12. 1, Jan., 1930, 68-80.

392. Inomata Tsunao 猪俣津南雄, Kyūbō no nōson 窮乏の農村 (Poverty in the rural areas), Tōkyō, Kaizōsha, 1934.

393. Noro Eitarō 野呂榮太郎, "Kushida-shi jidairon no handōsei 櫛田氏地代論の反動性 (Reactionary nature of Mr. Kushida's theory of land rent)," Chūō kōron (Central review), Oct., 1931.

394. Yamada Moritarō 山田盛太郎, "Meiji ishin ni okeru nōgyōjō no shohenkaku 明治維新に於ける農業上の諸変革 (Agricultural reforms in the Meiji Restoration)," in Nihon shihonshugi hattatsushi kōza (No. 370), 1933, v. 7, 28 pp.

395. Yamada Katsujirō 山田盛次郎, "Nōgyō ni okeru shihonshugi no hattatsu 農業における資本主義の發達 (Development of capitalism in agriculture)," in Nihon shihonshugi hattatsushi kōza (No. 370), 1933, v. 7, 58 pp.

In the general field of tenancy another debate has been concerned with the nature of the shin-jinushi (new landlords) of the Tokugawa Period. The new landlords were those who acquired forfeited land or newly exploited land. Tsuchiya interpreted these new landlords to be the forerunners of what he called the capitalistic management of agriculture. This was opposed by members of the Kōza School such as Hattori and Kobayashi Yoshimasa. These men found the new landlords to occupy a position almost the same as that of the feudal lords.

The important writings on this aspect of the controversy are the following, the last two being by independent critics:

396. Tsuchiya Takao 土屋喬雄, Kinsei Nihon nōson keizaishiron 近世日本農村經濟史論 (On the agricultural economy in modern Japan), Tōkyō, Kaizōsha, 1933.
Written in cooperation with One Michio.

397. Tsuchiya Takao 土屋喬雄, Nihon shihonshugi ronshū 日本資本主義論集 (Collection of articles on Japanese capitalism), Tōkyō, Ikuseisha, 1937, 370 pp.; repr., Tōkyō, Kōdosha, 1947.

398. Hattori Shisō 服部之總, "Ishinshi hōhōronjō no shomondai 維新史方法論上の諸問題 (Various problems in the methodology of study of Restoration history)," Rekishi kagaku (History science), Sept., 1933.

See also entries 403, 418, 419.

Another feature of the controversy was initiated by Hattori's work Meiji no kakumei to hankakumei (Revolution and anti-revolution in the Meiji period), one of the volumes of Nihon shihonshugi hattatsushi kōza (No. 370). He asked why Japan and China had followed different paths in development after their opening to the world, the former being an independent country and the latter a semi-colonial country. For his answer he looked into the development of Japanese manufacture during late Tokugawa times and reached the conclusion that the Japanese economy had already attained the stage, in Marxian terminology, of manufacture in the strict sense. The conventional interpretation, to which he himself had adhered in the past, was that handicraft and rural domestic industry were predominant in late Tokugawa Japan. By means of his new interpretation Hattori undertook to explain the opening of Japan to the world not only as a result of the expansion of Western capitalism but also as a result of the inherent pressure of the relatively developed stage of Japanese manufacture which had come to require markets abroad. The difference in the development of China from that of Japan was thus to be explained not so much by a balance of power among Western countries which happened to work in Japan's favor but rather by the absence of this stage of manufacture in China and its presence in Tokugawa Japan.

Tsuchiya raised doubts as to the acceptability of Hattori's point of view in his article Tokugawa jidai no manyufakucha (Manufacture in the Tokugawa period) which appeared in Kaizō in September, 1933. Tsuchiya took the position that there was a lack of satisfactory evidence to support Hattori's conclusions.

399. Tsuchiya Takao 土屋喬雄, "Tokugawa jidai no manyufakucha 徳川時代のマニュファクチュア (Manufacturing in the Tokugawa period)," Kaizō (Reform), 15. 9, Sept., 1933, 2-21.

400. Tsuchiya Takao 土屋喬雄, "Ishinshi kenkyū no chūshin ronten--- bakumatsu manyu no shomondai 維新史研究の中心論点一幕末マニュの諸問題 (Central point in the study of the history of the Restoration: problems of manufacturing in the late Tokugawa period)," Kaizō (Reform), 16. 1, Jan., 1934, 195-207.

401. Tsuchiya Takao 土屋喬雄, "Nihon manyufakucha zusetsu 日本マニュファクチュア圖說 (Illustrations of Japanese manufacturing)," Rekishigaku kenkyū (Study of history), Feb., 1934, 195-207.

402. Tsuchiya Takao 土屋喬雄, "Tokugawa jidai no orimonogyō ni okeru toiyasei kanai kōgyō 徳川時代の織物業における問屋制家内工業 (Home industry and the putting-out system in the Tokugawa textile industry)," Keizai (Economics), July-Aug., 1934.

See also entry 397.

403. Hattori Shisō 服部之総, "Meiji no kakumei to hankakumei 明治の革命と反革命 (Revolution and anti-revolution in the Meiji period)," in Nihon shihonshugi hattatsushi kōza (No. 370), 1933, v. 5, 59 pp.

404. Hattori Shisō 服部之総, "Hōhō oyobi zairyō no mondai 方法及び材料の問題 (Problems of methods and materials)," Rekishi kagaku (History science), 2. 8, Oct., 1933, 2-23.

405. Hattori Shisō 服部之総, "Gen-manyu jidai no rekishiteki jōken 厳マニユ時代の歴史的條件 (Historical conditions of the period of manufacturing in the strict sense)," Rekishi kagaku (History science), Mar. and April, 1934.

406. Hattori Shisō 服部之総, "Bakumatsu Akita-han no momen shijō oyobi momen kigyō 幕末秋田藩の木棉市場及木棉機業 (Cotton market and the cotton yarn industry of the Akita clan in the late Tokugawa period)," Rekishi kagaku (History science), 4. 3, Mar., 1935, 39-74; 4. 5, May, 1935, 133-147; 4. 8, July, 1935, 120-159.

407. Hattori Shisō 服部之総, Ishinshi no hōhōron 維新史の方法論 (Methodology of the study of the history of the Restoration), Tōkyō, Hakuyōsha, 1934.

408. Hirano Yoshitarō 平野義太郎, "Jiyū minken 自由民權 (Liberty and people's rights)," Kaizō (Reform), 15. 12, Dec., 1933, 2-22.

See also entries 398, 846, 847, 866.

In 1934 Yamada Moritarō published his famous work Nihon shihonshugi no bunseki (Analysis of Japanese capitalism) which is often called the Bible of his followers. This volume contained, in rearranged and supplemented form, his writings which had appeared in the Nihon shihonshugi hattatsushi kōza (No. 370).

At about the same time Hirano Yoshitarō published his Nihon shihonshugi shakai no kikō (Structure of Japanese capitalist society) (No. 411). This work was along the same lines as that of Yamada.

These two works dealt with all phases of the debates which have been referred to above. They undertook to explain the whole process of Japanese economic development in accordance with their own theories. Since they constitute the most systematic and comprehensive representation of the point of view they may well be called the crystalization of the ideology of the Kōza School. After their publication debates tended to run in terms of attack upon and defense of these books either in general or in particular features.

409. Yamada Moritarō 山田盛太郎, Nihon shihonshugi bunseki 日本資本主義分析 (Analysis of Japanese capitalism), Tōkyō, Iwanami Shoten, 1934.

410. Yamada Katsujirō 山田勝次郎, Kome to mayu no keizai kōzō 米と繭の經濟構造 (Economic structure of rice and cocoon production), Tōkyō, Iwanami Shoten, 1942.

411. Hirano Yoshitarō 平野義太郎, Nihon shihonshugi shakai no kikō 日本資本主義社會の機構 (Structure of Japanese capitalist society), Tōkyō, Iwanami Shoten, 1934.

412. Hirano Yoshitarō 平野義太郎, "Nihon ni okeru teichingin 日本における低賃金 (Low wages in Japan)," Chūō kōron (Central review), Sept., 1934.

413. Hirano Yoshitarō 平野義太郎, "Nihon no fukugyō: kanai kōgyō 農家の副業・家内工業 (Subsidiary work: home industry of farmers)," Keizai hyōron (Economic review), Oct., 1934.

414. Hirano Yoshitarō 平野義太郎, "Nihon shihonshugi no tokushitsu 日本資本主義の特質 (Characteristic features of Japanese capitalism)," Chūō kōron (Central review), 50. 10, Oct., 1935, 1-44.

415. Hirano Yoshitarō 平野義太郎, "Han-hōken jidai ron 半封建地代論 (On the semi-feudal land rental)," Kaizō (Reform), 17. 12, Dec., 1935, 2-19.

416. Hirano Yoshitarō 平野義太郎, "Kokunai shijō no kyōaisei 國内市場の狭隘性 (Narrowness of the national market)," Chūō kōron (Central review), Apr., 1936.

417. Hirano Yoshitarō 平野義太郎, "Ajiyateki nōgyō shakai to Nihon no nōgyō アジヤ的農業社會と日本の農業 (Asiatic agricultural society and Japanese agriculture)," Shisō (Thoughts), June, 1936.

418. Kimura Sōnosuke 木村莊之助, Nihon kosaku-seido-ron (jōkan) 日本小作制度論—上巻 (On the Japanese tenant system---volume one), Tōkyō, Sōbunkaku, 1936.

419. Toda Shintarō 戸田慎太郎, Nihon nōgyōron 日本農業論 (On the agriculture of Japan), Tōkyō, Sōbunkaku, 1936.

See also entries 723, 729, 853, 1157.

420. Sakisaka Itsurō 向坂逸郎, *Nihon shihonshugi no shomondai* 日本資本主義の諸問題 (Problems of Japanese capitalism), Tōkyō, Ikuseisha, 1937; Tōkyō, Kōdosha, 1947.

421. Sakisaka Itsurō 向坂逸郎, "Nihon ni okeru hōken seiryoku no mondai 日本における封建勢力の問題 (Problems of feudal power in Japan)," *Senku* (Pioneer), Oct., 1935.

422. Sakisaka Itsurō 向坂逸郎, "'Nihon shihonshugi bunseki' ni okeru hōhōron"日本資本主義分析"における方法論 (Methodology used in 'Analysis of Japanese capitalism')," *Kaizō* (Reform), 17. 10, Oct., 1935, 65-82.

423. Sakisaka Itsurō 向坂逸郎, "Nōson ni okeru kaikyū bunka no katei 農村における階級分化の過程 (Process of class differentiation in agricultural society)," *Chūō kōron* (Central review), 50. 11, Nov., 1936, 44-60.

424. Tsuchiya Takao 土屋喬雄, "Yamada-shi 'bunseki' ni okeru fueki-rōdō-ron hihan 山田氏「分析」における賦役勞動論批判 (Critique on the theory of forced labor in Mr. Yamada's 'Analysis')," *Kaizō* (Reform), Jan., 1936.

425. Tsuchiya Takao 土屋喬雄, *Nihon shihonshugi hattatsushi gaisetsu* 日本資本主義發達史概説 (Outline of the development of Japanese capitalism), Tōkyō, Yūhikaku, 1937; 1947.

426. Inomata Tsunao 猪俣津南雄, "Hōken isei ronsō ni yosete 封建遺制論争によせて (To the controversy over remains of feudalism)," *Chūō kōron* (Central review), 51. 10, Oct., 1936, 106-125.

427. Inomata Tsunao 猪俣津南雄, *Nihon ni okeru nōgyō kyōkō to sangyō kumiai* 日本に於ける農業恐慌と産業組合 (Agricultural crises and industrial cooperatives in Japan), Tōkyō, Gakugeisha, 1935.

See also entries 318, 354, 366, 718.

The controversy was suspended by the arrest of the leading members of the Kōza School in 1936 and those of the Rōnō School in 1937. When it was revived after World War II the political, economic and social circumstances were quite different from those of the earlier debates. It is hardly surprising to find that the controversy took on new features, among them an emphasis on the political aspects. The importance of its political implications may be regarded as a revival of an original feature of the controversy.

The recent literature of the Kōza School include:

428. Hattori Shisō 服部之総, *Meiji no kakumei* 明治の革命 (Revolution in the Meiji period), Tōkyō, Nihon Hyōronsha, 1951.

429. Inoue Harumaru 井上晴丸 and Usami Seijirō 宇佐美誠次郎, *Kiki ni okeru Nihon shihonshugi no kōzō* 危機における日本資本主義の構造 (Structure of Japanese capitalism in its critical stage), Tōkyō, Iwanami Shoten, 1951.

430. Hirano Yoshitarō 平野義太郎, *Nihon shihonshugi no kōzō* 日本資本主義の構造 (Structure of Japanese capitalism), Tōkyō, Nihon Hyōronsha, 1949.

431. Kamiyama Shigeo 神山茂夫, *Nihon shihonshugi bunseki no kihon mondai* 日本資本主義分析の基本問題 (Basic problems in the analysis of Japanese capitalism), Tōkyō, Iwasaki Shoten, 1947.

432. Toda Shintarō 戸田慎太郎, *Tennōsei no keizaiteki kiso bunseki* 天皇制の經濟的基礎分析 (Analysis of the economic basis of the Tennō system), Tōkyō, San'ichi Shobō, 1947.

433. Toyoda Shirō 豊田四郎, *Nihon shihonshugi hattatsushi* 日本資本主義發達史 (Development of capitalism in Japan), Tōkyō, Rōdō Bunkasha, 1949.

See also entries 248, 720, 740, 854.

The post-war writings of those who are generally regarded as of the Rōnō School are presented below:

434. Ikumi Takuichi 井汲卓一, *Nihon shihonshugi-ron* 日本資本主義論 (On Japanese capitalism), Tōkyō, Kureha Shoten, 1947.

435. Ōuchi Hyōe 大内兵衛, Sakisaka Itsurō 向坂逸郎, Tsuchiya Takao 土屋喬雄, and Takahashi Masao 高橋正雄, *Nihon shihonshugi no kenkyū* 日本資本主義の研究 (Study of Japanese capitalism), Tōkyō, Rōdōsha, 1948, 2 v.

See also entries 369, 737.

The following three works present the general history of this controversy. The first two are by pro-Kōza writers and the last by a pro-Rōnō writer.

436. Uchida Jōkichi 内田穰吉, *Nihon shihonshugi ronsō* 日本資本主義論争 (Controversy on Japanese capitalism), Tōkyō, Seiwa Shoten, 1937; Tōkyō, Shinkō Shuppansha, 1949, 2 v.

437. Shakai Keizai Rōdō Kenkyūsho 社會經濟勞動研究所 (Research Institute for Social Economics and Labor), Nihon shihonshugi ronsōshi 日本資本主義論爭史 (History of the controversy over Japanese capitalism), Tōkyō, Itō Shoten, 1947.

438. Tsushima Tadayuki 對島忠行, Nihon shihonshugi ronsōshi-ron 日本資本主義論爭史論 (On the history of the controversy over Japanese capitalism), Tōkyō, Kōdosha, 1948.

7. Colonial Economy

a. Formosa

439. Taiwan Ginkō 台灣銀行 (The Bank of Taiwan), Taiwan Ginkō yonjūnenshi 台灣銀行四十年誌 (Forty years' history of the Bank of Taiwan), Tōkyō, Taiwan Ginkō, 1939.
History of the semi-governmental financial institution during the Japanese administration.

440. Taiwan Seitō Kabushiki Kaisha 台灣製糖株式會社 (Taiwan Sugar Refining Company), Taiwan seitō kabushiki kaisha shi 台灣製糖株式會社史 (History of the Taiwan Sugar Refining Company), Taiwan Seitō Kabushiki Kaisha, 1939, 347+111 pp.
History of the largest corporation in the field of sugar refining in Formosa, which was related to the Mitsui zaibatsu. Contains a chronological table.

441. Taiwan Sōtokufu 台灣総督府 (Government-General of Taiwan), Taiwan keizai jijō 台灣經濟事情 (Economic situation of Formosa), Taiwan Sōtokufu, 1934.

442. Taiwan Sōtokufu 台灣総督府 (Government-General of Taiwan), Taiwan tōchi gaiyō 台灣統治概要 (Outline of the government of Formosa), Taiwan Sōtokufu, 1945.

443. Yanaibara Takao 矢内原忠雄, Teikokushugika no Taiwan 帝國主義下の台灣 (Formosa under imperialism), Tōkyō, Iwanami Shoten, 1929.
The author is professor of economics in Tōkyō University. He is a well-known expert on colonial policies and population problems.

b. Korea

444. Chōsen Ginkō 朝鮮銀行 (The Bank of Chōsen), Chōsen Ginkō nijūnenshi 朝鮮銀行二十年史 (Twenty years' history of the Bank of Chōsen), Chōsen Ginkō, 1934.
History of a semi-governmental financial institution during the Japanese administration. Contains a chapter on economic development in Korea and Manchuria, with a chronological table and a list of ordinances.

445. Chōsen Shigakkai 朝鮮史學會 (The Society for Korean History), Chōsenshi kōwa 朝鮮史講話 (Lectures on Korean history), Keijō, Chōsen Kenkyūkai, 1923-24, 3 v.

446. Chōsen Shokusan Ginkō 朝鮮殖產銀行 (Industrial Bank of Chōsen), Chōsen no kome 朝鮮の米 (Rice in Korea), Keijō, Chōsen Shokusan Ginkō, 1928.

447. Chōsen Shokusan Ginkō 朝鮮殖產銀行 (Industrial Bank of Chōsen), Chōsen no menka 朝鮮の棉花 (Raw cotton in Korea), Keijō, Chōsen Shokusan Ginkō, 1929.

448. Chōsen Sōtokufu 朝鮮総督府 (Government-General of Chōsen), Chōsen no shijō keizai 朝鮮の市場經濟 (The market economy of Korea), Keijō, Chōsen Sōtokufu, 1929.

449. Chōsen Sōtokufu 朝鮮総督府 (Government-General of Chōsen), Chōsen no jinkō genshō 朝鮮の人口現象 (Population phenomena in Korea), Keijō, Chōsen Sōtokufu, 1927.

450. Chōsen Sōtokufu 朝鮮総督府 (Government-General of Chōsen), Chōsen sembaishi 朝鮮專賣史 (History of monopolies in Korea), 1936, 3 v.
A history of fiscal monopolies in Korea including tobacco, ginseng, salt, and opium.

451. Chōsen Sōtokufu 朝鮮総督府 (Government-General of Chōsen), Chōsen no keizai jijō 朝鮮經濟事情 (Economic situation of Korea), Keijō, Chōsen Sōtokufu, 1937.

452. Chōsen Sōtokufu 朝鮮総督府 (Government-General of Chōsen), Chōsen sōran 朝鮮総覧 (General survey of Korea), Keijō, Chōsen Zasshisha, 1933.

453. Chōsen Sōtokufu 朝鮮総督府 (Government-General of Chōsen), Shisei sanjūnenshi 施政三十年史 (Thirty years' history of the administration of Korea), Keijō, Chōsen Sōtokufu, 1940, 932+66 pp.

454. Chōsen Tetsudōshi Hensan Iinkai 朝鮮鐵道史編纂委員會 (Commission for the Compilation of Korean Railway History), Chōsen tetsudōshi (daiikkan) 朝鮮鐵道史(第一巻) (History of railways in Korea, volume one), Keijō, Chōsen Sōtokufu Tetsudōkyoku, 1937.

455. Haku Nan'un 白南雲, Chōsen shakai keizaishi 朝鮮社會經濟史 (Social economic history of Korea), Tōkyō, Kaizōsha, 1933.
An introduction to methodology in the study of Korean economic history is followed by chapters on primitive and early times.

456. Haku Nan'un 白南雲, Chōsen hōken shakai keizaishi, jōkan 朝鮮封建社會經濟史・上巻 (Social economic history of feudal Korea, volume one), Tōkyō, Kaizōsha, 1937.
Deals with the development of Korea from the slavery system in Shiragi 新羅 to the Rhee 李 Dynasty through the feudal society of Kōrai 高麗 and compares its characteristics with those of Japan and European countries.

457. Honda Hideo 本田秀夫, ed., Chōsen shokusan ginkō nijūnenshi 朝鮮殖産銀行二十年志 (Twenty years' history of the Industrial Bank of Korea), Tōkyō, Chōsen Shokusan Ginkō, 1933, 292+115 pp.
Traces the history of the development of the bank from its establishment to 1937.

458. Itani Zen'ichi 猪谷善一, Chōsen keizaishi 朝鮮經濟史 (Economic history of Korea), Tōkyō, Taitōkaku, 1928.
Collection of the author's articles relating to the Korean economy before and after her annexation to Japan. Includes a bibliography of literature relating to Korean economic history.

459. Keijō Teikoku Daigaku Hōbungakubu 京城帝國大學法文學部 (College of Law and Literature of Keijō Imperial University), Chōsen shakai keizaishi kenkyū 朝鮮社會經濟史研究 (Studies in social economic history of Korea), Tōkyō, Kaizōsha, 1933.
Among the articles in this collection of essays by members of the faculty are: "The process of the establishment of modern capitalism in Korea," by Yomo Hiroshi; "Rural conditions toward the end of the Rhee Dynasty," by Ōuchi Takeji; "Essay in traditional agricultural society in Korea," by Moritani Katsumi.

460. Keijō Teikoku Daigaku Hōbungakubu 京城帝國大學法文學部 (College of Law and Literature of Keijō Imperial University), Chōsen keizai no kenkyū 朝鮮經濟の研究 (Study of the economy of Korea), Tōkyō, Tōkō Shoin, 1929.
A collection of articles on this subject including: "The Korean economy through the market," by Yomo Hiroshi; "The tenancy problem in Korea," by Tsugaki Kuranosuke; "The problem of Korean labor," by Yamada Fumio; "Public finance in Korea toward the end of the Rhee Dynasty," by Suzuki Takeo.

461. Takahashi Kamekichi 高橋亀吉, Gendai Chōsen keizairon 現代朝鮮經濟論 (On the contemporary economy of Korea), Tōkyō, Chikura Shobō, 1935.

See also entry 1116.

c. Sakhalin

462. Karafutochō 樺太廳 (Board of Karafuto), Karafuto shokumin no enkaku 樺太殖民の沿革 (Colonial development of Sakhalin), Toyohara, Karafutochō, 1929.
Outline of immigration into Sakhalin before and after its possession by Japan.

463. Karafutochō 樺太廳 (Board of Karafuto), Karafuto enkakushi 樺太沿革史 (Development of Sakhalin), Toyohara, Karafutochō, 1924.

464. Karafutochō 樺太廳 (Board of Karafuto), Karafuto no seisan 樺太の生産 (Production in Sakhalin), Toyohara, Karafutochō, 1934.

d. Others

465. Dairen Shōkō Kaigisho 大連商工會議所 (Chamber of Commerce of Dairen), Dairen keizai nenshi senkyūhyakusanjūichinen 大連經濟年史一九三一年 (Annual economic history of Dairen, 1931), Dairen, Dairen Shōkō Kaigisho, 1931.

466. Yanaibara Tadao 矢内原忠雄, Nan'yō guntō no kenkyū 南洋群島の研究 (Study of the South Sea Islands), Tōkyō, Iwanami Shoten, 1935.

See also entry 1118.

8. The Post-War Economic Situation

An extensive literature has appeared since the end of the war in 1945 which is concerned with the economic situation, with reconstruction and stabilization, and with speculation as to the future. The attempt has been made to select representative works which deal with the general problems of the Japanese economy. Works dealing with special fields are to be found under appropriate headings.

467. Asahi Shimbunsha 朝日新聞社 (Asahi Newspaper), Kiki ni aegu Nihon keizai 危機にあえぐ日本經濟 (Japanese economy in a crisis), Ōsaka, Asahi Shimbunsha, 1948.
The 1947 edition of Asahi keizai nenshi (Asahi economic yearbook).

468. Hoashi Kei 帆足計, Nihon sangyō fukkō e no michi 日本産業復興への道 (Path to the reconstruction of Japanese industry), Tōkyō, Shinshō Shuppansha, 1947.
The author was the secretary-general of the Japanese Council of Industrial Associations.

469. Inaba Shūzō 稲葉秀三, Nihon keizai no genjitsu 日本經濟の現實 (Realities of the Japanese economy), Tōkyō, Jiji Tsūshinsha, 1949.
The author was at the time an official of the Economic Stabilization Board and was influential in planning for stabilization and reconstruction.

470. Itagaki Shoten 板垣書店, Keizai hakusho 經濟白書 (The economic white paper), Tōkyō, Itagaki Shoten, 2 v.
A collection of economic reports by agencies of the Japanese government. The 1949 edition contains three reports on the economy in general by the Keizai Antei Hombu (Economic Stabilization Board), a paper on labor by the Rōdōshō (Ministry of Labor), one on local finance by the Chihō Zaisei Iinkai 地方財政委員會 (Local Finance Commission), one on railways by the Un'yushō and a report on war damage by the Keizai Antei Hombu. The 1950 edition contains a report on the economy in general by the Keizai Antei Hombu, one on construction by the Kensetsushō 建設省 (Ministry of Construction) and one on foreign trade by the Tsūshō Sangyōshō (Ministry of International Trade and Industry).

471. Jiji Tsūshinsha 時事通信社 (Jiji Press), Waga kuni sangyō no gensei 我國產業の現勢 (Current situation of our industry), Tōkyō, Jiji Tsūshinsha, 1948.

472. Kawasaki Misaburō 川崎巳三郎, Sengo keizai no kihon mondai 戰後經濟の基本問題 (Fundamental problems of post-war economy), Tōkyō, Kaizōsha, 1948.
A collection of articles on the problem of post-war inflation from the Marxist viewpoint. Chapter one contains two articles on the theoretical approach. Chapter two deals, in three articles, with the relation between wages and prices. Chapter three deals with the economic crisis and two chapters deal with political problems. The author was at the time a lecturer in Hitotsubashi University and a member of the Japanese Communist Party.

473. Keizai Antei Hombu 經濟安定本部 (Economic Stabilization Board), Tenkanki Nihon keizai no jittai 轉換期日本經濟の實態 (Actual situation of the Japanese economy in a transitional period), Tōkyō, Taiheisha, 1949.

474. Mochikabukaisha Seiri Iinkai 持株會社整理委員會 (Holding Companies Liquidation Committee), Sengo keizai no saihensei 戰後經濟の再編成 (Re-organization of post-war economy), Tōkyō, Jiyū Shobō, 1949.
A collection of articles written by distinguished economists and other social scientists on the democratization of the economy of Japan: "General introduction," by Suzuki Takeo; "Liquidation of zaibatsu," by Minobe Ryōkichi; "Democratization of public enterprises," by Rōyama Masamichi; "Democratization of agriculture," by Kondō Yasuo; "Labor relations," by Nakayama Ichirō; "Enlightening of laborers," by Ōkōchi Kazuo.

475. Nakayama Ichirō 中山伊知郎, Keizai saiken no kadai 經濟再建の課題 (Requirements for economic reconstruction), Tōkyō, Kamakura Bunko, 1948.
Contains thirteen articles relating to the Japanese post-war economic conditions and the theoretical and practical problems of reconstruction.
The author, the president of Hitotsubashi University, is a leading economist in contemporary Japan and also one of the commissioners of the Chūō Rōdō Iinkai (Central Committee on Labor Relations).

476. Nakayama Ichirō 中山伊知郎, Sengo keizai no tembō 戰後經濟の展望 (Perspectives of the post-war economy), Tōkyō, Hakujitsu Shoin, 1947.

477. Ōkita Saburō 大來佐武郎, Nihon no keizai suijun 日本の經濟水準 (Standard of the Japanese economy), Tōkyō, Tōzai Shuppansha, 1948.
The author was the chief of the Keizai Antei Hombu Chōsaka (Research Section of the Economic Stabilization Board) and the editor of the white papers on the economy of Japan.

478. Ōkita Saburō 大來佐武郎, Senkyūhyakugojūnen Nihon keizai no bunseki to tembō 1950年日本經濟の分析と展望 (Analysis and perspectives of the Japanese economy in 1950), Tōkyō, Jitsugyō no Nihonsha, 1950.

479. Ōkōchi Kazuo 大河内一男, ed., Sengo shakai no jittai bunseki 戰後社會の實態分析 (Analysis of the post-war social situation), Tōkyō, Nihon Hyōronsha, 1950.
The editor is a professor of Tōkyō University, a distinguished specialist in labor relations and social policy.

480. Ōkōchi Kazuo 大河内一男, Shinjō Hiroshi 新庄博, Toyozaki Minoru 豊崎稔, and Katayama Kenji 片山謙二, Keizai saiken no shomondai 經濟再建の諸問題 (Problems in economic reconstruction), Ōsaka, Hakugei Shobō, 1947.

481. Ōsaka Shōka Daigaku Keizai Kenkyūjo 大阪商科大學經濟研究所 (The Institute for Economic Research of the Ōsaka Commercial College), Sengo Nihon keizai no shomondai 戰後日本經濟の諸問題 (Problems in the post-war economy of Japan), Ōsaka, Murakami Kōeidō, 1948.

482. Shimamoto Tōru 島本融, Nihon keizai no saiken 日本經濟の再建 (Reconstruction of the Japanese economy), Tōkyō, Yūhikaku, 1948.
The author was a responsible official of the Bukkachō 物價廳 (Price Board) during the post-war inflationary period.

483. Suzuki Takeo 鈴木武雄, Atarashii keizai no taidō 新しい經濟の胎動 (Quickening of the new economy), Tōkyō, Dōyūsha, 1948.
The author is a professor at Tōkyō University.

484. Tōkyō Daigaku Keizai Gakubu 東京大學經濟學部 (College of Economics of Tōkyō University), ed., Sengo Nihon keizai no shomondai 戰後日本經濟の諸問題 (Problems in the post-war economy of Japan), Tōkyō, Yūhikaku, 1949.
Collection of articles which deal with the various fields of Japanese economy. Written by faculty members of the College of Economics of Tōkyō University such as: Ōuchi Hyōe, Arisawa Hiromi, Yamada Moritarō.

485. Tsuchiya Kiyoshi 土屋清, Nihon sengo keizai ron 日本戰後經濟論 (On the post-war economy of Japan), Tōkyō, Masu Shobō, 1948.
The author is a well-known editorial writer of the Asahi, which is generally considered as one of the best newspapers in Japan.

486. Tsuru Shigeto 都留重人, Antei to jiritsu no tame ni 安定と自立のために (For stabilization and independence), Tōkyō, Reimei Shobō, 1949.
The author was vice-president of the Keizai Antei Hombu (Economic Stabilization Board) and is now professor of economics at Hitotsubashi University. This is a colletion of his articles dealing with the possibility of stabilizing the Japanese economy and increasing production under conditions of independence. The author reaches the conclusion that a system of planned economy is required.

9. Biographical Studies

a. Business leaders since the Meiji Restoration

487. Godai Ryūsaku 五代龍作, Godai Tomoatsu den 五代友厚傳 (Biography of Godai Tomoatsu), privately pr., 1933.
Godai Tomoatsu (1835-1885) was a leading business man in the early Meiji Period who contributed greatly to the development of the Japanese economy, especially of Ōsaka.
A biographical work based on letters from and to Godai. Included are 13 chapters, providing a source of important information on both political and economic affairs from the end of the Tokugawa to the early Meiji Period.

488. Hirose Saihei 廣瀬宰平, Hansei monogatari 半世物語 (The story of half my life), pr. by the family, 1895, 2 v.
Hirose Saihei was a most important figure in the development of Sumitomo zaibatsu. He maintained and expanded the Besshi Kōzan 別子鑛山 (Besshi Mineral Industry) before and after the Meiji Restoration era. This book, written by Hirose himself, can be considered a part of the history of the Sumitomos.

489. Okada Sumio 岡田純夫, ed., Shibusawa-ō wa kataru 澁沢翁は語る (Viscount Shibusawa speaks), Tōkyo, pr. by the Okada family, 1932.
A biographical work based on a collection of stories told by Shibusawa himself.

490. Shimoda Masami 下田將美, ed., Fujiwara Ginjirō kaiko hachijūnen 藤原銀次郎回顧八十年 (Recollections of the eighty years' life of Fujiwara Ginjirō), Tōkyō, Kōdansha, 1949.
Fujiwara Ginjirō is a leading figure in the Japanese industrial field. His contribution to the war economy as Minister of Commerce and Industry in 1940 is particularly significant.

491. Shiraishi Kitarō 白石喜太郎, Shibusawa Eiichi ō 澁沢榮一翁 (Life of Viscount Shibusawa), Tōkyō, Tōkō Shoin, 1933.
An extensive work on the life of Shibusawa (1840-1931) based on his speeches, deeds and contributions, by one who was personally associated with him.

492. Shirayanagi Shūko 白柳秀湖, Iwasaki Yatarō den 岩崎彌太郎傳 (Biography of Iwasaki Yatarō), Tōkyō, Chōbunkaku, 1942.
Iwasaki Yatarō (1834-1885), the founder of the Mitsubishi zaibatsu, played an important role at the beginning of the Meiji Period by contributing to the development of the domination of the zaibatsu system in the Japanese economy.

493. Shirayanagi Shūko 白柳秀湖, Nakamigawa Hikojirō den 中上川彦次郎傳 (Life of Nakamigawa Hikojirō), Tōkyō, Iwanami Shoten, 1940.
Nakamigawa (1854-1901) was the most important figure in the managerial group associated with the Mitsui zaibatsu during the Meiji Period. Three of the seven chapters in this work are especially valuable sources of information: chapter one on Nakamigawa's position in the history of Japanese industry, chapter two on the Mitsui group in the history of the public finance of the Meiji Period and chapter three on Nakamigawa's reform of the Mitsui group.

494. Tōgō Yutaka 東郷豊, Ikeda Seihin 池田成彬 (Life of Ikeda Seihin), Tōkyō, Konnichi no Mondaisha, 1938, 229
Ikeda Seihin contributed to the development and expansion of the Mitsui zaibatsu as a talented managing director.

495. Yano Fumio 矢野文夫, Yasuda Zenjirō den 安田善次郎傳 (Life of Yasuda Zenjirō), Tōkyō, Yasuda Hozensha, 1925.
Yasuda Zenjirō (1838-1921) was one of the most influential figures in the financial circles in Japan from the end of the 19th to the beginning of the 20th century and the founder of Yasuda Bank.

b. Leaders in the Field of Economic Policy

496. Inoue Ronsō Hensankai 井上論叢編纂會 (Society for the Compilation of the Writings of Inoue), Inoue Junnosuke den 井上準之助傳 (Biography of Inoue Junnosuke), Tōkyō, Inoue Ronsō Hensankai, 1935, 904 pp.
Biography of a well-known banker who was Finance Minister in the late 1920s and was responsible for the return to the gold standard in January, 1930.

497. Ōkubo Toshikazu 大久保利和, Ōkubo Toshimichi bunsho 大久保利通文書 (Papers of Ōkubo Toshimichi), pr. by the Ōkubo family, 1927-31, 10 v.
Ōkubo (1832-1878) is an important figure widely responsible for economic policies during the early years of Meiji. The work is an extensive biography based on a collection of letters, recommendations and memoranda which constitute a valuable source of information.

498. Okutani Matsuji 奥谷松治, Shinagawa Yajirō den 品川彌二郎傳 (Biography of Shinagawa Yajirō), Tōkyō, Kōyō Shoin, 1940.
Shinagawa (1843-1900) was one of the introducers of the industrial cooperative movement during the Meiji Period.

499. Rikken Seiyūkai Hombu 立憲政友會本部 (Headquarters of Rikken Seiyūkai Party), Takahashi Korekiyo ō hachijūnenshi 高橋是清翁八十年史 (Eighty years' life history of Takahashi Korekiyo), Tōkyō, 1934.
This work and entry 501 present the life of a well-known financial and political leader who was Minister of Finance during practically the whole of the period from December, 1931 until his assassination in February, 1936. He introduced and administered the so-called reflation policy after the re-establishment of the gold embargo. Takahashi's dates are from 1854 to 1936.

500. Sawada Akira 沢田章, Segai Inoue kō jireki ishin zaiseidan 世外井上公事歴維新財政談 (An account of Inoue Kaoru's Restoration financial policies), Tōkyō, 1921, 3 v.
Inoue Kaoru was an important leader, during the post-Restoration period, not only from the political but from the economic viewpoint. He was significant as the modernizer of Japanese public finance.

501. Takahashi Korekiyo 高橋是清, Takahashi Korekiyo jiden 高橋是清自傳 (Autobiography of Takahashi Korekiyo), Tōkyō, Chikura Shobō, 1936.

502. Tokutomi Iichirō 徳富猪一郎, Kōshaku Matsukata Masayoshi den 侯爵松方正義傳 (Life of Marquis Matsukata Masayoshi), Tōkyō, Kōshaku Matsukata Masayoshi den Hakkōsho, 1935, 2 v.
Matsukata Masayoshi (1835-1924) was an important political leader during the Meiji Period who helped to create the governmental organization in support of the Japanese economy. Chapters of special interest in volume one deal with his great contribution to the reform of the land tax and his readjustment of the currency system, in volume two with his period of services as Minister of Finance and with the early consitutional period.

503. Tokutomi Iichirō 徳富猪一郎, Ōkubo Kōtō sensei 大久保甲東先生 (Ōkubo Toshimichi), Tōkyō, Min'yūsha, 1927.
An account of Ōkubo's life (1832-1878) by a well-known historian.

504. Watanabe Ikujirō 渡辺幾治郎, Bunsho yori mitaru Ōkuma Shigenobu kō 文書より観たる大隈重信侯 (Marquis Ōkuma, as seen through documents), Tōkyō, Waseda Daigaku Shuppambu, 1932.

c. Collections of Biographical Studies

505. Tsuchiya Takao 土屋喬雄, Nihon shihonshugi shijō no shidōshatachi 日本資本主義史上の指導者達 (Leaders in the history of Japanese capitalism), Tōkyō, Iwanami Shoten, 1939.
A brief biographical study by a contemporary scholar of the important economic leaders from the viewpoint of the development of Japanese capitalism. Those included are Ōkubo Toshimichi, Matsukata Masayoshi, Takahashi Korekiyo, Shibusawa Eiichi, Godai Tomoatsu, Fukuzawa Yukichi, etc.

Chapter VII

Public Finance

Public finance occupies a central place in every feudal economy. In feudal Japan it was at the heart of economic policy. The interest in public finance in the Tokugawa period is easily understood. The truth is that public finance was so identified with general economics in the minds of the writers of this period that they often failed to give it separate treatment. The few works on the Tokugawa period which are listed below should be supplemented by reference to the literature on economic history and on the economic thought of this earlier time. Specialization on public finance, as a special field of study and research, was suggested by the practice of Western economists and the Japanese literature included attention to Western writer, Adolph Wagner for example, and conditions in Western countries.

In Japan factual and statistical information has been available for detailed studies in this field. There are many technical features of the subject, legal features for example, and many special aspects, such as fiscal monopolies. As a result of these conditions an extensive literature has come into existence. It includes historical works that run to fifteen or twenty volumes, general works that present every point of view from laissez faire to socialism, and special works on the taxation of salt or tobacco. It has been thought desirable to provide separate lists on law and on budget practice.

Modern public finance, under the name of fiscal policy, has become nearly as inclusive as feudal public finance. Thus, a general work on the plan which is associated with Mr. Dodge's name is listed in this chapter and it seems proper to list it here. At the same time the plan involved money, banking, prices, international finance, and the balance of international payments. Public finance is similar to the other specific fields of economics in that it cannot be adequately viewed in isolation.

1. Bibliographies

No publications devoted entirely to the bibliography of public finance are reported here. Certain general treatises, however, provide substantial and useful lists of works on public finance. Among them are the following, with a reference in each case to the number which the entry carries in this work:

Ōuchi Hyōe 大内兵衛, Zaiseigaku taikō 財政學大綱 (Principles of public finance) (No. 521).

Itō Han'ya 井藤半彌, Zaiseigaku gairon 財政學概論 (Introduction to public finance) (No. 512).

Itō Han'ya 井藤半彌, Zaiseigaku kenkyū 財政學研究 (Studies in public finance) (No. 513).

2. History of the Study of Public Finance

506. Abe Ken'ichi 阿部賢一, Zaiseigakushi 財政學史 (History of the study of public finance), Tōkyō, Kaizōsha, 1929.
Deals with important theories of public finance from the 18th century to the present.

507. Ide Fumio 井手文雄, Kotengakuha no zaiseiron 古典學派の財政論 (Public finance of the classical school), Tōkyō, Jitsugyō no Nihonsha, 1948.
Deals with the fiscal theory of Adam Smith and with Ricardo's redemption fund theory.

508. Kimura Gen'ichi 木村元一, Zaiseigaku---sono mondai ryōiki no hatten 財政學—その問題領域の發展 (Public finance: development of the scope of the subject), Tōkyō, Shunjūsha, 1949.
Deals with theories from the period of mercantilism to present-day capitalism. The author puts emphasis on the historical basis of these theories considering both the history of public finance and the history of method in this field.

509. Shima Yasuhiko 島恭彦, Kinsei sozei shisōshi 近世租税思想史 (History of thought on taxation in the modern age), Tōkyō, Yūhikaku, 1938.
Deals with theories of taxation in England and France during the 17th and 18th centuries.

510. Takagi Juichi 高木壽一, Kinsei zaisei shisōshi 近世財政思想史 (History of thought on public finance in the modern age), Tōkyō, Hokuryūkan, 1949.
Deals with the various theories of public finance from the period of the establishment of modern states to 1930.

3. General Theory of Public Finance

511. Hijikata Seibi 土方成美, Zaiseigaku genri 財政學原理 (Principles of public finance), Tōkyō, Tōyō Shuppansha, 1935.
The relation between public finance and the national economy is emphasized.

512. Itō Han'ya 井藤半彌, Zaiseigaku gairon 財政學概論 (Outline of public finance), Tōkyō, Nihon Hyōronsha, 1948.
Devoted chiefly to a theoretical study of the subject.

513. Itō Han'ya 井藤半彌, Zaiseigaku kenkyū 財政學研究 (Studies in public finance), Tōkyō, Chikura Shobō, 1950.
A collection of the author's articles relating to specific topics in the field. Has a valuable annotated bibliography.

514. Iwano Chōjirō 岩野晁次郎, Zaisei no keizai riron 財政の經濟理論 (Economic theory of public finance), Tōkyō, Seiya Shoten, 1949.
Deals with fiscal policy as business cycle policy and is devoted chiefly to introducing Keynesian doctrine.

515. Kambe Masao 神戸正雄, Zentei zaiseigaku taikō 全訂・財政學大綱 (Principles of public finance, revised), Tōkyō, Nihon Hyōronsha, 1941.

516. Kimura Kihachirō 木村禧八郎, Shakaishugi zaiseiron 社會主義財政論 (Socialist public finance), Tōkyō, Rōdōbunkasha, 1948.

517. Nagata Kiyoshi 永田清, Gendai zaiseigaku no riron 現代財政學の理論 (Theory of contemporary public finance), Tōkyō, Iwanami Shoten, 1937.
An introduction to Western theories of public finance after World War I.

518. Nagata Kiyoshi 永田清, Zaiseigaku no tenkai 財政學の展開 (Development of public finance), Tōkyō, Nihon Hyōronsha, 1942.
Criticism of the traditional theory of public finance.

519. Ogawa Gōtarō 小川郷太郎 and Shiomi Saburō 汐見三郎, Zaiseigaku (kaiteiban) 財政學（改訂版）(Public finance; revised edition), Tōkyō, Yūhikaku, rev. ed., 1940.

520. Ōhata Bunshichi 大畑文七, Zaiseigaku josetsu 財政學序説 (Introduction to public finance), Tōkyō, Yūhikaku, 1939.
Attention is put on the relation of public finance to social, economic, and political matters.

521. Ōuchi Hyōe 大内兵衛, Zaiseigaku taikō 財政學大綱 (General principles of public finance), Tōkyō, Iwanami Shoten, 1930-31, 2 v.
The author belongs to the socialist school. Two of three volumes have been published so far. Volume one deals with the accounting system and expenditures of the government. Volume two deals with the theory of taxation.

522. Shima Yasuhiko 島恭彦, Zaiseigaku gairon 財政學概論 (Outline of public finance), Tōkyō, Mikasa Shobō, 1950.
Presents a theory of public finance from a socialist point of view.

523. Taguchi Ukichi 田口卯吉, Zaisei 財政 (Public finance), Tōkyō, Taguchi Ukichi Zenshū Kankōkai, 1928.
Written in the late 19th century. The author was an early leader in economics in Japan and noted for his emphasis on laissez faire.

524. Uchiike Renkichi 内池廉吉, Zaiseigaku gairon 財政學概論 (Outline of public finance), Tōkyō, Dōbunkan, 1927.

4. Special Theoretical Works

a. Methodological Studies

525. Hijikata Seibi 土方成美, Zaiseigaku no kiso gainen---keizaishakai to zaisei genshō 財政學の基礎概念―經濟社會と財政現象 (Basic concepts of public finance: economic society and public financial phenomena), Tōkyō, Iwanami Shoten, 1923.
Deals with the method and with the interrelation between public finance and economy in general.

526. Itō Han'ya 井藤半彌, Zaiseigaku genri---zaisei seisaku sōron 財政學原理―財政政策総論 (Principles of public finance: general treatise on public finance policy), Tōkyō, Ganshōdō, 1931.
A study of the interrelation between public finance and philosophy.

b. Taxation and Public Bonds

527. Andō Haruo 安藤春夫, Kokka keizai to kōsai keizai 國家經濟と公債經濟 (National economy and the economy of public bonds), Tōkyō, Dōbunkan, 1936.
Valuable study of the theory of the shifting of the burden of public bond issues.

528. Fujita Takeo 藤田武夫, Kindai sozei seido 近代租税制度 (Modern taxation systems), Tōkyō, Kawade Shobō, 1948.

529. Itō Han'ya 井藤半彌, Sozei gensoku gakusetsu no kōzō to seisei 租税原則學説の構造と生成 (Structure and development of the theory of taxation), Tōkyō, Ganshōdō, 1935.

530. Kambe Masao 神戸正雄, Sozei kenkyū 租税研究 (Studies of tax), Kyōto, Kōbundō, 1919-30, 10 v.
A collection of the author's valuable and exhaustive works on taxation. Deals with highly detailed problems of taxation.

531. Matsuno Kengo 松野賢吾, Sozei tenka ron 租税轉嫁論 (On the shifting of tax burdens), Tōkyō, Ganshōdō, 1943.
Theoretical, detailed and careful study of this subject.

532. Shiomi Saburō 汐見三郎, Sozei ron 租税論 (On taxation), Tōkyō, Yūhikaku, 1948.
Revised edition of a part of the author's earlier work which was written with the cooperation of Ogawa.

5. History of Japanese Public Finance

a. Before the Meiji Restoration

The two following works deal with the history of Japanese public finance from ancient times to the Tokugawa Period. Both are chiefly concerned with the taxation system and other financial institutions.

533. Honjō Eijirō 本庄榮治郎, Nihon zaiseishi 日本財政史 (History of public finance in Japan), Tōkyō, Kaizōsha, 1925.

534. Tsuchiya Takao 土屋喬雄, Nihon zaiseishi 日本財政史 (History of Japanese public finance), Tōkyō, Kaizōsha, 1930.

b. After the Meiji Restoration

535. Fujita Takeo 藤田武夫, Nihon shihonshugi to zaisei 日本資本主義と財政 (Japanese capitalism and public finance), Tōkyō, Jitsugyō no Nihonsha, 1949.
Description of Japanese public finance to the Manchurian affair in connection with the development of Japanese capitalism.

536. Hijikata Seibi 土方成美, Zaiseishi 財政史 (History of public finance), Tōkyō, Tōyō Keizaisha, 1940.
The first half of this work deals with the general history of public finance after the Meiji Restoration. The second half is concerned with specific history such as government expenditure, taxation and local finance.

537. Katsu Masanori 勝正憲, Nihon zeisei kaikakushi 日本税政改革史 (History of the reform of the taxation system in Japan), Tōkyō, Chikura Shobō, 1938.
Analysis mainly of the reform of the taxation system during and after the Meiji Period.

538. Kazehaya Yasoji 風早八十二, Zaiseishi 財政史 (History of public finance) [=v. 1 of Nihon shihonshugi hattatsushi kōza (Lectures on the development of Japanese capitalism) (No. 370)], Tōkyō, Iwanami Shoten, 1932.
Marxian analysis of the history of Japanese public finance.

539. Meiji Zaiseishi Hensankai 明治財政史編纂會 (Society for the Compilation of the History of Public Finance in the Meiji Period), Meiji zaiseishi 明治財政史 (History of public finance in the Meiji period), Tōkyō, Maruzen Shoten, 1904-05, 15 v.
A highly detailed history of public finance from the beginning of the Meiji Period to the 35th year of Meiji (1902). Covers all fields.

540. Ōkurashō 大藏省 (Ministry of Finance), Meiji Taishō zaiseishi 明治大正財政史 (History of public finance in the Meiji and Taishō periods), Tōkyō, Zaisei Keizai Gakkai, 1936-40, 20 v.
An exhaustive official history of public finance throughout the Meiji and Taishō Periods. Yoshikawa Hidezō was in charge of this edition.

541. Ōkurashō Shuzeikyoku 大藏省主税局 (Tax Bureau of the Ministry of Finance), Naikokuzei no zeiritsu oyobi nōki ni kansuru enkaku tekiyō 内國税の税率及び納期に關する沿革摘要 (Summarized history of the rate and the fixed date of internal taxes), Tōkyō, Ōkurashō Shuzeikyoku, 1949.
Convenient and valuable materials dealing with the changes in the institutions of taxation such as the tax rate and the fixed date of tax collection from the beginning of the Meiji Period to 1948.

542. Ōkurashō Shuzeikyoku 大藏省主税局 (Tax Bureau of the Ministry of Finance), Chisoshi 地租史 (History of the land tax), Tōkyō, Ōkurashō, 1901.
Official report on the details of the land tax reform in the early Meiji Period.

543. Ōuchi Hyōe 大内兵衛, Nihon zaiseiron---kōsaihen 日本財政論—公債篇 (On Japanese public finance: public bonds), Tōkyō, Kaizōsha, 1932, 253+131 pp.
Well-known work on the history of Japanese public bonds from the Meiji Restoration to the Manchurian affair. Deals not only with the institutional problems but also the economic and social influences of bond policy. With valuable statistical tables in the appendix.

544. Suzuki Mosaburō 鈴木茂三郎, Zaisei dokuhon 財政讀本 (Reading in public finance), Tōkyō, Jitsugyō Kyōkasho Kabushiki Kaisha, 1949.
Explanation and criticism of Japanese public finance from the viewpoint of socialism.

545. Yoshikawa Hidezō 吉川秀造, Nihon zaiseishi 日本財政史 (History of Japanese public finance), Tōkyō, Nihon Hyōronsha, 1940.
Deals with the history of Japanese public finance during the period from the Meiji Restoration to the post-war economy after World War I.

c. Public Finance during the Period of World War II

546. Itō Han'ya 井藤半彌, Zōho senji zaisei kōwa 增補戰時財政講話 (Lectures on war-time public finance, enlarged and revised), Tōkyō, Ganshōdō, 1941.
Deals with the problems of public finance during the war period.

547. Shionoya Tsuzure 塩野谷九十九, Zaisei shishutsu to sensō keizaiseisaku ni tsuite 財政支出と戰爭經濟政策について (On government expenditure and war-time economic policies), Tōkyō, Tōyō Keizai Shimpōsha, 1948.

548. Takagi Juichi 高木壽一, Sensō zaisei no keizai riron 戰爭財政の經濟理論 (Economic theory of war-time public finance), Tōkyō, Hokuryūkan, 1943.

549. Takagi Juichi 高木壽一, Senji zaisei ron 戰時財政論 (Theory of war-time public finance), Tōkyō, Nihon Hyōronsha, 1934.

6. Particular Factual Studies

550. Aoki Tokuzō 青木得三 and Yamaguchi Tadao 山口忠夫, Kokka zaisei to kokumin keizai 國家財政と國民經濟 (Public finance and the national economy), Tōkyō, Yūhikaku, 1941.
A factual study of the interrelation between public finance and the national economy. Emphasis is on the relation between governmental expenditure and the Japanese economy in general.

551. Higuchi Gorō 樋口午朗, Sengo zaisei seisaku to kokumin keizai kanjō 戰後財政政策と國民經濟勘定 (Post-war financial policies and the national accounts), Tōkyō, Tōyō Keizaisha, 1950.
A statistical analysis of the interrelation among public finance, national income, and other fields of the national economy during the post-war period in Japan.

552. Ōuchi Hyōe 大内兵衛, Teikokushugi sensō to sengo no zaisei mondai 帝國主義戰爭と戰後の財政問題 (Imperialistic war and post-war public financial problems), Tōkyō, Iwanami Shoten, 1948.
Criticism of the war-time and post-war public financial policies by a well-known socialist scholar.

553. Ōuchi Hyōe 大内兵衛, Sengo Nihon zaisei no ayunda michi 戰後日本財政の歩んだ道 (Paths of Japanese public finance during the post-war period), Tōkyō, Jiji Tsūshinsha, 1950.
A collection of the author's articles which criticize the policies of the Japanese government during the post-war period. Chiefly but not exclusively concerned with public finance.

554. Shiomi Saburō 汐見三郎, Zaisei tōkei 財政統計 (Public financial statistics), Tōkyō, Daiichi Shuppan Kabushiki Kaisha, 1946.
Explanation of statistics relating to the national and local finance of Japan. Also includes the international comparison of financial statistics.

555. Shiomi Saburō 汐見三郎, Nihon zaisei no tokushumondai 日本財政の特殊問題 (Specific problems of Japanese public finance), Tōkyō, Yūhikaku, 1926.
An elaborate factual study of the seasonal fluctuation of Japanese public finance and the shift of the burden of the tax on sake.

556. Suzuki Takeo 鈴木武雄, Dojji rain---antei yori jiritsu e no shomondai ドッヂライン―安定より自立への諸問題 (Dodge line: various problems underlying the transition from stability to self-sustenance), Tōkyō, Jiji Tsūshinsha, 1950.
Deals with the drastic fiscal policy to stabilize the Japanese economy in 1949, recommended by Mr. Joseph M. Dodge. Its main points consist of balancing the budget, cutting off the subsidies to business, rigid banking policy, and strict control over the management of American Aid funds.

7. Local Finance

557. Fujita Takeo 藤田武夫, Nihon chihō zaisei seido no seiritsu 日本地方財政制度の成立 (Establishment of the Japanese local financial system), Tōkyō, Iwanami Shoten, 1941.
Deals with the period from late Tokugawa to the establishment of the modern prefectural system in Japan in 1888. Characteristics of the system, the author says, are : the fact that it was established not by internal impulse but by external pressure, the fact that the central government was highly influential in the local administration, the poor financial condition of local units, and the neglect of the importance of towns and villages in comparison with the prefecture.

558. Fujita Takeo 藤田武夫, Nihon chihō zaisei hattenshi 日本地方財政發展史 (History of the development of Japanese local finance), Tōkyō, Kawade Shobō, 1949.
Deals with the development of the finance of local autonomous entities from 1888 to 1940. A continuation of the preceding work.

559. Fujita Takeo 藤田武夫, Gendai chihō zaisei no riron--- chihō zaisei to kokka zaisei no kanren 現代地方財政の理論―地方財政と國家財政の關連 (Theory of contemporary local finance: the interrelation between local finance and national finance), Tōkyō, Kōbunsha, 1950.
A theoretical work on the principles of local finance.

560. Fujitani Kenji 藤谷謙二, Chihō zaiseiron 地方財政論 (On local finance), Tōkyō, Ryūginsha, 1944.
A collection of the author's articles which deal with the general problems of local finance.

561. Tanaka Kōtarō 田中廣太郎, Chihōzei kenkyū 地方税研究 (Study of local taxation), Tōkyō, Ryōsho Fukyūkai, 1928, 3 v.
Exhaustive studies of both general and particular local taxation.

8. Fiscal Monopolies

562. Horie Yasuzō 堀江保藏, Waga kuni kinsei no sembai seido 我國近世の專賣制度 (Monopoly system in the modern age [Tokugawa period] of our country), Tōkyō, Nihon Hyōronsha, 1933.
Deals with monopolies during the Tokugawa Period. The first half of this work is concerned with problems of a general nature and the second half with the monopolies of wax, ginseng, iron industry and iron products under certain feudal lords.

563. Sembaikyoku 專賣局 (Monopoly Bureau), Sembaishi (dai-isshū) 專賣史(第一輯) (History of government monopolies), Tōkyō, Sembaikyoku, 1937, 8 v.
The tobacco monopoly is dealt with in the first four volumes, the fifth deals with salt, and the sixth with camphor. The remaining volumes deal with accounts and laws and ordinances.

564. Shima Yasuhiko 島恭彦, Nihon shihonshugi to kokuyū tetsudō 日本資本主義と國有鐵道 (Japanese capitalism and governmental railroads), Tōkyō, Nihon Hyōronsha, 1950.
Deals with the government-owned railroads as a fiscal monopoly.

565. Takenaka Tatsuo 竹中龍雄, Nihon kōkigyō seiritsushi 日本公企業成立史 (Foundation of Japanese public enterprises), Tōkyō, Daidō Shoin, 1939.
Deals with public enterprises managed by cities, such as water supply, gas supply, canals, etc.

9. The Budget: National and Local

566. Chihō Jichichō Zaiseibu 地方自治廳財政部 (Finance Division, Local Autonomy Board), Chihō zaisei benran 地方財政便覧 (Handbook on local finance), 1949 +.
Compilation of statistics relating to the public finance of local autonomous entities.

567. Ōkurashō Shukeikyoku 大藏省主計局 (Budget Bureau, Ministry of Finance), Teikoku no yosan 帝國の予算 (Budget of the Japanese empire), Tōkyō, Chōyōkai, 1925 +, annual.
A pre-war annual publication of the Ministry of Finance explaining the governmental budget of the year.

568. Ōkurashō Shukeikyoku 大藏省主計局 (Budget Bureau, Ministry of Finance), Yosan no setsumei 予算の説明 (Commentary on the budget), Tōkyō, Okura Zaimukyoku, 1947 +, annual.
Explanation of the administration's draft of the budget of the year. Usually published immediately after the submission of the budget request by the administration to the Diet.

569. Ōkurashō Shukeikyoku 大藏省主計局 (Budget Bureau, Ministry of Finance), Kuni no yosan---sono kōzō to haikei 國の予算 — その構造と背景 (National budget: its structure and background), Tōkyō, Hakuyōsha, 1949.
An explanation in detail of the administration's draft of the budget for the year.

570. Shūgiin Jimukyoku 衆議院事務局 (Secretariat of the House of Representatives), Teikoku Gikai yosan'an 帝國議會予算案 (Draft of the budget in the Imperial Diet), Tōkyō, 1890 +, annual.
Pre-war annual publication of the Secretariat of the House of Representatives explaining the administration's proposed national budget.

571. Shūgiin Jimukyoku 衆議院事務局 (Secretariat of the House of Representatives), Teikoku Gikai kessan 帝國議會決算 (Settlement account in the Imperial Diet), Tōkyō, 1890 +, annual.
Pre-war annual publication of the Secretariat of the House of Representatives dealing with the statement of national accounts.

572. Shūgiin Jimukyoku 衆議院事務局 (Secretariat of the House of Representatives), Yosan sankōsho 予算参考書 (Reference materials on the budget), Tōkyō, 1890 +, annual.
Annual publication of the Secretariat of the House of Representatives of the reference materials relating to the national budget.

10. Laws and Ordinances relating to Public Finance

573. Chihō Jichichō Zaiseibu 地方自治廳財政部 (Finance Division, Local Autonomy Board), Chihō zeihō, chihō zaiseihō kankei hōreishū 地方税法・地方財政法関係法令集 (Collection of laws and ordinances relating to the local taxation act and local finance act), Tōkyō, Chihō Zaimu Kyōkai, 1950.

574. Fujita Takeo 藤田武夫, Chihō zaiseihō kaisetsu 地方財政法解説 (Commentary on the local finance act), Ōsaka, Hōritsu Bunkasha, 1948.
Commentary on the basic law which regulates the public finances of local autonomous entities.

575. Hirai Heiji 平井平治, Kaitei yosan kessan seido yōron 改訂予算決算制度要論 (Outline of the system of national budget and its settlement, revised), Tōkyō, Ōkura Zaimu Kyōkai, 1950.

576. Kōno Kazuyuki 河野一之, Yosan kessan seido 予算決算制度 (System of national budget and its settlement), Tōkyō, Gakuyō Shobō, 1950.
This work and the preceding one explain the current national treasury operations. They are written by government officials engaged in financial administration.

577. Okuno Masasuke 奥野正亮 and Shibata Mamoru 柴田護, Chihō zaiseihō kōwa 地方財政法講話 (Lecture on the local finance law), Tōkyō, Chihō Zaimu Kyōkai, 1949.
Commentary by appropriate officials on the basic law which regulates the public finances of the local autonomous entities.

578. Ōkurashō Shukeikyoku 大藏省主計局 (Budget Bureau, Ministry of Finance), Zaisei kankei hōreishū 財政関係法令集 (Collection of laws and ordinances relating to public finances), Tōkyō, Ōkura Zaimu Kyōkai, 1948.

579. Ōkurashō Shuzeikyoku 大藏税主計局 (Tax Bureau, Ministry of Finance), Sozei hōki ruishū 租税法規類集 (Collection of laws and ordinances relating to taxation), Tōkyō, Ōkura Zaimu Kyōkai, 1948, 1950.

11. Materials

580. Ōkurashō 大藏省, Tokugawa rizai kaiyō 德川理財會要 (Public financial and economic administration in the Tokugawa period), Tōkyō, Hakutosha, 1932.

A compilation of materials relating to the administration of public finance by the Tokugawa government. This work appeared in Takimoto, ed., Nihon keizai taiten (No. 273).

581. Ōuchi Hyōe 大内兵衛 and Tsuchiya Takao 土屋喬雄, Meiji zenki zaisei keizai shiryō shūsei 明治前期財政經濟史料集成 (A collection of public financial and economic data on the first half of the Meiji period), Tōkyō, Kaizōsha, 1931-33, 21 v.

A collection of official reports, studies and records relating to institutions and administration in the field of public finance from the Meiji Restoration to the establishment of the Diet. There are separate volumes on the history of the Ministry of Finance, the income and expenditure of the national treasury, the land tax system, the termination of the system of feudal fiefs, research on the monetary system, and recommendations for industrialization.

582. Katsu Awa 勝安房, ed., Suijinroku 吹塵錄 (Collection of materials), and Suijin yoroku 吹塵余錄 (Collection of materials--- continued), Tōkyō, Ōkurashō, 1890; repr. in v. 3-5 of Katsu zenshū 勝全集 (The complete works of Katsu), Tōkyō, Kaizōsha, 1927.

A collection of records and studies by individuals in the field of the public finances of the Tokugawa period. Compiled with annotation and critical comments by Katsu Awa, an influential subject of the Shogunate.

583. Takahashi Kamekichi 高橋亀吉, ed., Zaisei keizai nijūgonenshi 財政經濟二十五年誌 (Twenty-five years' history of public finance and economy), Tōkyō, Jitsugyō no Sekaisha, 1932, 8 v.

A collection of materials relating to the economy and public finance of the country after the Russo-Japanese war comprising official records of the Imperial Diet, policy statements by political parties, reports of commissions, and reports of banks and corporations.

584. Ōkurashō 大藏省 (Ministry of Finance), Nihon zaisei keizai shiryō 日本財政經濟史料 (Historical materials relating to the Japanese public finance and economy), Tōkyō, Zaisei Keizai Gakkai, 1922-25, 11 v.

Chapter VIII

Money and Banking

In Japan, as in Western countries, the study of money and of banking has been in large measure a response to the needs of the country. The course of events set a series of financial problems. The efforts to meet these problems are revealed in the writings of the economists, such as are listed below, and in the monetary and banking organization of Japan.

The first of this series of problems to be reflected in the writings reported here is that of explaining the rise and spread, during the Tokugawa period, of a money economy in a country that looked upon rice not only as a measure of value and a means of payment but also as a symbol of a correct ideology, a proper outlook. If a rice economy may be contrasted with a money economy so may the point of view of feudal lord and samurai with that of merchant and exchange banker. A second and a less general problem of the Tokugawa period was presented by the practice of the debasement of coins by feudal lords. There was a lively interest in money and prices in Japan before the opening of the country.

After the Meiji Restoration the general problem was that of the best monetary and banking system for the country after its acceptance of world trade and in support of its program of industrialization. The literature seems to show that a modern monetary system was more easily achieved than a modern banking system. Characteristic features of the Japanese economy are revealed in the works on banking. These works discuss the importance of the government as a collector and investor of savings, the need for special banks with government backing, and self-financing on the part of the zaibatsu.

A more recent succession of financial problems began with the boom of World War I and its aftermath of depression. These were followed by the earthquake of 1923 and the banking crisis of 1927. Then came the return to gold in 1930, the rejection of gold in 1931, the financing of the war, the post-war inflation and stabilization, and the current search for policy appropriate to Japan's new status in a profoundly disturbed Far East and a divided world.

The literature is more controversial as the current period is approached. The repeal of the gold embargo and its reimposition, together with the Takahashi policy of "reflation," brought about a great debate. Its importance is reflected in the writings which have been selected for presentation.

During the post-war years there has been difference of opinion over the explanation and significance of inflation. In this discussion the Marxist writers have played some part though they have usually had relatively little to say on monetary and banking matters.

The theoretical work reported below is to be seen against the historical background which has been outlined. The general literature and the studies of particular subjects listed in this chapter should be supplemented by attention to the related fields of public finance and international trade and to the statistical information of the third chapter.

1. Bibliographies

585. Hōsei Daigaku Keizaigakubu Kenkyūshitsu 法政大學經濟學部研究室 (Research Seminar in the Economics College of Hōsei University), "Torihikijo bunken mokuroku 取引所文献目錄 (Catalogue of written works on the stock exchange)," Hōsei Daigaku ronshū 法政大學論集 (Economic review of Hōsei University), v. 4, no. 2, 1929.

586. "'Kin-yushutsu kaikin mondai' kankei mokuroku「金輸出解禁問題」関係目錄(Catalogue of literature relating to the problem of the lifting of the gold embargo)," Naigai chōsa shiryō 内外調査資料 (Domestic and foreign research materials), v. 1, no. 5, 1929.

587. Ryū Shintarō 笠信太郎, "Marukusu shugi kaheiron ni kansuru bunken マルクス主義貨幣論に関する文献 (Literature relating to Marxian monetary theory)," Shinkō kagaku no hata no moto ni 新興科學の旗の下に (Under the flag of the new science), v. 1, no. 3, 1928.

588. Suzuki Naoji 鈴木直二, Kome ni kansuru bunken kaisetsu 米に関する文献解説(Annotated bibliography of works relating to rice), Tōkyō, Ganshōdō, 1939.
This is a list of all the items in the Suzuki Beikoku Bunko 鈴木米穀文庫 (Suzuki Library on Rice). The first part deals with the technology of rice production and the second with social and economic problems associated with rice.

589. Takagaki Torajirō 高垣寅次郎, Ginkōron 銀行論 (Theory of banking), Tōkyō, Nihon Hyōronsha, 1930, (No. 622), "Ginkōron sankō bunken shūroku 銀行論参考文献輯錄 (List of works relating to banking theory)."

590. Takashima Saichirō 高島佐一郎, Kin'yū seisaku 金融政策 (Banking policy), Tōkyō, Kaizōsha, 1931 (No. 623), "Kin'yū seisaku ni kansuru hompō bunken 金融政策に関する本邦文献 (Japanese works relating to banking policies)."

591. Tōkyō Shōkō Kaigisho 東京商工會議所 (Chamber of Commerce of Tōkyō), Kin-yushutsu kaikin mondai ni kansuru sankō shiryō 金輸出解禁問題に関する参考資料 (Reference materials on the problem of lifting of the gold embargo), Tōkyō, Nihon Kōmin Gakkai, 1927.

2. Theory of Money and of Prices

a. Money

592. Araki Kōtarō 荒木光太郎, Kahei gairon 貨幣概論(Monetary theory), Tōkyō, Yūhikaku, 1936.

593. Hashizume Akio 橋爪明男, Kaheiron 貨幣論 (Monetary theory), Tōkyō, Nihon Hyōronsha, 1929.

594. Inomata Tsunao 猪俣津南雄, Kahei shin'yō oyobi infureishon no riron 貨幣信用及びインフレーションの理論 (Theory of money, credit, and inflation), Tōkyō, Kaizōsha, 1933, 369 pp.; repr., Tōkyō, Dōyūsha, 1948.

595. Kitō Nisaburō 鬼頭仁三郎, Kahei to rishi no dōtai 貨幣と利子の動態 (Dynamic analysis of money and interest), Tōkyō, Iwanami Shoten, 1942.

596. Masai Keiji 正井敬次, Kahei kachi no kenkyū 貨幣價値の研究 (Studies in the value of money), Tōkyō, Nihon Hyōronsha, 1935.

597. Ryū Shintarō 笠信太郎, Kin, kahei, shihei---kahei mondai no hihan 金，貨幣，紙幣 — 貨幣問題の批判 (Gold, coin, and paper money: essays on monetary problems), Tōkyō, Ōhata Shoten, 1933.

598. Takada Yasuma 高田保馬, Kahei no riron 貨幣の理論 (Theory of money), Tōkyō, Iwanami Shoten, 1930.

599. Takagaki Torajirō 高垣寅次郎, Kahei no seisei 貨幣の生成 (Growth of money), Tōkyō, Dōbunkan, 1926.
This and the two following works are taken from the author's general treatise on money, Kahei no riron (Theory of money) (No. 598).

600. Takagaki Torajirō 高垣寅次郎, Kahei no shokunō 貨幣の職能 (Function of money), Tōkyō, Dōbunkan, 1927.

601. Takagaki Torajirō 高垣寅次郎, Kahei no honshitsu 貨幣の本質 (Nature of money), Tōkyō, Dōbunkan, 1927.

602. Yamazaki Kakujirō 山崎覺次郎, Kahei mondai zakkan 貨幣問題雜觀(Miscellaneous views on monetary problems), Tōkyō, Yūhikaku, 1933.
A collection of articles written by a well-known economist who was a leading figure in the field of monetary theory.

b. Price

603. Kitō Nisaburō 鬼頭仁三郎, Bukka no riron 物價の理論 (Theory of price), Tōkyō, Keizai Shimpōsha, 1948.

604. Miyata Kiyozō 宮田喜代藏, Heika kirisage no riron 平價切下の理論 (Theory of devaluation), Nagoya, Reimei Shobō, 1947.

605. Shinjō Hiroshi 新庄博, Tsūka-antei no kenkyū 通貨安定の研究 (Study of currency stabilization), Ōsaka, Sangyō Keizai Shimbunsha, 1948.

606. Inomata Tsunao 猪俣津南雄, Infureishon no kiso riron インフレーションの基礎理論 (Fundamental theory of inflation), Tōkyō, Kaizōsha, 1933.

607. Takada Yasuma 高田保馬, Infureishon no kaimei インフレーションの解明 (Analysis of inflation), Kyōto, Seki Shobō, 1947.

608. Yamaguchi Shigeru 山口茂, Kakaku suijun no kihon riron 價格水準の基本理論 (Basic theories on the price level), Tōkyō, Ganshōdō, 1943.

3. The Monetary System

609. Araki Kōtarō 荒木光太郎, Kanei seido gaisetsu 貨幣制度概説 (Outline of the monetary system), Tōkyō, Nihon Hyōronsha, 1933.

An exposition of the basic concepts is followed by an account of the monetary systems of various countries.

610. Tanaka Kinji 田中金司, Kin hon'isei to chūō ginkō seisaku 金本位制と中央銀行政策 (The gold standard system and central bank policy), Tōkyō, Hōbunkan, 1929.

611. Takagaki Torajirō 高垣寅次郎, Kahei seido sōsetsu 貨幣制度総説 (General treatise on monetary systems), Tōkyō, Nihon Hyōronsha, 1929.

612. Tōyō Keizai Shimpōsha 東洋經濟新報社, Kin hon'isei no kenkyū 金本位制の研究 (Study of the gold standard system), Tōkyō, Tōyō Keizai Shuppambu, 1932.

A collection of articles by leading economists and writers on economics such as Yamazaki Kakujirō, Kawakami Hajime and Takashima Saichirō.

4. Monetary and Banking Policy

613. Fukai Eigo 深井英五, Tsūka chōsetsuron 通貨調節論 (On the control of money), Tōkyō, Nihon Hyōronsha, 1929.

A general account of the subject. The author is a well-known banker and was the president of the Bank of Japan.

614. Okinaka Tsuneyuki 沖中恒幸, Kin'yū chōseiron 金融調整論 (On the control of banking), Tōkyō, Chikura Shobō, 1938.

615. Ryū Shintarō 笠信太郎, Tsūka shin'yō tōsei hihan 通貨信用統制批判 (Critical account of the control of currency and credit), Tōkyō, Kaizōsha, 1934.

Deals with the relation of credit control to prices, production activities, foreign trade, consumption, and public finance.

616. Takashima Saichirō 高島佐一郎, Kin'yū tōseiron 金融統制論 (On the control of banking), Tōkyō, Chikura Shobō, 1931.

See also entry 244.

5. Banking

617. Aoki Tokuzō 青木得三, Tokushu kin'yū kikanron 特殊金融機關論 (On the special banking organizations) [=v. 20 of Gendai kin'yū zenshū 現代金融全集 (Series on contemporary financial economics)], Tōkyō, Kaizōsha, 1935.

618. Izeki Takao 井関孝雄, Chūshō shōkōgyō shomin kin'yūron 中小商工業庶民金融論 (On money-lending to the medium and small commercial and manufacturing enterprises and to individuals) [=v. 5 of Gendai kin'yū zenshū 現代金融全集 (Series on contemporary financial economics)], Tōkyō, Kaizōsha, 1935.

619. Izeki Takao 井関孝雄, Chūshō kin'yū no taikei 中小金融の体系 (System of financing medium and small-scale enterprises), Tōkyō, Ganshōdō, 1950.

620. Matsuzaki Hisashi 松崎壽, Hompō chūshō kōgyō kin'yūron 本邦中小工業金融論 (On the financing of medium and small manufacturing enterprises in Japan), Tōkyō, Bungadō, 1934.

A factual as well as critical account of financing facilities and methods for medium and small-scale industries.

621. Okurashō Kin'yū Seido Chōsakai 大藏省金融制度調査會 (Research Committee on Banking, Ministry of Finance), *Shin-kin'yū seido no kenkyū* 新金融制度の研究 (Study of the new banking system), Tōkyō, Itagaki Shoten, 1948.

622. Takagaki Torajirō 高垣寅次郎, *Ginkōron* 銀行論 (On banking), Tōkyō, Nihon Hyōronsha, 1930.

623. Takashima Saichirō 高島佐一郎, *Kin'yū seisaku* 金融政策 (Banking policy), Tōkyō, Kaizōsha, 1931.

624. Tanaka Kinji 田中金司, *Chūō ginkō, Nihon Ginkōron* 中央銀行・日本銀行論 (On the central bank and Bank of Japan), Tōkyō, Kaizōsha, 1936.

625. Yoshino Toshihiko 吉野俊彦, *Waga kuni kin'yū seido no kenkyū* 我國金融制度の研究 (Study of the Japanese banking system), Tōkyō, Jitsugyō no Nihonsha, 1952.

6. International Finance

626. Hattori Bunshirō 服部文四郎, *Nihon no kokusai kin'yū* 日本の國際金融 (International finance of Japan)[=v. 42 of *Keizaigaku zenshū* 經濟學全集 (Anthology of economics)], Tōkyō, Kaizōsha, 1930.

627. Inoue Junnosuke 井上準之助, *Waga kokusai kin'yū no genjō oyobi kaizensaku* 我國際金融の現狀及改善策 (Japan's present financial situation and proposals for its improvement), Tōkyō, Iwanami Shoten, 1926.
The author gives special attention to World War I and the period after the great earthquake.

628. Kanno Watarō 菅野和太郎, *Tsūshōgaisha, kawasegaisha* 通商會社・爲替會社 (The trading company and the exchange company), in Honjō, ed., *Meiji ishin keizaishi kenkyū*, Tōkyō, Kaizōsha, 1930 (No. 653).
Deals with the establishment and development of these companies in the early Meiji period.

629. Kimbara Kennosuke 金原賢之助, *Kokusai kin'yū sōron* 國際金融總論 (Introduction to international finance)[=v. 1 of *Sekai keizai mondai sōsho* 世界經濟問題叢書 (Series on world economic problems)], Tōkyō, Dōbunkan, 1931.

630. Kitō Nisaburō 鬼頭仁三郎, *Kokusai shihon idōron* 國際資本移動論 (On the international flow of capital), 1939; repr., Tōkyō, Ginza Shuppansha, 1948.

631. Taniguchi Yoshihiko 谷口吉彦, *Kawase riron to kawase mondai* 爲替理論と爲替問題 (Theory and problems of foreign exchange), Tōkyō, Chikura Shobō, 1933.

See also entries 893-897, 901-903.

7. History of Money and Banking

a. General

632. Akashi Teruo 明石照男, *Meiji ginkōshi* 明治銀行史 (History of banking in the Meiji period), Tōkyō, Kaizōsha, 1935.

633. Inoue Junnosuke 井上準之助, *Sengo ni okeru waga kuni no keizai oyobi kin'yū* 戰後に於ける我國の經濟及金融 (Post-war economy and finance in Japan), Tōkyō, Iwanami Shoten, ed. 5, 1926.
The five chapters include an account of the crisis of 1920, an assessment of the position of the Bank of Japan, and comment on a possible return to the gold standard.

634. Ishibashi Tanzan 石橋湛山, *Nihon kin'yūshi* 日本金融史 (History of Japanese banking), Tōkyō, Kaizōsha, 1936.
Deals with the period from early Meiji to the crisis of 1927.

635. Kurusu Takeo 粟栖赳夫, *Shintaku hōki oyobi shintaku kaisha hattatsushi* 信託法規及信託會社發達史 (Laws and ordinances relating to trusts and the history of the development of the trust company), Tōkyō, Bungadō, 1922.

636. Kurusu Takeo 粟栖赳夫, *Nihon kin'yū seido hattatsu no kenkyū* 日本金融制度發達の研究 (Study of the development of the financial system in Japan), Tōkyō, Keimeisha, 1929.
Deals with banking during the Tokugawa period and with the bank and the trust company after the Meiji Restoration.

637. Matsuyoshi Sadao 松好貞夫, *Nihon ryōgae kin'yū shiwa* 日本兩替金融史話 (History of money and banking in Japan), Tōkyō, Bungei Shunjūsha, 1932.

638. Mitsui Takamasa 三井高維, *Shinkō ryōgae nendaiki kanken* 新稿兩替年代記關鍵 (Guide to the chronological history of the money exchange business), Tōkyō, Iwanami Shoten, 1933, 2 v.
The first volume consists of materials on the subject from a compilation of such materials by the exchange guild in Edo and covers the organization and regulations of the guild as well as prices. The second volume carries the author's comments on the source materials.

639. Nomura Junnosuke 野村順之助, Nihon kin'yū shihcn hattatsushi 日本金融資本發達史 (History of the development of Japanese financial capital), Tōkyō, Kyōseikaku, 1931.
Deals with the development of Japanese banking after the Meiji period from the viewpoint of historical materialism.

640. Obata Atsushi 小葉田淳, Nihon kahei ryūtsūshi 日本貨幣流通史 (History of the circulation of money in Japan), Tōkyō, Tōkō Shoin, 1930.
This work presents the development of the circulation of money from the Middle Age to the early Tokugawa period. It is reported to have been revised and enlarged in 1943.

641. Okada Sumio 岡田純夫, Hompō ginkōshi 本邦銀行史 (History of banks in Japan), Tōkyō, Shibun Shoin, 1930-31.

642. Ōsaka Ryōgaeshō Kumiai 大阪両替商組合 (Ōsaka Exchange Guild), Ryōgaeshō enkakushi 両替商沿革史 (History of development of the exchange guild), Ōsaka Ryōgaeshō Kumiai, 1903.
The first section deals with the origin of the guild, its development, its relations with the Shogunate and other aspects. The second section contains the laws and ordinances relating to money over the years 1608-1872.

643. Takahashi Kamekichi 高橋亀吉, Nihon kin'yūron 日本金融論 (On Japanese banking), Tōkyō, Keizai Shuppambu, 1931.
Deals with the current situation of Japanese banking including the position of the zaibatsu, of trust companies, of insurance companies, of the Ōkurashō Yokimbu 大蔵省預金部 (Deposit Division of the Finance Ministry), the Japanese money market, the Japanese capital market, the control of bankers over industry and the function of the Bank of Japan. In the last chapter, the author offers certain reforms of the Japanese banking system.

644. Takimoto Seiichi 滝本誠一, Nihon kaheishi 日本貨幣史 (History of money in Japan), Kokushi Kōshūkai, 1923, 238 pp.; Tōkyō, Shunjūsha, 1929.
Deals with Japanese monetary history from ancient times to the Tokugawa period.

645. Tōyō Keizai Shimpōsha 東洋經濟新報社 (Oriental Economist News Company), Kin'yū rokujūnenshi 金融六十年史 (Sixty years' history of banking), Tōkyō, Tōyō Keizai Shimpōsha, 1924.
Deals with the history of Japanese banking during the period from the Meiji Restoration to the first World War.

646. Ishihama Tomoyuki 石浜知行, Tokushu kin'yū kikanshiron 特殊金融機関史論 (On the history of special banking organizations), Tōkyō, Ikuseisha, 1937.
Deals with special banking institutions such as the Nihon Ginkō 日本銀行 (Bank of Japan), the Ōkurashō Yokimbu 大蔵省預金部 (Deposit Division of the Finance Ministry), the Nihon Kangyō Ginkō 日本勧業銀行 (Japan Hypothec Bank), the Nihon Kōgyō Ginkō 日本興業銀行 (Japan Industrial Bank), several colonial banks, the Sangyō Kumiai Chūō Kinko 産業組合中央金庫 (Central Treasury of Industrial Cooperatives).

647. Yoshida Kensuke 吉田賢輔 and Honjō Eijirō 本庄栄治郎, Dainihon kaheishi 大日本貨幣史 (History of Japanese money), Tōkyō, Chōyōkai, 1925-26, 8 v.
An expanded edition of the Ōkurashō or Finance Ministry's earlier compilation on Japanese monetary history to 1875.

b. History of Banks and Other Financial Institutions

648. Hokkaidō Takushoku Ginkō 北海道拓殖銀行 (Colonial Bank of Hokkaidō), Hokkaidō kin'yū enkaku ippan 北海道金融沿革一斑 (Summary of the development of finance in Hokkaidō), Sapporo, Hokkaidō Takushoku Ginkō, 1911.

649. Ōkurashō Kin'yū Seido Chōsakai 大蔵省金融制度調査會 (Research Committee on the Banking System, Ministry of Finance), Kin'yū kikan hattatsushi 金融機関發達史 (Development of financial organs), Tōkyō, Itagaki Shoten, 1949.
Report of a committee of experts on banking problems. There is a brief account of the development of sixteen banking institutions---governmental, semi-governmental and private---and of the history of life insurance, trust companies, and security brokerage.

650. Sangyō Kumiai Chūō Kinko 産業組合中央金庫 (Central Treasury of the Industrial Cooperatives), Sangyō Kumiai Chūō Kinko jūnenshi 産業組合中央金庫十年誌 (Ten years' history of the Central Treasury of the Industrial Cooperatives), Tōkyō, Sangyō Kumiai Chūō Kinko, 1934.

See also entries 1104, 1106, 1129, 1130, 1136-1138, 1142, 1145, 1148-1150.

651. Sugimoto Masayuki 杉本正幸, Zenkoku nōkō ginkō hattatsushi 全國農工銀行發達史 (History of the development of banks of agriculture and industry in Japan), Tōkyō, Zenkoku Nōkō Ginkō Hattatsushi Hakkōsho, 1924.

652. Zōheikyoku 造幣局 (The Mint Bureau), Zōheikyoku rokujūnenshi 造幣局六十年誌 (Sixty years' history of the Mint Bureau), Ōsaka, Zōheikyoku, 1931.

8. Special Problems

a. The Reform of the Monetary System During the Meiji Period

653. Horie Yasuzō 堀江保蔵, Meiji yonen no heisei kaikaku 明治四年の幣制改革 (Monetary reform in 1871), in Honjō Eijirō, ed., Meiji ishin keizaishi kenkyū 明治維新經濟史研究 (Studies of the economic history of the Meiji Restoration), Tōkyō, Kaizōsha, 1930.

654. Kahei Seido Chōsakai 貨幣制度調査會 (Monetary System Research Commission), Kahei seido chōsakai hōkoku 貨幣制度調査會報告 (Report of the Monetary System Research Commission), Tōkyō, 1895.
The report of a commission appointed at an earlier date. It describes not only the monetary system of Japan but of other countries as well. Appendices provide a table of gold-silver price ratios and other materials relating to money, prices, and foreign trade.

655. Ōkurashō 大藏省 (Finance Ministry), Meiji kasei kōyō 明治貨政考要 (Summary of monetary policy in the Meiji period), Tōkyō, Ōkurashō, 1887, 3 v.
Provides important information concerning monetary administration during the period from 1867 to 1881.

656. Ōkurashō 大藏省 (Finance Ministry), Meiji sanjūnen heisei kaikaku shimatsu gaiyō 明治三十年幣制改革始末概要 (Particulars of the monetary reform in 1897), Tōkyō, Ōkurashō.
Presents the development of the Japanese monetary system after the Meiji Restoration and the details of the establishment of the gold standard in 1897.

657. Ōkurashō 大藏省 (Finance Ministry), Shihei seiri shimatsu 紙幣整理始末 (Particulars of the paper currency readjustment), Tōkyō, Ōkurashō, 1890.
Report of the Ministry to the Prime Minister on the control of governmental currency and of the disposition of paper currency issued by feudal lords during the period from 1881 to 1885.

b. The Gold Embargo

658. Fukai Eigo 深井英五, Kin hon'i ridatsugo no tsūka seisaku 金本位離脱後の通貨政策 (Monetary policy after leaving the gold standard), Tōkyō, Chikura Shobō, 1938.

659. Fukai Eigo 深井英五, Tsūka mondai to shite no kin kaikin 通貨問題としての金解禁 (Lifting of the gold embargo as a monetary problem), Tōkyō, Nihon Hyōronsha, 1929.
Deals with the debate over the return to the gold standard and related matters.

660. Ginkō Mondai Kenkyūkai 銀行問題研究會 (Research Society for Banking Problems), Kin yushutsu kinshishi ---kin kaikin mondai no riron to jissen 金輸出禁止史 — 金解禁問題の理論と實踐 (History of the gold embargo: theory and practice relating to problems of lifting the gold embargo), Tōkyō, Ginkō Mondai Kenkyūkai, 1929.
Among the subjects presented: the Japanese economy under the gold embargo, the prospect of return to the gold standard and relevant examples from foreign countries.

661. Hijikata Seibi 土方成美, Kin kaikin 金解禁 (Lifting of the gold embargo), Tōkyō, Nihon Hyōronsha, 1929.

662. Inomata Tsunao 猪俣津南雄, "Kin yushutsu saikinshi mondai hihan 金輸出再禁止問題批判 (Critical commentary on the problems relating to the re-embargo of gold)," Kaizō, 12.12, Dec., 1930, 94-117.
This and the next item present the return to gold, 1930-31, from the Marxist viewpoint.

663. Inomata Tsunao 猪俣津南雄, "Kin saikin o hihan-suru 金再禁を批判する (Critical commentary on the re-embargo of gold)," Chūō kōron, v. 47, no. 2, 1932.

664. Inoue Ronsō Hensankai 井上論叢編纂會 (Society for the Compilation of the Writings of Inoue), Inoue Junnosuke ronsō 井上準之助論叢 (The works of Inoue Junnosuke), Tōkyō, 1935, 4 v.
The collected writings of the Finance Minister in the Minseitō cabinet which brought about the return of Japan to the gold standard in 1930. Certain of these writings are separately listed below.

665. Inoue Junnosuke 井上準之助, "Kawase sōba no kaifuku to kin kaikin mondai 為替相場の回復と金解禁問題 (Recovery of exchange rates and the problem of the return to the gold standard)," Kokka Gakkai zasshi, v. 40, no. 7, 1926.

666. Inoue Junnosuke 井上準之助, Kin kaikin---zen-Nihon ni sakebu 金解禁—全日本に叫ぶ (Return to the gold standard: call to the whole of Japan), Tōkyō, Senshinsha, 1929.

667. Inoue Junnosuke 井上準之助 and Katsu Masanori 勝正憲, Kokumin keizai no tatenaoshi to kin kaikin 國民經濟の立直しと金解禁 (Reestablishment of national economy and the return to the gold standard), Tōkyō, Chikura Shobō, 1929.

668. Inoue Junnosuke 井上準之助, "Kin kaikin ni michibiku seifu narabi ni minkan no kakugo 金解禁に導く政府並に民間の覺悟 (Preparation of government and business for the return to the gold standard)," Zaisei keizai jichō, v. 16, no. 7, 1929.

669. Inoue Junnosuke 井上準之助, "Kin kaikin ni wa zaisei kinshuku ga kyūmu 金解禁には財政緊縮が急務 (Urgency in the curtailment of public finance in connection with the return to the gold standard)," Daiyamondo, v. 17, no. 19-20, 1929.

670. Inoue Junnosuke 井上準之助, "Kin kaikin no keizaikai ni ataeru eikyō 金解禁の經濟界に与える影響 (Expected influence of the return to the gold standard on business)," *Chūō kōron*, v. 44, no. 9, 1929.

671. Inoue Junnosuke 井上準之助, "Kokumin keizai no tatenaoshi to kin kaikin no kekkō ni tsuite kokumin ni uttō 國民經濟の立直しと金解禁の決行について國民に訴ふ (Appeal to the nation on the re-establishment of the national economy and the return to the gold standard)," *Tōkyō Kōjō Konwakai*, no. 43, 1929; also in *Ginkō ronsō*, v. 13, no. 3, 1929.

672. Inoue Junnosuke 井上準之助, "*Kyūheika kin kaikinron* 歸平價金解禁論 (Return to the gold standard at the old par)," *Kaizō*, v. 11, no. 9, 1929.

673. Inoue Junnosuke 井上準之助, "Kin kaikin no hi ni atatte 金解禁の日に当って (On the day of the return to gold standard)," *Ginkō ronsō*, v. 14, no. 2, 1930.

674. Inoue Junnosuke 井上準之助, *Kin kaikin zengo no keizai jijō* 金解禁前後の經濟事情 (Economic situation before and after the return to the gold standard), ? privately published, 1930.

675. Inoue Junnosuke 井上準之助, "Kin kaikin isshūnengo no kansō 金解禁一週年後の感想 (Thoughts on the first anniversary of the return to the gold standard)," *Tōkyō Kōjō Konwakai kaihō*, no. 53, 1931.

676. Inoue Junnosuke 井上準之助, "Kin no yushutsu saikinshi ni tsuite 金の輸出再禁止について (On the re-embargo of gold)," *Keizai geppō*, v. 3, no. 12, 1931.

677. Inoue Junnosuke 井上準之助, *Kin saikinshi to waga zaikai no zento* 金再禁止と我財界の前途 (Re-embargo of gold and the future of business), Tōkyō, Chikura Shobō, 1932.

678. Inoue Junnosuke 井上準之助, "Kin saikinshi wa mōdan 金再禁止は妄断 (The re-embargo of gold is a mistaken decision)," *Hoken oyobi kin'yū*, v. 9, no. 1, 1932.

679. Ishibashi Tanzan 石橋湛山, *Kin kaikin no eikyō to taisaku---shin-heika kaikin no teishō* 金解禁の影響と對策—新平價解禁の提唱 (The effect and policy of returning to the gold standard: proposal for returning to the gold standard at a new par), Tōkyō, Tōyō Keizai Shimpōsha, 1929.

680. Kimura Kihachirō 木村禧八郎, *Infureishon to Nihon keizai no kiki* インフレーションと日本經濟の危機 (Inflation and crisis in the Japanese economy), Tōkyō, Seibunkan, 1932.

681. Mitsuchi Chūzō 三土忠造, *Kin kaikin to kinshuku seisaku no hihan, fu: kin kaikin to nōson* 金解禁と緊縮政策の批判 附：金解禁と農村 (Critical comment on the return to the gold standard and on the retrenchment policy; appendix: return to the gold standard and the agricultural community), Tōkyō, Hōbunkan, 1929.

682. Nihon Ginkō Chōsakyoku 日本銀行調査局 (Bureau of Research of the Bank of Japan), *Kin yushutsu kinshi o chūshin to shitaru saikin jūnenkan ni okeru waga kuni zaikai no tembō* 金輸出禁止を中心としたる最近十年間に於ける我國財界の展望 (General view of the last ten years of business in Japan with special attention on the problem of leaving the gold standard), in Zenkoku Keizai Chōsakikan Rengōkai 全國經濟調査機關連合會 (All-Japan Association of Organizations concerned with Economic Surveys), *Nihon keizai no saikin jūnen* (The last ten years of the Japanese economy), Tōkyō, Kaizōsha, 1931.

683. Takahashi Kamekichi 高橋亀吉, *Kin yushutsu saikinshiron---fukeiki dakai no kihon taisaku* 金輸出再禁止論—不景氣打開の基本對策 (On the re-embargo of gold: the basic measure to meet the depression), Tōkyō, Senshinsha, 1930.

684. Takahashi Kamekichi 高橋亀吉, *Sekai hakyoku to Nihon keizai no henkaku---kin yushutsu kinshi to sono kōka* 世界破局と日本經濟の變革—金輸出禁止と其効果 (World crisis and the reform of the Japanese economy---the gold embargo and its effect), Tōkyō, Chikura Shobō, 1931.

685. Takahashi Korekiyo 高橋是清, "Kin saikinshi dankō wa jikyoku kyūkyū no daiippo 金再禁止断行は時局急救の第一歩 (Decision in favor of the gold re-embargo is the first step to relieve the current crisis)," *Tōkyō Kōjō Konwakai kaihō*, no. 63, 1932.

A statement by the Finance Minister of the Seiyūkai cabinet which undertook the re-embargo in December, 1931.

c. Inflation after World War II

686. Arizawa Hiromi 有沢廣巳, *Infureishon to shakaika* インフレーションと社會化 (Inflation and socialization), Tōkyō, Nihon Hyōronsha, 1948.

687. Daiyamondosha ダイヤモンド社, *Nihon infure to sengo keizai* 日本インフレと戦後經濟 (Japanese inflation and her post-war economy), Tōkyō, Daiyamondosha, 1947.

688. Hosono Kōichi 細野孝一, *Infureishon no jisshōteki kenkyū* インフレーションの實証的研究 (Factual study of inflation), Tōkyō, Chikura Shobō, 1947.

689. Kimura Kihachirō 木村禧八郎, *Infureishon no kenkyū* インフレーションの研究 (Study of inflation), Tōkyō, Ginza Shuppansha, 1948.

690. Ōuchi Hyōe 大内兵衛 , Wakimura Yoshitarō 脇村義太郎 , Arizawa Hiromi 有澤廣巳 , Minobe Ryōkichi 美濃部亮吉 , and Takahashi Masao 高橋正雄 , *Nihon infureishon no kenkyū* 日本インフレーションの研究 (Study of inflation in Japan), Tōkyō, Kōdosha, 1946.

691. Takahashi Taizō 高橋泰藏 , *Infureishon shinkō no hōsoku to gendankai* インフレーション進行の方則と現段階 (Principles of the development of inflation and its present stage), Tōkyō, Tōyō Keizai Shimpōsha, 1948.

692. Tsuru Shigeto 都留重人 , *Sengo Nihon no infureishon* 戦後日本のインフレーション (Inflation in post-war Japan), Tōkyō, Iwanami Shoten, 1949.

693. Yamaguchi Shigeru 山口茂 and Higuchi Gorō 樋口午郎 , *Nihon infureishon no bunseki* 日本インフレーションの分析 (Analysis of Japanese inflation), Tōkyō, Tōyō Keizai Shimpōsha, 1948.

694. Yoshino Toshihiko 吉野俊彦 , *Infureishon no keizaigaku* インフレーションの經濟學 (The economics of inflation), Tōkyō, Jiji Tsūshinsha, 1948.

See also entries 467, 470, 472, 475, 482.

d. The Problems of the Price of Rice

695. Honjō Eijirō 本庄榮治郎 , *Jōheisō no kenkyū* 常平倉の研究 (Study on *jōheisō*---official storehouses of rice to protect the rice market from great fluctuations of price), Kyōto, Naigai Shuppan Kabushiki Kaisha, 1925.
Consists of two parts: the first part deals with the origin and development of *jōheisō*, and the second, with the *jōheisō* developed in Mito.

696. Honjō Eijirō 本庄榮治郎 , *Tokugawa bakufu no beika chōsetsu* 徳川幕府の米價調節 (The control of the price of rice by the Tokugawa government), Tōkyō, Kōbundō, 1924.
Discusses such subjects as fluctuation of rice price during the Tokugawa period, the method and development of control of price by the Shogunate government. Provides statistics of rice price and of population during the Tokugawa period in the appendices.

697. Ishihara Yasuhide 石原保秀 , *Beika no hensen* 米價の變遷 (Fluctuations of the price of rice), Tōkyō, Ken'yoku Chōseikai, 1925.
Deals with fluctuations of the price of rice from the Middle Ages to 1924.

698. Ishihara Yasuhide 石原保秀 , *Beika no hensen (zokuhen), fu: hompō korai no bukka chōsetsu* 米價の變遷(續編),附:本邦古來の物價調節 (Fluctuation of the price of rice, continued; appendix: price control from ancient times), Tōkyō, Ken'yoku Chōseikai, 1935.
A supplemental volume to the above (no. 697). Contains statistics on fluctuation of rice price from 1925 to 1935.

699. Naimushō Chihōkyoku 内務省地方局 (The Local Bureau of the Ministry of Domestic Affairs), *Tokugawa bakufu no beikoku ni taisuru seisaku* 徳川幕府の米穀に對する政策 (Rice policy of the Tokugawa government), Tōkyō, Naimushō Chihōkyoku, 1919.
Contains a survey of inflationary trends in the price of rice at the beginning of the 18th century and an analysis of the Kyōho rice uprising and its settlement.

700. Nishizawa Kiichi 西澤基一 , *Beikokuhō jisseki chōsa* 米穀法實績調査 (Research on the enforcement of the Rice Act), Ōsaka, Ōsaka Shōka Daigaku Keizai Kenkyūsho, 1930.
Contains a brief survey of the control of the price of rice before the enactment of the Rice Act in 1921, and detailed research on the results of the Act during ten years after its enactment.

701. Nōrinshō Beikokubu 農林省米穀部 (The Rice Bureau of the Agriculture Ministry), *Beikokuhō no enkaku* 米穀法の沿革 (Particulars relating to the Rice Act), Tōkyō, Nōrinshō Beikokubu, 1933.
Deals with the development of the Rice Act from 1920 to 1932.

702. Ōkurashō Rizaikyoku 大藏省理財局 (The Financial Bureau of the Finance Ministry), *Meiji nenkan beika chōsetsu enkakushi* 明治年間米價調節沿革史 (History of the control of the price of rice during the Meiji period), Tōkyō, Ōkurashō Rizaikyoku, 1919.
A detailed explanatory work on the price of rice and the control policy up to the year, 1890.

703. Suzuki Naoji 鈴木直二 , ed., *Beikokuhō seitei no keii shiryō* 米穀法制定の經緯資料 (Materials relating to the enactment of the Rice Act), Tōkyō, Ganshōdō, 1938.
Materials included are divided according to three periods: the high price period of 1912-13, the low price period of 1924-26, and the high price period of 1927-28.

704. Suzuki Naoji 鈴木直二 , *Ōsaka ni okeru bakumatsu beika hendōshi* 大阪に於ける幕末米價變動史 (History of fluctuation in the price of rice in Ōsaka during the last days of the shogunate), Tōkyō, Shikai Shobō, 1935.
A work based on the study of "daily price-list" of Daimonjiya (a representative Ōsaka merchant) which recorded the price of rice in Ōsaka after 1834.

705. Zenkoku Torihikijo Dōmei Rengōkai 全國取引所同盟連合會 (National Federation of Associations of Stock Exchanges), *Beikokuhō ni kansuru sankō shiryō* 米穀法に関する参考資料 (Materials relating to the Rice Act), Zenkoku Torihikisho Rengōkai, 1928, 2 v.
A summarized history of the control of the price of rice is followed by the relevant laws and ordinances, an estimate of the effect of the Rice Act, and the views of officials, of scholars, of men of affairs, and of the newspapers.

Chapter IX

Agriculture and Other Primary Industries

Japanese literature on agriculture covers a wide field. It may express traditional respect for farming as communion with nature and, at the other extreme, it may report some experiment on seed disinfection. The attempt has been made here to select useful works that deal with the economics of agriculture from the point of view of history, fact, or analysis. This chapter offers also a limited number of references on mining, fishing, and forestry.

The Japanese economist has brought out in his exposition of the general problems of agriculture certain features characteristic of Japan. There is the great importance of rice. This means that water is necessary and mechanization difficult. The great population of Japan makes for operations on a small scale. Concentration of ownership has made for high rentals. Certain writers emphasize the significance of feudal traditions and attitudes. These features taken together make for a high product per unit of area and low product per man.

The history of agriculture has been intensively studied at all times. The Tokugawa period, which had produced its own historians, was studied during the early years of Meiji as a basis for new policy. After some years attention was turned to the relation between agriculture and industry during the industrialization of the country.

The land reform since World War II has been and is now being examined by the agricultural economists. There has been some use of historical comparison. The analysis of the economist has, however, tended to give great weight to the effect of the land reform on productivity. The prospect for increased output per man is applied to the land reform and to other current proposals in the field of agriculture. There is current interest, for example, in the mechanization of agriculture as a means of raising incomes.

The attention of the student of the economics of agriculture is called to the many official and unofficial sources of statistical information reported in the third chapter.

1. Bibliographies

706. Arima Nōson Mondai Kenkyūsho 有馬農村問題研究所 (Arima Research Institute for Agricultural Problems), Nōson mondai bunken shiryō 農村問題文献資料 (List of books and materials relating to agricultural problems), Tōkyō, Nihon Hyōronsha, 1925.

707. Nōrinshō Toshokan 農林省圖書館 (The Library of the Ministry of Agriculture and Forestry), Nōrinshō kankōbutsu mokuroku 農林省刊行物目錄 (Catalog of publications of the Ministry of Agriculture and Forestry), Tōkyō, Nōrinshō, 1948.

A list of the publications of the Ministry classified by bureau and section. The date of publication is given.

708. Nōrinshō Toshokan 農林省圖書館 (The Library of the Ministry of Agriculture and Forestry), Nōrinshō toshokan zōsho mokuroku dai ikkan 農林省圖書館藏書目錄第一巻 (Catalog of the library of the Ministry of Agriculture and Forestry), Tōkyō, Nōrinshō, 1950.

A list of about 8000 books on agriculture and other primary industries which are in the library of the Ministry.

709. Ōno Shirō 大野史朗, Nōgaku bunken mokuroku 農學文献目錄 (Catalog of literature on agricultural science), Tōkyō, Meibundō, 1930-31, 2 v.

A list of works relating to agriculture in general. Volume one covers publications to 1924 and volume two, the period 1925-29.

710. Ono Takeo 小野武夫, Nōmin shiryō kaisetsu 農民史料解説 (Comments on materials relating to the history of farmers) [=v. 6 of the Nihon shihonshugi hattatsushi kōza (Lectures on the development of Japanese capitalism) (No. 370)], Tōkyō, Iwanami Shoten, 1933.

The periods before and after the Meiji Restoration are dealt with in separate parts.

711. Ōuchi Tsutomu 大内力, ed., Nōson zaisei bunken mokuroku 農村財政文献目錄 (Catalog of literature on the relation of agriculture to public finance), Tōkyō, Nōrinshō, Nōgyō Sōgō Kenkyūsho, 1950.

712. Zenkoku Nōgyōkai 全國農業會 (National Federation of Agricultural Associations), Zenkoku Nōgyōkai chōsa kankō tosho mokuroku 全國農業會調査刊行圖書目錄 (Catalog of publications of research works by the Zenkoku Nōgyōkai), Tōkyō, Zenkoku Nōgyōkai Chōsabu, 1948.

2. General Problems of Agriculture

713. Azuma Tōsaku 我妻東策, Nōson sangyō kikōshi 農村産業機構史 (History of structural change in agricultural industry), Tōkyō, Sōbunkaku, 1937.

The author deals with the causes and the process of change in the structure of economic activities in the countryside after the rise of modern industrialism in Japan. He selects for study thirty-four activities which declined during the period and thirty-seven which prospered.

714. Baba Keinosuke 馬場啓之助, ed., Sanshigyō no keizaiteki bunseki 蠶絲業の經濟的分析 (Economic analysis of the silk reeling industry), Tōkyō, Nihon Hyōronsha, 1951.
Report of the survey of this industry in Yamanashi, Gumma, and Nagano prefectures carried out by the Nōrinshō Sōgō Kenkyūjo 農林省綜合研究所 (Research Institute of the Ministry of Agriculture and Forestry).

715. Furushima Toshio 古島敏雄, Kinsei Nihon nōgyō no kiso kōzō 近世日本農業の基礎構造 (Basic structure of Japanese agriculture in the modern [Tokugawa] age), Tōkyō, Nihon Hyōronsha, 1952.

716. Honjō Eijirō 本庄栄治郎, Waga kuni kinsei no nōson mondai 我國近世の農村問題 (Problems of the rural village in the modern [Tokugawa] period), Tōkyō, Kaizōsha, 1930.
Specific problems of the Japanese farmer during the Tokugawa period are presented. There are chapters on the land tax, basic problems of farm policy, the decline in population, the system of tenancy, and peasants' uprisings.

717. Inamura Ryūichi 稲村隆一, Nihon ni okeru nōson mondai 日本に於ける農村問題 (Rural problems in Japan), Tōkyō, Ikuseisha, 1938.
Discusses the reform of the land system at the time of the Meiji Restoration and the development of capitalism in Japanese agriculture.

718. Inomata Tsunao 猪俣津南雄, Nōson mondai nyūmon 農村問題入門 (Introduction to agricultural problems), Tōkyō, Chūō Kōronsha, 1937; Tōkyō, Kōdosha, 1948.
A representative Marxian interpretation of the problems of agriculture and the rural village.

719. Inoue Harumaru 井上晴丸, Nōgyō mondai nyūmon 農業問題入門 (Introduction to agricultural problems), Tōkyō, Nōgyō Gijutsu Kyōkai, 1948.
An interpretation of Japanese agricultural problems by a Marxian economist.

720. Kamiyama Shigeo 神山茂夫, Nihon nōgyō ni okeru shihonshugi no hattatsu 日本農業における資本主義の發達 (Development of capitalism in Japanese agriculture), Tōkyō, Jitsugyō no Nihonsha, 1947.
An influential member of the Japanese Communist Party deals with the relation of agriculture to the development of capitalist economy in Japan in a book which was written in 1940 but did not become openly available until later. It is regarded by many as the viewpoint of the Party. Among the subjects are problem of theory, commercialized agriculture, the problems of agricultural labor, land ownership and tenancy, small scale farming, and the place of agriculture in the national economy.

721. Kimura Yasuji 木村靖二, Nihon nōgyō kyōkō no bunseki 日本農業恐慌の分析 (Analysis of the crisis in Japanese agriculture), Tōkyō, Hakuyōsha, 1948.
The author attempts an explanation of the agricultural crisis of 1930. There is a detailed examination by prefectures. The crisis is held by the author to have brought about the extension of specialization and capitalism with decreased benefit to the farm population. There is some attention to the post-war period. Marxist influence is evident.

722. Koike Motoyuki 小池基之, Nihon nōgyō to suiden 日本農業と水田 (Japanese agriculture and the paddy field), Tōkyō, Nihon Hyōronsha, 1946.
Deals with the technical problems of rice production in Japanese paddy fields and with the characteristics of Japanese agricultural labor which are inherent in such production.

723. Koike Motoyuki 小池基之, Nihon nōgyō kōzōron 日本農業構造論 (On the structure of Japanese agriculture), Tōkyō, Jichōsha, 1948.

724. Kondō Yasuo 近藤康男, Nihon nōgyō keizairon 日本農業經濟論 (Treatise on Japanese agricultural economy), Tōkyō, Nihon Hyōronsha, 1947.
Deals with the fundamentals of Japanese agricultural production and with their influence on its development as shown in its history since the Meiji period.

725. Kondō Yasuo 近藤康男, Nōgyō mondai kōwa 農業問題講話 (Lectures on agricultural problems), Tōkyō, Yamakawa Shoten, 1947.

726. Kondō Yasuo 近藤康男, Nōgyō seisaku 農業政策 (Agricultural policy), Tōkyō, Yūhikaku, 1950.

727. Kondō Yasuo 近藤康男, Ryūan 硫安 (Ammonium sulphate), Tōkyō, Nihon Hyōronsha, 1951.
The relation of Japanese agriculture to the Japanese economy is presented as shown in the development of the production of ammonium sulphate. The volume carries the sub-title, Nihon shihonshugi to hiryōkōgyō (Japanese capitalism and the fertilizer industry).

728. Kondō Yasuo 近藤康男, Sengo no nōgyō mondai 戦後の農業問題 (Agricultural problems in the post-war period), Tōkyō, Nihon Hyōronsha, 1951.
A collection of articles by a leading agricultural economist.

729. Kurihara Hyakuju 栗原百壽, Nihon nōgyō no kisokōzō 日本農業の基礎構造 (The fundamental structure of Japanese agriculture), Tōkyō, Chūō Kōronsha, 1948.
There is detailed description, with much statistical information, under such headings as: the structure of land ownership, agricultural production, the productivity of labor and land. The period covered is from the Meiji Restoration to about 1940.

730. Kurihara Hyakuju 栗原百壽, Nihon nōgyō no hatten kōzō 日本農業の發展構造 (The developing structure of Japanese economy), Tōkyō, Nihon Hyōronsha, 1949.

A successor of the author's Nihon nōgyō no kisokōzō (no. 729), bringing materials up to date from 1940. The author deals with such subjects as the disintegration of class structure, the redistribution of income among farm groups, changes in the ownership of farm land, changes in the scale of farming, and the structure of production.

731. Nasu Hiroshi 那須皓, Nihon nōgyōron 日本農業論 (Japanese agriculture), Tōkyō, Chikura Shobō, 1929.

This is a work by a well-known economist on agriculture who was highly influential in the field of agricultural administration in pre-war Japan.

732. Nōrinshō Kambō Chōsaka 農林省官房調査課 (Research Section, Minister's Secretariat, Agriculture and Forestry Ministry), Tenkanki ni tatsu Nihon nōgyō 轉換期に立つ日本農業 (Japanese agriculture in a period of transition), Tōkyō, Jitsugyō no Nihonsha, 1952.

The viewpoint of the Ministry toward agricultural problems together with much statistical information.

733. Nōrinshō Nōseikyoku 農林省農政局 (Bureau of Agricultural Administration, Ministry of Agriculture and Forestry), Nōka no sozei futan ni kansuru chōsa hōkoku 農家の租税負担に関する調査報告 (Report on the tax burden of farmers), Tōkyō, Nōrinshō, 1949.

734. Ono Takeo 小野武夫, Ishin nōson shakai shiron 維新農村社會史論 (On the social history of rural districts during the period of the Meiji Restoration), Tōkyō, Tōkō Shoin, 1932.

Deals with the changes in the social system in rural districts of the time. Contains valuable materials relating to the land system.

735. Ono Takeo 小野武夫, Nōson kikō no bunretsu katei 農村機構の分裂過程 (Process of the disintegration of agricultural society), Tōkyō, Kaizōsha, 1928.

The author presents what may be called a history of social disintegration in the countryside from the beginning of the Meiji period. Attention is given also to the political aspects and to the reform of the land system.

736. Ono Takeo 小野武夫, Nōson shakaishi ronkō 農村社會史論考 (Articles on the history of agrarian society), Tōkyō, Ganshōdō, 1927.

A collection of the author's articles relating to changes in the structure of agricultural society during the Tokugawa period. Contains subjects such as farmers' uprisings, passive resistance of farmers in the feudal period, development of modern land ownership, and changes in the tenancy system.

737. Ōuchi Tsutomu 大内力, Nihon shihonshugi no nōgyō mondai 日本資本主義の農業問題 (Agricultural problems of Japanese capitalism), Tōkyō, Nihon Hyōronsha, 1947.

This work presents an economic analysis of Japanese agriculture with appropriate critical commentary and factual information.

738. Ōuchi Tsutomu 大内力, Nihon nōgyō no zaiseigaku 日本農業の財政學 (Public finance in relation to Japanese agriculture), Tōkyō, Tōdai Kyōdō Kumiai Shuppambu, 1950.

739. Ōuchi Tsutomu 大内力, Nihon nōgyō no ronri 日本農業の論理 (Logic of Japanese agriculture), Tōkyō, Nihon Hyōronsha, 1949.

A collection of the author's articles dealing with his methodological viewpoint.

740. Toda Shintarō 戸田慎太郎, Nihon shihonshugi to Nihon nōgyō no hatten 日本資本主義と日本農業の發展 (Japanese capitalism and the development of Japanese agriculture), Tōkyō, Nihon Hyōronsha, 1947.

741. Tōhata Seiichi 東畑精一, Nihon nōgyō no tenkai katei 日本農業の展開過程 (Process of the development of Japanese agriculture), Tōkyō, Iwanami Shoten, 1936; repr. 1947.

The author is generally regarded as a leading figure among agricultural economists. The book gives a well-balanced general view of Japanese agriculture and its problems after the Meiji period. One of the best books in the field.

742. Tōura Shōji 東浦庄治, Nihon nōgyō gairon 日本農業概論 (Outline of Japanese agriculture), Tōkyō, Iwanami Shoten, 1934.

743. Uno Kōzō 宇野弘藏, Nōgyō mondai joron 農業問題序論 (Introduction to agricultural problems), Tōkyō, Kaizōsha, 1947.

744. Uno Kōzō 宇野弘藏, Suzuki Kōichirō 鈴木鴻一郎, Ōuchi Tsutomu 大内力, and Saitō Haruzō 齋藤晴造, Nihon ni okeru nōgyō to shihonshugi 日本に於ける農業と資本主義 (Agriculture and capitalism in Japan), Tōkyō, Jitsugyō no Nihonsha, 1948.

745. Watanabe Shin'ichi 渡辺信一, Nihon nōson jinkōron 日本農村人口論 (On the Japanese agricultural population), Tōkyō, Nankōdō, 1933.

746. Yokoi Tokitaka 横井時敬, Shōnō ni kansuru kenkyū 小農に関する研究 (Study of small scale farms), 1924.

An early but valuable work on the small scale farmers.

747. Yoshioka Kin'ichi 吉岡金市, *Nihon nōgyō rōdōron* 日本農業勞働論 (On Japanese agricultural labor), Tōkyō, Jichōsha, 1939.

748. Yutaka Masao 硲正夫, *Nihon nōgyō no shomondai* 日本農業の諸問題 (Problems of Japanese agriculture), Tōkyō, Kisetsusha, 1948.

See also entries 356, 381-395, 409-427, 431, 432, 435, 960.

3. History

749. Azuma Tōsaku 我妻東策, *Meiji zenki nōseishi no shomondai* 明治前期農政史の諸問題 (Problems of agricultural administration in the first half of the Meiji period), Tōkyō, Mibu Shoin, 1936.
Deals with the development of local administration and local land systems, the land tax, grants-in-aid, and policy toward stock-farming during the early Meiji period.

750. Azuma Tōsaku 我妻東策, *Nisshin Nichiro senji no nōgyō seisaku* 日清日露戰時の農業政策 (Agricultural policy during the periods of the Sino-Japanese and the Russo-Japanese wars), Tōkyō, Ikuseisha, 1938.

751. Fumin Kyōkai 富民協會 (Association for a Prosperous People), ed., *Shōwa nōgyō hattatsushi* 昭和農業發達史 (Development of agriculture in the Shōwa era), Tōkyō, Fumin Kyōkai, 1937.
Fourteen articles by authors who are authorities in their particular fields. A chronology of important events in the history of agriculture, statistical tables and important laws are to be found in appendices.

752. Ishizaka Kitsuju 石坂橘樹, *Nihon nōgyō shiron* 日本農業史論 (On the history of Japanese agriculture), Tōkyō, Ganshōdō, 1926.

753. Kimura Yasuji 木村靖二, *Nōmin seikatsu no kenkyū* 農民生活の研究 (Study of the life of farmers), Tōkyō, Nishōdō, 1924.
There are chapters on agricultural policy during the Tokugawa period, on agricultural population, on the control of the farming class, and other related subjects.

754. Kimura Yasuji 木村靖二, *Nōson shakai keizaishi* 農村社會經濟史 (Social and economic history of the agricultural village), Tōkyō, Hakuyōsha, 1931.
Covers the period from the time of the family clan to that of the capitalist economy.

755. Nakamura Kichiji 中村吉治, *Kinsei shoki nōseishi kenkyū* 近世初期農政史研究 (Study of the history of agricultural administration in the early modern era), Tōkyō, Iwanami Shoten, 1938.
Deals with such problems as tribute, compulsory labor, population control, maintenance of civil status and policies for the relief and encouragement of rural villages. The period covered ends with early Tokugawa.

756. Nihon Rekishi Chiri Gakkai 日本歷史地理學會 (Japanese Historical Geography Society), "Nihon nōminshi 日本農民史 (History of the Japanese farmer)," *Rekishi chiri* (Historical geography), Tōkyō, Nihon Rekishi Chiri Gakkai, v. 44, no. 3, 1924.
Sixteen articles by authorities, including the life of the farmer during the Middle Age by Nishioka Toranosuke, the problems of poverty of the farm village by Shiba Shinotarō and the movement of agricultural population by Miwa Jusō.

757. Nōrinshō Nōmukyoku 農林省農務局 (The Bureau of Agricultural Affairs of the Ministry of Agriculture and Forestry), ed. and rev., *Dainihon nōseishi* 大日本農政史 (History of Japanese agricultural administration), Tōkyō, Bungei Shunjūsha, 1932.
A revised edition of *Dainihon nōsei ruihen* (no. 759).

758. Nōshōmushō 農商務省 (Agriculture and Commerce Ministry), *Dainihon nōshi* 大日本農史 (Agricultural history of Japan), Tōkyō, Nōshōmushō, 1890-91, 3 v.
A collection of source material on the agriculture of Japan and its administration arranged chronologically and covering the whole period from pre-historical times to the present.

759. Nōshōmushō 農商務省 (Ministry of Agriculture and Commerce), *Dainihon nōsei ruihen* 大日本農政類編 (Compilation of data on Japanese agricultural administration), Tōkyō, Nōshōmushō, 1897, 1 v.
Revised and enlarged edition of the preceding work.

760. Ono Takeo 小野武夫, *Nōmin keizaishi kenkyū* 農民經濟史研究 (Study of the history of farm economy), Tōkyō, Ganshōdō, 1924.
A collection of the author's articles dealing chiefly with the land and tenant system.

761. Ono Takeo 小野武夫, *Tokugawa jidai no nōka keizai* 德川時代の農家經濟 (Farm economy in the Tokugawa period), Tōkyō, Ganshōdō, 1926.
A compilation of factual data on agriculture during the Tokugawa period, including prices of land and rice, division of the crop between landlord and tenant, the life of the farmer, etc.

762. Ono Takeo 小野武夫, *Kindai Nihon nōson hattatsushiron* 近代日本農村發達史論 (On the development of Japanese agricultural villages in the modern era), Tōkyō, Hodaka Shobō, 1950.

763. Sakurai Takeo 櫻井武雄 , Kindai Nihon nōseishi 近代日本農政史 (History of Japanese agricultural administration in the modern age), Tōkyō, Sekai Shoin, 1947.

764. Takigawa Seijirō 滝川政治郎 , Hōseishijō yori mitaru Nihon nōmin no seikatsu---ritsuryō jidai 法制史上より観たる日本農民の生活 — 律令時代 (Life of the Japanese farmer from the viewpoint of legal history: early period of penal and administrative codes), Tōkyō, Dōjinsha Shoten, 1926-27, 2 v.

Deals with the economic and social state of farmers during the Nara period. The first volume deals with social classes, the land system, etc. The second volume presents observations on expenditures, taxation, military service, the concentration of land holdings, and the development of the feudal system.

765. Tamagawa Haruzō 玉川治三 , Nihon nōminshi 日本農民史 (History of the Japanese farmer), Tōkyō, Seibidō, 1935.

Deals with the subject from the Nara to the Tokugawa periods.

766. Tōyō Keizai Kenkyūbu 東洋經濟研究部 (Research Section, the Oriental Economist), ed., Meiji Taishō nōson keizai no hensen 明治大正農村經濟の變遷 (The development of agricultural economy in the Meiji and Taishō periods), Tōkyō, Tōyō Keizaisha, 1926, 292+165 pp.

767. Yanagida Kunio 柳田國男 , Nihon nōminshi 日本農民史 (History of the Japanese farmer), Tōkyō, Tōkō Shoin, 1940.

The author is a well-known scholar in the field of Japanese folk-lore.

4. Peasant Uprisings and Movements among Farmers

768. Aoki Keiichirō 青木恵一郎 , Nihon nōmin undōshi 日本農民運動史 (History of farmers' movements in Japan), Tōkyō, Minshū Hyōronsha, 1947.

769. Hasegawa Yoshio 長谷川美雄 , Nōmin undō no shiteki kōsatsu 農民運動の史的考察 (Historical survey of agrarian movements), Tōkyō, Nihon Nōson Shinkōkai, 1924.

770. Kimura Yasuji 木村靖二 , Nihon nōmin sōdōshi 日本農民騷動史 (History of the riots of Japanese farmers), Tōkyō, Nishōdō Shoten, 1925.

771. Kimura Yasuji 木村靖二 , Nihon nōmin sōtoshi 日本農民争斗史 (History of the struggles of Japanese farmers), Tōkyō, Hakuyōsha, 1930.

Deals with agrarian uprisings in four periods: the feudal period, the fall of the feudal age, the early capitalistic period, and the age of highly developed capitalism.

772. Kimura Yasuji 木村靖二 , Kindai Nihon nōmin undō hattatsushi 近代日本農民運動發達史 (The development of the agrarian movement in modern Japan), Tōkyō, Hakuyōsha, 1931.

773. Kuroda Hisao 黒田壽男 and Ikeda Tsuneo 池田恒雄 , Nihon nōmin kumiai undōshi 日本農民組合運動史 (History of Japanese farmers' cooperatives), Tōkyō, Shinchi Shobō, 1949.

774. Kokushō Iwao 黒正巖 , Hyakushō ikki no kenkyū 百姓一揆の研究 (Study of farmers' riots), Tōkyō, Iwanami Shoten, 1928.

A study of the decline of Japanese feudalism by means of an examination of the more than 500 agrarian uprisings during the whole of the Tokugawa period.

775. Kokushō Iwao 黒正巖 , Hyakushō ikki gaikan oyobi nempyō 百姓一揆概觀及年表 (General view of agrarian riots with a chronological table), Tōkyō, Nihon Hyōronsha, 1937.

Points out the non-revolutionary characteristics of traditional Japanese agrarian uprisings. The chronological table covers the period from 1603 to 1867.

776. Kokushō Iwao 黒正巖 , Hyakushō ikki shidan 百姓一揆史談 (Anecdotal history of farmers' riots), Tōkyō, Nihon Hyōronsha, 1929.

777. Ono Takeo 小野武夫 , Tokugawa jidai hyakushō ikki sōdan 徳川時代百姓一揆叢談 (Stories of farmers' riots in the Tokugawa period), Tōkyō, Tōkō Shoin, 1927, 2 v.

A compilation of extensive materials concerning agrarian uprisings during the Tokugawa period.

778. Ono Takeo 小野武夫 , Ishin nōmin hōkitan 維新農民蜂起譚 (Stories of farmers' rebellions during the Restoration), Tōkyō, Kaizōsha, 1930.

A collection of historical data concerned with agrarian uprisings in the early Meiji period.

779. Tamura Eitarō 田村榮太郎 , Kindai Nihon nōmin undō shiron 近代日本農民運動史論 (On the history of the farmers' movements of Japan in the modern age), Tōkyō, Getsuyō Shobō, 1948.

780. Tamura Eitarō 田村榮太郎 , Hōkenseika no nōmin ikki 封建制下の農民一揆 (Agrarian riots under the feudal system), Tōkyō, Sōbunkaku, 1933.

781. Tsuchiya Takao 土屋喬雄 and Ono Takeo 小野武夫 , Meiji shonen nōmin sōjōroku 明治初年農民騷擾録 (Agrarian disturbances in the early Meiji period), Tōkyō, Namboku Shoin, 1931.

A collection of valuable information. Contains a chronological table of agrarian uprisings in the early Meiji period.

5. Land System and Tenancy

782. Ariga Kizaemon 有賀喜左衛門, Nōson shakai no kenkyū---nago no fueki 農村社會の研究—名子の賦役 (Study of agricultural society: compulsory service of nago), Tōkyō, Kawade Shobō, 1938.
The term nago is applied in Japan to tenants in a position similar to that of serfdom, of whom compulsory labor is required. This is a general account of such tenancy showing the nature and significance of the system of compulsory labor.

783. Ariga Kizaemon 有賀喜左衛門, Nihon kazoku seido to kosaku seido 日本家族制度と小作制度 (The family system and tenancy system in Japan), Tōkyō, Kawade Shobō, 1944.

784. Hosokawa Kiichi 細川亀一, Nihon jiryō shōen keizaishi 日本寺領荘園經濟史 (Economic history of the Japanese temple manor), Tōkyō, Hakuyōsha, 1932.
This work presents an exposition of the temple manor, its nature, establishment,organization, military system, and its system of serfdom.

785. Imai Rintarō 今井林太郎, Nihon shōenseiron 日本荘園制論 (On the Japanese manor system), Tōkyō, Mikasa Shobō, 1939.

786. Nakada Kaoru 中田薫, Shōen no kenkyū 荘園の研究 (Study of the manor system), Tōkyō, Shōkō Shoin, 1948.

787. Nomura Iwao 野村岩夫, Kankō kosakuken ni kansuru kenkyū 慣行小作權に関する研究 (Research on customary tenant-rights), Tōkyō, Kyōchōkai, 1937.

788. Nōrinshō Nōmukyoku 農林省農務局 (The Bureau of Agricultural Affairs, the Ministry of Agriculture and Forestry), Kosaku sōgi no gaiyō 小作爭議の概要 (Survey of tenant's disputes), Tōkyō, Nōrinshō, 1930.
Commentary and statistics on tenants' disputes year by year with information on landlords' associations, tenants' unions, and arbitration.

789. Ogura Takeichi 小倉武一, Tochirippō no shiteki kōsatsu 土地立法の史的考察 (Historical observations on land legislation), Tōkyō, Nōrinshō Nōgyō Sōgō Kenkyūsha, 1951.
The author, a government official in the Ministry of Agriculture and Forestry, begins his analysis of private ownership of land with the so-called shinjinushi (new landlords) of the late Tokugawa period.

790. Ono Takeo 小野武夫, Nihon shōen seido shiron 日本荘園制度史論 (Articles on the history of the Japanese manor system), Tōkyō, Yūhikaku, 1943.

791. Ono Takeo 小野武夫, Meiji izen tochi seido shiron 明治以前土地制度史論 (On the history of the land system before the Meiji period), Tōkyō, Yūhikaku, 1948.

792. Shimizu Mitsuo 清水三男, Chūsei shōen no kiso kōzō 中世荘園の基礎構造 (Basic structure of the manor in the Middle Age), Kyōto, Takagiri Shoin, 1949.

793. Fujima Seidai 藤間生大, Nihon shōenshi 日本荘園史 (History of the Japanese manor), Tōkyō, Kondō Shoten, 1947.

See also entries 381-395, 409-427.

6. Land Reform After World War II

794. Furushima Toshio 古島敏雄, Kaikaku tojō no Nihon nōgyō 改革途上の日本農業 (Japanese agriculture on the way toward reformation), Tōkyō, Hakuyō Shoten, 1949.

795. Itō Ritsu 伊藤律, Nōgyō kakumei no kihon mondai 農業革命の基本問題 (Basic problems of agricultural revolution), Tōkyō, Kenshinsha, 1948.

796. Hirano Yoshitarō 平野義太郎, Nōson kindaika e no michi 農村近代化への途 (Path to the modernization of agricultural society), Tōkyō, Chōryūsha, 1948.

797. Hirano Yoshitarō 平野義太郎, Nōgyō mondai to tochi kaikaku 農業問題と土地改革 (Agricultural problems and land reform), Tōkyō, Nihon Hyōronsha, 1948.

798. Jiji Tsūshinsha 時事通信社, under the supervision of the Nōrinshō 農林省 (Agriculture and Forestry Ministry), Shin nōchi seido kaisetsu 新農地制度解説 (Commentary on the new agricultural land system), Tōkyō, Jiji Tsūshinsha, 1947.
A commentary on the two acts which were the legal basis of the land reform after the second World War.

799. Katō Ichirō 加藤一郎 and Wagatsuma Sakae 我妻榮, Nōchihō no kaisetsu 農地法の解説 (Commentary on the Farm Land Act), Tōkyō, Nihon Hyōronsha, 1948.
A commentary by a leading lawyer.

800. Kimura Yasuji 木村靖二, Nōchihō zensho 農地法全書 (Guide to the Farm Land Act), Tōkyō, Hakuyōsha, 1948.

801. Kondō Yasuo 近藤康男 , Sengo no nōgyō mondai 戰後の農業問題 (Agricultural problems in the post-war period), Tōkyō, Nihon Hyōronsha, 1947.

802. Kondō Yasuo 近藤康男 , Tochi mondai no tenkai 土地問題の展開 (Development of the land problem), Tōkyō, Jichōsha, 1948.

803. Kondō Yasuo 近藤康男 , Nōchi kaikaku no shomondai 農地改革の諸問題 (Various problems of the land reform), Tōkyō, Yūhikaku, 1951.
A collection of articles which provide valuable materials on the effects of the land reform. Among the articles are: Real situation of illegal purchase and sale of land, survey of the land rental, and change of land ownership.

804. Mori Kiichi 森喜一 , Nihon no nōgyō kakumei---nōchi kaikaku to kyōkō 日本の農業革命 — 農地改革と恐慌 (Japanese agricultural revolution---land reform and crisis), Tōkyō, Hakuyōsha, 1949.

805. Nōchi Kaikaku Kiroku Iinkai 農地改革記錄委員會 (Committee for Recording the Course of the Land Reform), Nōchi kaikaku temmatsu gaiyō 農地改革顛末概要 (Survey of the course of the land reform), Tōkyō, Nōsei Chōsakai, 1951.
This is the most extensive and reliable report on the land reform of the post-war period. It was edited in compliance with the request of the Ministry of Agriculture and Forestry. The members of the committee, of which Professor Yamada Moritarō of Tōkyō University was chairman, were students of agricultural economy and officials of the Ministry. The report covers such subjects as brief history of the land system since ancient times and of land legislation after the Meiji Restoration, the legislation basic to the recent land reform, the detailed progress and results of the land reform and the problems remaining to be solved. This large work provides also valuable statistical and non-statistical materials.

806. Nōrinshō Kyōto Nōchi Jimukyoku 農林省京都農地事務局 (Kyōto Farm-land Office of the Agriculture and Forestry Ministry), Nōchi kaikaku ni yoru nōson hembō chōsa 農地改革による農村變貌調查 (Survey of the changes in agricultural villages after the land reform), Kyōto Nōchi Jimukyoku, 1950.
Provides valuable factual data relating to the results of the land reform.

807. Nōsei Chōsakai 農政調查會 (Research Association on Agricultural Administration), Okayama-ken Fujita Nōjō no kaihō temmatsu 岡山縣藤田農場の解放顛末 (Details of land reform at the Fujita farm in Okayama prefecture), Nōsei Chōsakai, 1950.
The Fujita farm was known for its centralized management and mechanization.

808. Ōnishi Toshio 大西俊夫 , Dainiji nōchi kaikaku seido no kaisetsu 第二次農地改革制度の解說 (Commentary on the second land reform), Tōkyō, Nihon Nōmin Kumiai, 1947.
A comment on the land reform. Presents the viewpoint of the farmers' associations.

809. Ōwada Keiki 大和田啓氣 , Nōchi kaikaku no kaisetsu 農地改革の解說 (Commentary on the land reform), Tōkyō, Nōminsha, 1946.
A commentary on the land reform by an official of the Agriculture and Forestry Ministry. The same author has published another work, Kaisei nōchihō no kaisetsu (Commentary on the amended Farm Land Act), 1947, which presents a commentary on the basic legislation of the land reform.

810. Sakurai Takeo 櫻井武雄, Nihon nōgyō no zento 日本農業の前途 (The future of Japanese agriculture), Tōkyō, Shinzembisha, 1948.

811. Sugama Seisaku 菅間正朔 , Nihon nōgyō kakumei no futatsu no michi 日本農業革命の二つの途 (Two ways toward Japanese agricultural revolution), Tōkyō, Kaizōsha, 1948.

812. Tōhata Seiichi 東畑精一, Nōchi o meguru jinushi to nōmin 農地をめぐる地主と農民 (Land owners and farmers on the problem of the farm), Tōkyō, Kantōsha, 1947.

See also entry 789.

7. Agricultural Technology

813. Fukaya Susumu 深谷進 , Nihon nōgyō kikaika no tokushitsu 日本農業機械化の特質 (Special features of the mechanization of Japanese agriculture), Tōkyō, Kisetsusha, 1948.

814. Fukushima Yōichi 福島要一 , Nōgyō gijutsuron 農業技術論 (On agricultural technology), Tōkyō, Shōkō Shoin, 1947.

815. Furushima Toshio 古島敏雄 , Nihon nōgyō gijutsushi 日本農業技術史 (History of technology in Japanese agriculture), Tōkyō, Jichōsha, 1949, 2 v.

816. Kimura Yasuji 木村靖二 , Nihon nōkigu hattatsushi 日本農機具發達史 (Development of machines and tools for agriculture in Japan), Nōgyō to Kikaisha, 1936.

817. Kinuma Sōki 生沼曹喜 , Kikaika nōson 機械化農村 (The mechanized farm), Tōkyō, Hihansha, 1949.
Deals with the two villages which are generally regarded as outstanding examples of mechanized agriculture in Japan.

818. Yoshioka Kin'ichi 吉岡金市, Nihon nōgyō no kikaika 日本農業の機械化 (Mechanization of Japanese agriculture), Tōkyō, Hakuyōsha, 1939.

819. Yoshioka Kin'ichi 吉岡金市, Suiden no kikaika 水田の機械化 (Mechanization of paddy field agriculture), Tōkyō, Hakuyōsha, 1946.

8. Mining

820. Kojima Keizō 小島慶三, Tankō no kokka kanri 炭鑛の國家管理 (The nationalization of coal mines), Tōkyō, Nihon Keizai Shimbunsha, 1948.
A commentary on the basic act for the nationalization of Japanese coal mines in the post-war period.

821. Kōzan Konwakai 鑛山懇話會 (Miners' Society), Nihon kōgyō hattatsushi 日本鑛業發達史 (Development of the Japanese mining industry), Tōkyō, Kōzan Konwakai, 1932, 3 v.
Highly detailed history of the subject. Provides materials relating to individual mines and companies.

822. Kuboyama Yūzō 久保山雄三, Sekitan kōgyō hattenshi 石炭鑛業發展史 (Development of coal mining), Tōkyō, Kōronsha, 1942.

823. Mitsubishi Keizai Kenkyūsho 三菱經濟研究所 (Mitsubishi Institute for Economic Research), Sekitan keizai no kihon mondai 石炭經濟の基本問題 (Basic problems of the economy of coal), Tōkyō, Mitsubishi Keizai Kenkyūsho, 1947.

824. Nihon Sekiyu Kabushiki Kaisha 日本石油株式會社 (Japan Petroleum Company), Nihon sekiyushi 日本石油史 (History of petroleum in Japan), Nihon Sekiyu Kabushiki Kaisha, 1914.

825. Nishio Keitarō 西尾銈太郎, Nihon kōgyō shiyō 日本鑛業史要 (Summary of Japanese mining history), Jūichikumi Shuppambu, 1943.

826. Yanase Tetsuya 柳瀬徹也, Waga kuni chūshō tankō no jūzoku keitai 我國中小炭鑛の從屬形態 (Control over medium and small scale coal mines in Japan), Tōkyō, Itō Shoten, 1946.

9. Fishing

827. Katayama Fusakichi 片山房吉, Dainihon suisanshi 大日本水產史 (History of the Japanese marine product industry), Tōkyō, Nōgyō to Suisansha, 1937.
There is a short list of reference works in the appendix.

828. Kuwata Tōichi 桑田透一, Gaikan Nihon suisanshi 概觀日本水產史 (Outline of the history of the Japanese marine products industry), Tōkyō, Umi to Sorasha, 1943.

829. Nōrinshō Suisankyoku 農林省水產局 (Bureau of Marine Products, Ministry of Agriculture and Forestry), Kyūhan jidai no Nihon gyogyō seido 舊藩時代の日本漁業制度 (Fisheries system during the Tokugawa period), Tōkyō, Nōgyō to Suisansha, 1933.
A collection of materials relating to the subject.

830. Suisanchō Keizaika 水產廳經濟課 (Economic Section of the Marine Products Board), Gyogyō seido no kaikaku 漁業制度の改革 (Reform of the fishing system), Tōkyō, Nihon Keizai Shimbunsha, 1950.
Governmental report on the subject in the post-war period.

831. Yamaguchi Kazuo 山口和雄, Nihon gyogyō keizaishi kenkyū 日本漁業經濟史研究 (Study of the economic history of Japanese fishing), Tōkyō, Hokuryūkan, 1948.

10. Forestry

832. Dainihon Sanrinkai 大日本山林會 (Japanese Forestry Association), Meiji ringyō isshi 明治林業逸史 (History of forestry in the Meiji period) and Meiji ringyō isshi zokuhen 明治林業逸史續篇 (Supplementary volume to the history of forestry in the Meiji period), Tōkyō, Dainihon Sanrinkai, 1931, 2 v.

833. Endō Yasutarō 遠藤安太郎, Nihon sanrinshi 日本山林史 (History of Japanese forestry), Tōkyō, Nihon Sanrin, 1934-36, 3 v.

834. Matsunami Shūjitsu 松波秀實, Meiji ringyō shiyō 明治林業史要, Meiji ringyō shiyō kōshū 明治林業史要後輯 (History of forestry in the Meiji period, later edition), Tōkyō, Dainihon Sanrinkai, 1919, 2 v.

835. Nōrinshō 農林省 (Agriculture and Forestry Ministry), Nihon rinseishi shiryō 日本林制史資料 (Materials relating to the history of the regulation of forestry in Japan), Tōkyō, Chōyōkai, 1932-34, 20 v.

Chapter X

Manufacturing

Manufacturing is a fundamental factor in the economy of contemporary Japan and industrial development has played a great role in the modern economic history of the country. No aspect of economics can be presented without listing works that deal in some measure with manufacturing. Agriculture must be seen in its relation to industry and the mechanization of agriculture is, from one point of view, a branch of manufacturing. Labor problems are largely the problems of the industrial worker. The international trade of the country has included heavy exports of manufactured goods. These observations on well-known facts are but a preface to the statement that works on manufacturing in the broadest sense are to be found listed under every chapter heading and to the further statement that the term, manufacturing, is here given a narrow interpretation. This was necessary to bring the list of works cited down to a reasonable length.

The writings on theory, which come first, are limited to those on the economics of manufacturing and do not include general location theory which, in any case, seems not to have been given great attention in Japan. Works on the history of manufactures and factual studies in this field offer a further example of a narrow interpretation. Some excellent general works are included but most of the writings deal with history and fact for particular industries.

Small scale industry is a subject to which Japanese economists have given a great deal of attention for a variety of reasons. Small scale operations are much in evidence in Japan. Their varied forms and traditional organization whet the curiosity. Small and medium scale industrial enterprises have been the subject of much research and of some controversy. There has been reference in the writings to feudalism to the family, to unemployment, and to fluctuation in economic activity. The writings on technology are, in most cases, either the examination of technological change or the estimate of current technical effectiveness in particular industries. The economics of technological change is a matter of growing interest in Japan but it is not one to which great attention was given in the past. Current technical effectiveness is likely to be dealt with by engineers and industrial technicians rather than economists. Recent interest has been stimulated by problems of reconstruction. Writings upon the general aspects of the rise of modern industry, it should be said once more, are to be looked for under many headings and especially in the chapter on economic history.

1. Theoretical Works

836. Isobe Kiichi 磯部喜一, Gendai kōgyō seisakuron 現代工業政策論 (On contemporary policy toward manufacturing), Tōkyō, Yūhikaku, 1949.

837. Kambayashi Teijirō 上林貞治郎, Kōgyō keizairon 工業經濟論 (Treatise on the economics of manufacturing), Tōkyō, Mikasa Shobō, 1950.

838. Shizuta Hitoshi 静田均, Kōgyō keizai gairon 工業經濟概論 (Treatise on the economics of manufacturing), Tōkyō, Yūhikaku, 1950.

839. Yamanaka Tokutarō 山中篤太郎, Kōgyō seisakuron 工業政策論 (On policy toward manufacturing), Tōkyō, Shinkigensha, 1950.

840. Yonezawa Jibun 米澤治文, Kōgyō keizai no kihon mondai 工業經濟の基本問題 (Basic problems in the economics of manufacturing), Tōkyō, Jitsugyō no Nihonsha, 1950.

See also entries 955, 956.

2. Historical and Factual Studies

841. Akashi Hiroshi 明石弘, Kindai sanshigyō hattatsushi 近代蠶絲業發達史 (Development of the modern silk-reeling industry), Tōkyō, Meibundō, 1939.

842. Bōseki Rengōkai 紡績聯合會 (Federation of Associations of the Cotton Spinning Industry), Hompō mengyō no hattatsu 本邦棉業の發達 (The development of the Japanese cotton industry), Bōseki Rengōkai, 1932.

843. Dainihon Sanshikai 大日本蠶絲會 (Japanese Silk Reeling Association), Nihon sanshigyōshi 日本蠶絲業史 (History of the Japanese silk-reeling industry), Tōkyō, Dainihon Sanshikai, 1935-36, 5 v.
An historical account of the export of raw silk, silk-reeling, sericulture, government policy and certain technical features of the industry.

844. Dainihon Yōgyō Kyōkai 大日本窯業協會 (Japan Ceramic Association), Nihon yōgyō taikan 日本窯業大觀 (General view of the Japanese ceramic industry), Tōkyō, Dainihon Yōgyō Kyōkai, 1933.

845. Fujita Gorō 藤田五郎, Nihon kindai sangyō no seisei 日本近代產業の生成 (Growth of modern industries in Japan), Tōkyō, Nihon Hyōronsha, 1948.

846. Hattori Shisō 服部之総 and Shinobu Seizaburō 信夫清三郎 , Meiji senshoku keizaishi 明治染織經濟史 (History of the dyeing and yarn industry in the Meiji period), Tōkyō, Hakuyōsha, 1937.

847. Hattori Shisō 服部之総 and Shinobu Seizaburō 信夫清三郎 , Nihon manyufakucha shiron 日本マニユファクチユア史論 (On the history of Japanese manufacture), Tōkyō, Ikuseisha, 1937.
This is an account of the position of manufacturing in the Japanese economy during the late Tokugawa period. Hattori deals in the first section with the raw cotton market and the cotton weaving industry in Akita. In the second section Shinobu deals with the weaving of Kurumegasuri, a particular kind of cloth produced in Kyūshū.

848. Horie Eiichi 堀江英一 , Kindai sangyōshi kenkyū 近代產業史研究 (Study of the history of modern industry), Tōkyō, Nihon Hyōronsha, 1948.
A study of the development of the silk weaving industry in the later Tokugawa period and the development of the domestic market for it.

849. Iijima Manji 飯島幡司 , Nihon bōsekishi 日本紡績史 (History of Japanese cotton spinning industry), Ōsaka, Sōgensha, 1949.
Deals chiefly with the history of technology and business aspects of the industry. Provides valuable material and information.

850. Kambayashi Teijirō 上林貞治郎 , Nihon kōgyō hattatsu shiron 日本工業發達史論 (On the development of Japanese industry), Tōkyō, Gakusei Shobō, 1948.

851. Kameyama Naoto 亀山直人 , Kagaku kōgyō gairon 化學工業概論 (General remarks on the chemical industry), Tōkyō, Nihon Hyōronsha, 1949.
A general work by a well-known chemist.

852. Kinugawa Taichi 絹川太一 , Hompō menshi bōsekishi 本邦綿絲紡績史 (History of the spinning of cotton yarn in Japan), Ōsaka, Nihon Mengyō Kurabu, 1937-39, 4 v.

853. Kobayashi Yoshimasa 小林良正 , Nihon sangyō no kōsei 日本產業の構成 (Structure of Japanese industry), Tōkyō, Hakuyōsha, 1935; 1949.

854. Kobayashi Yoshimasa 小林良正 , Nihon shihonshugi no seisei to sono kiban 日本資本主義の生成とその基盤 (Origin, formation, and background of Japanese capitalism), Tōkyō, Nihon Hyōronsha, 1949.
Deals with the Japanese cotton industry in the late Tokugawa period and with its reorganization after the Meiji Restoration.

855. Kōgakkai 工學會 (Engineering Institute), Meiji kōgyōshi 明治工業史 (Industrial history of the Meiji era), Tōkyō, Kōgakkai, 1920-32, 10 v.
An extensive work on the subject covering the fields of chemical industry, shipbuilding, railways, construction, electric industry, military industry, steel industry, mining and machine industry.

856. Kōno Shinji 河野信治 , Nihon tōgyō hattatsushi 日本糖業發達史 (Development of sugar industry in Japan), Tōgyō Hattatsushi Hensan Jimusho, 1930-31, 3 v.
Consists of three volumes dealing with: production and consumption in the industry and with the contributions of the leading persons.

857. Matsuo Otojirō 松尾音次郎 , ed., Waga kuni shōkōgyō no genzai oyobi shōrai 我國商工業の現在及將來 (The present and future of Japanese commerce and industry), Tōkyō, Hokubunkan, 1914.
A history, sponsored by the Nōshōmushō 農商務省 (Ministry of Agriculture and Commerce), which deals with the degree of business concentration in a number of industries, such as textiles, paper, sugar refining, etc.

858. Moriya Norio 守屋典郎 , Bōseki seisanhi bunseki 紡績生產費分析 (Analysis of costs in cotton spinning), Tōkyō, Nihon Hyōronsha, 1948.
A valuable account of the development of the Japanese cotton spinning industry and its cost structure.

859. Nawa Tōichi 名和統一 , Nihon bōsekigyō no shiteki bunseki 日本紡績業の史的分析 (Historical analysis of the Japanese cotton spinning industry), Tōkyō, Chōryūsha, 1948.

860. Nihon Bōseki Kyōkai 日本紡績協會 (Japan Cotton Spinning Association), Nihon bōsekigyō no fukkō 日本紡績業の復興 (Reconstruction of the Japanese cotton spinning industry), Ōsaka, Nihon Bōseki Kyōkai, 1948.

861. Nihon Chisso Hiryō Kabushiki Kaisha 日本窒素肥料株式會社 (The Japan Nitrogenous Fertilizer Company), Nihon chisso hiryō jigyō taikan 日本窒素肥料事業大觀 (General survey of the Japanese nitrogenous fertilizer industry), Korea, Nihon Chisso Hiryō Kabushiki Kaisha, 1937.

862. Nihon Jinken Rengō Tsūshinsha 日本人絹連合通信社 (Associated News Agency for Japanese Artificial Silk), Nihon jinken hattatsushi 日本人絹發達史 (The development of artificial silk in Japan), Tōkyō, Nihon Jinken Rengō Tsūshinsha, 1935.

863. Nōshōmushō 農商務省 (Ministry of Agriculture and Commerce), Kōgyō iken 興業意見 (Report on industrialization), Tōkyō, Nōshōmushō, 1884, 30 v.
An exhaustive research work which deals with Japanese industry in the early Meiji period, with natural resources and other sources of national power, and with principles of industrialization. Generally regarded as highly influential in the establishment of governmental policy at that time. The work is included in Meiji zenki zaisei keizaishi shiryō (no. 581).

864. Ōji Seishi Kabushiki Kaisha 王子製紙株式會社 (Ōji Paper Manufacturing Company), Nihon shigyō sōran 日本紙業綜覽 (General survey of the Japanese paper industry), Tōkyō, Ōji Seishi Kabushiki Kaisha, 1937.
Includes the histories of six paper manufacturing companies from the early Meiji period.

865. Mihei Takako 三瓶孝子, Nihon mengyō hattatsushi 日本綿業發達史 (The development of cotton spinning in Japan), Tōkyō, Keiō Shobō, 1941.

866. Shinobu Seizaburō 信夫清三郎, Kindai Nihon sangyōshi josetsu 近代日本產業史序說 (Introduction to the history of modern Japanese industry), Tōkyō, Nihon Hyōronsha, 1946.
Deals with the origin and the development of several consumption goods industries of modern Japan, such as silk weaving, cotton spinning, and sugar refining.

867. Shōji Otokichi 莊司乙吉, Bōseki sōgyō tanshukushi 紡績操業短縮史 (History of the curtailment of operations in the cotton textile industry), Ōsaka, Nihon Mengyō Kurabu, 1930.
Covers in detail the period from the first curtailment of operations in 1890 to the eleventh curtailment in 1930. Presents also the background of business and politics relating to the subject.

868. Takimoto Seiichi 滝本誠一 and Mukai Shikakatsu 向井鹿松, ed., Nihon sangyō shiryō taikei 日本產業資料大系 (Collection of materials on Japanese industry), Tōkyō, Chūgai Shōgyō Shimpō, 1926-27, 12 v.
An extensive collection of documents and other materials relating to Japanese industry. Covers not only the field of manufacturing but the fields of agriculture, fisheries, mining, commerce, transportation, and relevant institutions and governmental policies.

869. Tominaga Yūji 富永祐治, Hompō tekkōgyō to kanzei 本邦鐵鋼業と関税 (The Japanese steel industry and the tariff), Ōsaka, Ōsaka Shōka Daigaku Keizai Kenkyūjo, 1932.
Deals with the development of the Japanese steel industry and with the protective policy for this industry.

870. Tōyō Keizai Shimpōsha 東洋經濟新報社 (Oriental Economist), Hompō jūyō jigyōshi 本邦重要事業史 (History of important industries in Japan), Tōkyō, Tōyō Keizai Shimpōsha, 1923.
Deals with the development of textile, food, machinery, chemical, mining, transportation, and other industries.

871. Toyozaki Minoru 豊崎稔, Nihon kikai kōgyō no kiso kōzō 日本機械工業の基礎構造 (Basic structure of the Japanese machine industry), Tōkyō, Nihon Hyōronsha, 1949.
Study of the influence of the uneven development of Japanese industry on the making of machines.

872. Yokoi Tokifuyu 横井時冬, Nihon kōgyōshi 日本工業史 (History of Japanese industry), Tōkyō, Hakuyōsha, 1927.
An industrial history of Japan covering the period from ancient times to the first half of the Meiji period. Although it was written at an early date, it is still regarded as one of the outstanding works in the field. The first edition was published in 1898.

873. Zōsen Kyōkai 造船協會 (Association of the Shipbuilding Industry), Nihon kinsei zōsenshi (Taishō jidai) 日本近世造船史（大正時代） (History of shipbuilding in modern Japan: the Taishō period), Tōkyō, Zōsen Kyōkai, 1935, 2 v.

See also entries 397, 406, 409, 411, 1127, 1128, 1131-1133, 1135, 1139, 1140, 1144, 1147.

3. Small Scale Industries

874. Honjō Eijirō 本莊榮治郎, Nishijin no kenkyū 西陣の研究 (Study of Nishijin), Tōkyō, Kaizōsha, 1930.
Nishijin is a branch of the silk industry which is regarded as an excellent example of a field in which small scale operations have persisted. This is a general account.

875. Horie Eiichi 堀江英一 and Gotō Kiyoshi 後藤清, Nishijin kigyō no kenkyū---chūshō kōgyō no jittai 西陣機業の研究—中小工業の實態 (Studies of the Nishijin weaving industry: the real condition of medium and small scale industries), Tōkyō, Yūhikaku, 1950.

876. Isobe Kiichi 磯部喜一, ed., Chūshō kōgyō tōsei soshiki 中小工業統制組織 (Organization for the control of medium and small scale industries), Tōkyō, Yūhikaku, 1942, 2 v.
Deals with wartime control over medium and small scale industries.

877. Ninagawa Torazō 蜷川虎三, Chūshō kigyō mondai no kaiketsu 中小企業問題の解決 (The solution of the problems of medium and small scale industries), Tōkyō, Jiji Tsūshinsha, 1950.
The author, a well-known statistician, was the director of the Chūshō Kigyōchō 中小企業廳 (Board of Medium and Small Scale Enterprises) of the Japanese government.

878. Toyoda Shirō 豊田四郎, Nihon chūshō kōgyōron no seika 日本中小工業論の成果 (Result of studies of Japanese medium and small scale industries), Tōkyō, Aoki Shoten, 1948.

879. Yamanaka Tokutarō 山中篤太郎, ed., Chūshōkōgyō no shōraisei 中小工業の將來性 (The future prospects of medium and small scale industries), Tōkyō, Yūhikaku, 1942.

880. Yamanaka Tokutarō 山中篤太郎, Chūshō kōgyō no honshitsu to tenkai 中小工業の本質と展開 (The nature and development of medium and small scale industries), Tōkyō, Yūhikaku, 1948.
The author, who has written other works in this field, is regarded as a leading authority.

881. Yamanaka Tokutarō 山中篤太郎, Nihon keizai to chūshō kōgyō 日本經濟と中小工業 (Japanese economy and medium and small scale industries), Tōkyō, Heiwa Shobō, 1948.

882. Yamanaka Tokutarō 山中篤太郎, Chūshō kōgyō no shomondai 中小工業の諸問題 (Problems of the medium and small scale industries), Tōkyō, Itō Shoten, 1948.

883. Yamanaka Tokutarō 山中篤太郎, ed., Chūshō kōgyō to keizai hendō---Nihon Gakujutsu Shinkōkai Chūshō Sangyō Iinkai hōkoku 中小工業と經濟變動—日本學術振興會中小產業委員會報告 (Medium and small scale industries and the fluctuation of the economy: Report of the Committee on Medium and Small Scale Industries, Japanese Society for the Promotion of Academic Studies), Tōkyō, Kunimoto Shobō, 1950.
This is the final report of the Committee and emphasizes the general importance of medium and small scale industries. Attention is given to the place of these industries in the export trade. Among the subjects dealt with are the reorganization of small scale and medium industries during the war, the post-war situation of these industries, the copper metal-working industry, the small tool, metal, and machine industries, the role of smaller industries in foreign trade. A bibliography provides a list of publications during the years 1945-49.

884. Yamashiro Akira 山城章, Chūshō kōgyō to keiei gōrika 中小工業と經營合理化 (Medium and small scale industries and the rationalization of management), Tōkyō, Dōbunkan, 1949.

See also entries 618, 619, 620.

4. Technology

885. Kajinishi Mitsuhaya 梶西光速, Gijutsu hattatsushi---keikōgyō 技術發達史—輕工業 (History of the development of technology: light industry), Tōkyō, Kawade Shobō, 1948.

886. Kōgyō Gijutsuchō 工業技術廳 (Board of Industrial Technology), Gijutsu hakusho---waga kuni kōkōgyō gijutsu no genjō 研究白書—我國鑛工業技術の現狀 (White paper on technology: the present condition of Japanese industrial and mining technology), Tōkyō, Kōgyō Shimbunsha, 1949.
An official report on the condition of Japanese industrial technology. A brief general statement is followed by detailed description of current technology in several important fields of mining and manufacturing. Provides valuable statistics.

887. Kōgyō Gijutsuchō 工業技術廳 (Board of Industrial Technology), Kenkyū hakusho---waga kuni kōkōgyō ni okeru shiken kenkyū no genjō 研究白書—我國鑛工業における試驗研究の現狀 (White paper on research activities: the present situation of experiment and research activities in the Japanese mining and manufacturing industries), Tōkyō, Nikkan Kōgyō Shimbunsha, 1951.
Deals with current experiments and research activities in mining, steel, electric, machine, chemical, textile, and miscellaneous goods industries. There is a list of research institutions.

888. Okumura Masaji 奧村正二, Seisan gijutsushi 生產技術史 (History of the technology of production), Tōkyō, Itō Shoten, 1949.

889. Okumura Masaji 奧村正二, Gendai kikai gijutsuron 現代機械技術論 (On contemporary machine technology), Tōkyō, Hakuyōsha, 1949.

890. Saigusa Hiroto 三枝博音, Gijutsuka hyōden 技術家評傳 (Biographies of engineers), Tōkyō, Kagakushugi Kōgyōsha, 1940.
Brief studies of the lives of technical leaders of the Tokugawa Period, such as Hiraga Gennai, Ino Tadataka, Tanaka Hisashige, Ishikawa Seiryū, Ōshima Takatō, Egawa Tarōzaemon.

891. Saigusa Hiroto 三枝博音, Gijutsushi 技術史 (History of technology), Tōkyō, Tōyō Keizai Shimpōsha, 1940, 370+19 pp.
History of the development of machines from the stage of simple tools.

892. Yamamoto Saburō 山本三郎, Nihon kindai gijutsushi 日本近代技術史 (History of technology in modern Japan), Tōkyō, Mikasa Shobō, 1940.
Separate chapters deal with the techniques of the silk-reeling, cotton spinning, the iron and metal industries.

Chapter XI

International and Domestic Trade

Over the last century the international trade of Japan has been a factor of outstanding importance in the economy of the country. It has raised incomes, provided means for economic development, and influenced foreign policy. Comparison with the United Kingdom suggests itself to the observer. Both countries bear evidence of the profound effect of specialization and the extension of the international division of labor. Britain was never again the same after the Napoleonic Wars nor was Japan after the Meiji Restoration.

The economists of the two countries have differed in their reactions. The Japanese have given relatively more attention to history and the British to theory. In Japan this was due in some measure to the delight of the Japanese scholar in delving into the past. The Japanese scholar shares this enthusiasm with scholars everywhere but in Japan it seems to glow more brightly. But there are additional reasons for Japanese emphasis on history. There has been a desire to correct the over-emphasis on recent international trade by showing that such trade had worked an effect in earlier times, including the Tokugawa period, and by giving proper weight to the growth of domestic trade.

Works on the theory of international trade are presented in the first section of the chapter. Japanese writings are evidence of participation in the development of general theory and its adaptation to Japan. A few Marxist writers have endeavored to give new significance to the link between the labor theory of value and the theory of international trade. Greater interest attaches, however, to those who relate international trade to the nature of the economic development of the country, to its unbalanced development as some see it.

Historical and factual studies are presented in the three sections which follow. The richness of this literature has made selection difficult. Historical accounts of the trade in silk and tea have been included. Interest in policy appears throughout the list and it must be borne in mind that the financial and exchange aspects of policy appear under other chapter headings as well. The post-war period has been dominated by attention to the prospects for the future. Both official research groups and individual scholars now find themselves driven by circumstances to assess the possibilities before their country.

1. Foreign Trade Theory

893. Fujii Shigeru 藤井茂, Kokusai bōekiron 國際貿易論 (International trade theory), Tōkyō, Kunimoto Shobō, 1948.

894. Kitagawa Kazuo 北川一雄, Kokusai bōeki riron no kenkyū 國際貿易理論の研究 (Study of international trade theories), Tōkyō, Yūhikaku, 1948.
The emphasis is upon the nature and the effects of international specialization.

895. Kojima Kiyoshi 小島清, Jiyū bōeki riron no kenkyū 自由貿易理論の研究 (Study of free trade theory), Nagoya, Reimei Shobō, 1947.

896. Kojima Kiyoshi 小島清, Kokusai keizairon 國際經濟論 (Theory of international trade), Tōkyō, Shinkigensha, 1950.

897. Matsui Kiyoshi 松井清, Sekai keizaigaku hihan 世界經濟學批判 (World economics: a critical commentary), Tōkyō, Yūhikaku, 1948.
A revised and enlarged edition of his Bōeki riron no kenkyū (Study of the theory of foreign trade) published in 1938. This work is a critical account of the theory of international trade from the point of view of the labor theory of value. A chapter on methodology is followed by chapters on value and prices, on capital movements, and on the balance of payments.

898. Nawa Tōichi 名和統一, Kokusai kachiron kenkyū 國際價值論研究 (Study of international value theory), Tōkyō, Nihon Hyōronsha, 1949.
Study of foreign trade theory from the point of view of the labor theory of value.

899. Suzuki Takeo 鈴木武雄, Shijō riron 市場理論 (Theory of the market), Tōkyō, Kawade Shobō, 1948, 299 pp.

900. Taniguchi Yoshihiko 谷口吉彦, Bōeki tōsei no kenkyū 貿易統制の研究 (Study of foreign trade control), Tōkyō, Yūhikaku, 1935-37, 3 v.
Presents factual studies of the controlled foreign trade of Japan as well as general theoretical studies.

901. Tōdai Keizai Gakubu 東大經濟學部 (College of Economics, University of Tōkyō), Kokusai keizai no shomondai 國際經濟の諸問題 (Various problems in international trade), Tōkyō, Yūhikaku, 1949.

902. Yamamoto Yoneji 山本米治, Kawase kanriron 為替管理論 (On foreign exchange control), Tōkyō, Jitsugyō no Nihonsha, 1949.
Deals with the subject from the viewpoint of monetary policy. Refers to the history of the subject in foreign countries.

See also entries 626, 628, 630.

903. Yumoto Toyokichi 油本豊吉, Kokusai keizai sōron 國際經濟総論 (General account of international economics), Tōkyō, Kunimoto Shobō, 1948; ed. 2, 1949.
This work presents the author's lectures on the subject at Tōkyō University. The chief headings are: the concept of international trade, the structure of the international economy, and the theory of international economics.

904. Yumoto Toyokichi 油本豊吉, Damupinguron ダムピング論 (On dumping), Tōkyō, Nankōsha, 1938.
Deals with dumping and other related subjects such as the tariff, cartels, and transportation costs.

905. Yumoto Toyokichi 油本豊吉, Bōeki seisaku taikei 貿易政策大系 (General account of foreign trade policy), Tōkyō, Kōbunsha, 1949.

2. General History

906. Kanno Watarō 菅野和太郎, Nihon shōgyōshi 日本商業史 (History of commerce in Japan), Tōkyō, Nihon Hyōronsha, 1930.
The Tokugawa and earlier periods are briefly treated and there is a detailed account of the period after the Meiji Restoration.

907. Matsumoto Kiyoshi 松本清, Nihon sōkoshi 日本倉庫史 (History of warehousing in Japan), Tōkyō, Dainihon Shuppansha, 1937.
Covers the period from ancient times until after the Meiji Restoration.

908. Miyamoto Mataji 宮本又次, Nihon shōgyōshi 日本商業史 (History of Japanese commerce), Tōkyō, Ryūginsha, 1949.
A general account covering the whole period from ancient times to early Shōwa. An appendix presents a valuable bibliography. The author is a professor in Kyūshū University and published a work under a similar title in 1946.

909. Miyamoto Mataji 宮本又次, Nihon shōgyōshi kōwa 日本商業史講話 (Lectures on the history of Japanese trade), Tōkyō, Daiyamondosha, 1948.

910. Suganuma Teifū 菅沼貞風, Dainihon shōgyōshi 大日本商業史 (History of Japanese commerce), Tōkyō, Tōhō Kyōkai, 1892, 633+130 pp.; Iwanami Shoten, 1940.
Deals with the period from ancient times to the early part of Tokugawa. Provides excerpts from old documents.

911. Tokumasu Eitarō 徳増榮太郎, Nihon bōekishi 日本貿易史 (History of Japanese foreign trade), Tōkyō, Genrin Shobō, 1948.
A fairly brief general history of the subject.

912. Tsurumi Sakio 鶴見左吉雄, Nihon bōekishi kō 日本貿易史綱 (Outline history of Japanese foreign trade), Tōkyō, Ganshōdō, 1939.

913. Yokoi Tokifuyu 横井時冬, Nihon shōgyōshi 日本商業史 (History of commerce in Japan), Tōkyō, Kinkōdō, 1898; Hakuyōsha, 1926; Kaizōsha, 1929.
A history of domestic and foreign trade, of transportation, money and mining from ancient times to the end of the Tokugawa period.

914. Yokoi Tokifuyu 横井時冬, Ishingo no shōgyōshi 維新後の商業史 (History of commerce after the Restoration), Tōkyō, Kinkōdō, 1906.
This work by the same author as the preceding deals with the same subjects for the Meiji period.

3. Historical and Factual Studies for the Period before the Meiji Restoration

915. Akiyama Kenzō 秋山謙三, Nisshi kōshōshi kenkyū 日支交渉史研究 (Study of the historical relations between Japan and China), Tōkyō, Iwanami Shoten, 1939.
The author is a well-known historian.

916. Asai Torao 浅井虎夫, Shina Nihon tsūshōshi 支那日本通商史 (History of trade between China and Japan), Tōkyō, Kinkōdō, 1906.
Detailed historical account of the trade relations of the two countries.

917. Gunji Kiichi 郡司喜一, Tokugawa jidai no Nissen kokkō 徳川時代の日暹國交 (Relations between Japan and Siam in the Tokugawa period), Tōkyō, Tōa Keizai Chōsakyoku, 1938.

918. Kanno Watarō 菅野和太郎, Ōsaka keizaishi kenkyū 大阪經濟史研究 (Study of the economic history of Ōsaka), Kyōto, Kōbundō, 1935, 2 v.

919. Kawashima Motojirō 川島元次郎, Shuinsen bōekishi 朱印船貿易史 (History of the foreign trade by licensed ships), Kyōto, Naigai Shuppan Kabushiki Kaisha, 1921.
An account of trade under a system which was employed as a method of control in early Tokugawa times.

920. Kōda Naritomo 幸田成友, Edo to Ōsaka 江戸と大阪 (Edo and Osaka), Tōkyō, Fuzambō, 1934.

921. Kōda Naritomo 幸田成友, Nichiō tsūkōshi 日歐通交史 (History of the relations between Japan and Europe), Tōkyō, Iwanami Shoten, 1942.

922. Kokusho Kankōkai 國書刊行會 (Association for the Publication of Japanese Classics), Tokugawa jidai shōgyō sōsho 徳川時代商業叢書 (Collection of literature of the Tokugawa period on commerce), Tōkyō, Kokusho Kankōkai, 1913-14, 3 v.

923. Miyamoto Mataji 宮本又次, Kinsei shōgyō soshiki no kenkyū 近世商業組織の研究 (Studies of the trade system in the modern age), Tōkyō, Yūhikaku, 1939, 293+14 pp.
The first section of this work is devoted to commerce in the Tokugawa period and the second to the wholesale trade of the period.

924. Miyamoto Mataji 宮本又二, Kinsei shōnin ishiki no kenkyū 近世商人意識の研究 (Study of the spirit and outlook of merchants in the modern [Tokugawa] age), Tōkyō, Yūhikaku, 1942.

925. Nihon Rikishi Chiri Gakkai 日本歴史地理學會 (The Japan Historical Geography Society), Nihon shōninshi 日本商人史 (History of Japanese merchants), Tōkyō, Nihon Gakujutsu Fukyūkai, 1925.

A special edition of the periodical, Rekishi chiri, containing sixteen articles on the merchant in various periods of Japanese history.

926. Okamoto Yoshitomo 岡本良知 , Jūroku seiki Nichiō kōtsūshi no kenkyū 十六世紀日歐交通史の研究 (Study of relations between Japan and Europe in the 16th century), Tōkyō, Kobunsō, 1936, enl. ed., 1942.

927. Suzuki Naoji 鈴木直二 , Edo ni okeru kome torihiki no kenkyū 江戸における米取引の研究 (Study of the rice trade in Edo), Tōkyō, Shikai Shobō, 1935.

928. Suzuki Naoji 鈴木直二 , Tokugawa jidai no beikoku haikyū soshiki 徳川時代の米穀配給組織 (The rice distribution system in the Tokugawa period), Tōkyō, Ganshōdō, 1938.

929. Takamura Shōhei 高村象平 , Nichiho tsūkōshi 日葡通交史 (History of relations between Japan and Portugal), Tōkyō, Kokusai Kōtsū Bunka Kyōkai, 1942.

930. Toyama Usaburō 外山卯三郎 , Nichiran bōeki shōshi 日蘭貿易小史 (Brief history of trade between Japan and Holland), Tōkyō, Wakai Hitosha, 1942.

931. Toyoda Takeshi 豊田武 , Nihon shōninshi (chūsei-hen) 日本商人史（中世篇） (History of Japanese merchants: the middle age), Tōkyō, Tōkyōdō, 1949.

932. Yamaguchi Kazuo 山口和雄 , Bakumatsu bōekishi 幕末貿易史 (History of foreign trade in the late Tokugawa period), Tōkyō, Seikatsusha, 1947.

4. Historical and Factual Studies for the Period after the Meiji Restoration

933. Chagyō Kumiai Chūō Kaigisho 茶業組合中央會議所 (Central Council of the Tea Manufacturing Associations), Nihon chabōeki gaikan 日本茶貿易概觀 (Outline of Japanese foreign trade in tea), Tōkyō, Chagyō Kumiai Chūō Kaigisho, 1935.

934. Fujimoto Jitsuya 藤本實也 , Kaikō to kiito bōeki 開港と生絲貿易 (The opening of the country and the silk trade), Yokohama, Kaikō to Kiito Bōeki Kankōkai, 1939, 3 v.

A full and detailed account of the silk trade during the early Meiji period.

935. Hamada Tokutarō 濱田徳太郎 , ed., Nihon Bōeki Kyōkai gojūnenshi 日本貿易協會五十年史 (Fifty years' history of the Japanese Foreign Trade Association), Tōkyō, Nihon Bōeki Kyōkai, 1936.

936. Horie Yasuzō 堀江保藏 , Gaishi yunyū no kaiko to tembō 外資輸入の回顧と展望 (The past and future of foreign capital imports), Tōkyō, Yūhikaku, 1950.

History of the importation of capital into Japan beginning with the Meiji period with attention to future possibilities.

937. Kawashima Shintarō 川島信太郎 , Hompō tsūshō seisaku jōyakushi gairon 本邦通商政策條約史概論 (Outline of the history of trade policies and treaties of Japan), Tōkyō, Ganshōdō, 1941.

938. Matsui Kiyoshi 松井清 , Nihon bōekiron 日本貿易論 (On Japanese foreign trade), Tōkyō, Yūhikaku, 1950.

Historical analysis of Japanese foreign trade from the Meiji period. There is a brief discussion of methodology.

939. Nawa Tōichi 名和統一 , Nihon shihonshugi to bōeki mondai 日本資本主義と貿易問題 (Japanese capitalism and foreign trade problems), Tōkyō, Kōdosha, 1948.

940. Nōshōmushō Shōmukyoku Bōekika 農商務省商務局貿易課 (Foreign Trade Section, Bureau of Commercial Affairs, Agriculture and Commerce Ministry), Saikin nijūnen ni okeru hompō bōeki no hensen 最近二十年に於ける本邦貿易の變遷 (Development of Japanese foreign trade in the last twenty years), Tōkyō, Nōshōmushō, 1925.

An official report on Japanese foreign trade which covers the period from 1903 to 1923.

941. Taniguchi Yoshihiko 谷口吉彦 , Nihon bōeki seisaku 日本貿易政策 (Japanese foreign trade policy), Tōkyō, Chikura Shobō, 1937.

The development of foreign trade policy with attention to the development of trade.

942. Tōyō Keizai Shimpōsha 東洋經濟新報社 (Oriental Economist), Dainihon gaikoku bōeki gojūrokunen taishōhyō 大日本外國貿易五十六年對照表 (Comparative tables of fifty-six years' foreign trade of Japan), Tōkyō, Tōyō Keizai Shimpōsha, 1925.

Covers the period from 1868 to 1923.

943. Yoshimura Masaharu 吉村正晴 , Nihon bōekiron 日本貿易論 (On Japanese foreign trade), Tōkyō, Tōyō Keizai Shimpōsha, 1948.

The author sees the development of Japanese foreign trade as a result of the unbalanced economic development of Japan and rejects the narrowness of the domestic market as the sole explanation.

See also entry 627.

5. Foreign Trade after World War II

944. Keizai Antei Hombu Bōeki Seisaku Kenkyūkai 經濟安定本部貿易政策研究會 (Research Group on Foreign Trade Policy, Economic Stabilization Board), *Nihon bōeki to dampingu mondai* 日本貿易とダンピング問題 (Japanese foreign trade and the dumping problem), Tōkyō, Jitsugyō no Nihonsha, 1950.

945. Nihon Kōgyō Ginkō 日本興業銀行 (Industrial Bank of Japan), *Nihon no bōeki to yushutsu sangyō* 日本の貿易と輸出産業 (Japanese foreign trade and her export industry), Tōkyō, Jitsugyō no Nihonsha, 1952.
A study of the post-war world market in relation to important branches of Japanese industry. Valuable data are presented.

946. Gaimushō Tsūsanshō Kanri Bōeki Kenkyūkai 外務省通産省管理貿易研究會 (Research Group on Foreign Trade Control in the Foreign Ministry and the International Trade and Industry Ministry), *Sengo Nihon no bōeki kin'yū kyōtei* 戰後日本の貿易金融協定 (Agreements on trade and finance of post-war Japan), Tōkyō, Jitsugyō no Nihonsha, 1949.

947. Keizai Antei Hombu 經濟安定本部 (Economic Stabilization Board), *Bōeki to sono shōrai* 貿易とその將來 (Foreign trade and its future), Tōkyō, Hōjō Shoten, 1949.

948. Keizai Antei Hombu Bōeki Seisakuka 經濟安定本部貿易政策課 (Foreign Trade Policy Section, Economic Stabilization Board), *Kaigai shijō no bunseki to tembō* 海外市場の分析と展望 (Analysis of foreign markets and prospects for foreign trade), Tōkyō, Hōjō Shoten, 1949.

949. Nihon Keizai Kenkyūsho 日本經濟研究所 (Research Institute for the Japanese Economy), *Bōeki saikai to kaku sangyō no shōrai* 貿易再開と各産業の將來 (The renewal of trade and the future of certain industries), Tōkyō, Nihon Keizai Kenkyūsho, 1947.

Chapter XII

Population

Population has become a separate field of study which in recent decades has become the special domain of the demographer. But the interest of the economist has been persistent. In the West this interest goes back to Malthus and in Japan to the discussions during the Tokugawa period of the movement of people from the countryside to the city. The interest of the Japanese scholar has been stimulated in more recent decades by the increase in numbers and by the establishment in 1920 of a satisfactory census at five-year intervals. The increase has led to a reexamination of the more stable population of Tokugawa times and the census has provided the student with the information necessary for intensive work in the more recent period.

The general interest of the economist in population studies is re-inforced by a special interest in ceratin aspects such as the shift of population in response to economic opportunity, the size and nature of the labor force, the relation of population to unemployment, the occupational distribution of the population, and the effect of industrialization upon the rate of growth. These aspects have been taken into consideration in the selection of the works listed below. What has been said of other fields may be repeated here, namely, that the course of events has obliged Japanese students to give serious attention to the future.

950. Abe Gen'ichi 阿部源一, *Jinkō shokuryō seisaku no hatten keitai* 人口糧食政策の發展形態 (Development of population policies and food policies), Tōkyō, Sangyō Tosho, 1947.

951. Honjō Eijirō 本莊榮治郎, *Nihon jinkōshi* 日本人口史 (History of Japanese population), Tōkyō, Nihon Hyōronsha, 1941.
An enlarged edition of the same author's *Jinkō oyobi jinkō mondai* (Population and the population problem). Deals with the population in Japan from ancient times to the Meiji period. Special attention is paid to population problems during the Tokugawa period under such headings as concentration of population in cities, population control, and the theory of population during the Tokugawa period.

952. Jinkō Mondai Kenkyūsho 人口問題研究所 (Research Institute on Population Problems), *Jinkō seisaku no shiori* 人口政策の栞 (Guide to population policies), Tōkyō, Jinkō Mondai Kenkyūsho, 1941.
A brief analysis of the current situation of Japanese population.

953. Mainichi Shimbunsha Jinkō Mondai Chōsakai 毎日新聞社人口問題調査會 (Research Institute of the Mainichi Press on Population Problems), *Nihon no jinkō mondai* 日本の人口問題 (Population problems in Japan), Tōkyō, Mainichi Shimbunsha Jinkō Mondai Chōsakai, 1950.

954. Minami Ryōzaburō 南亮三郎, *Jinkōron hattenshi* 人口論發展史 (Development of the population theory), Tōkyō, Sanseidō, 1936.
Special attention is given to Japanese studies of population over the ten years before publication.

955. Minoguchi Tokijirō 美濃口時次郎, Kōgyō jinkōron 工業人口論 (On the industrial population), Tōkyō, Tōyō Keizaisha, 1948.
An general account of the source and development of the industrial labor force which is followed by factual studies for Britain, Germany, and Japan.

956. Minoguchi Tokijirō 美濃口時次郎, Nihon kōgyō rōdōryokuron 日本工業勞働力論 (On the labor resources in Japanese industry), Ōsaka, Kōbundō Shoten, 1943.

957. Minoguchi Tokijirō 美濃口時次郎, Jinkō riron no kenkyū 人口理論の研究 (Study of population theory), Tōkyō, Chūō Kōronsha, 1949.

958. Morita Yūzō 森田優三, Jinkō zōka no bunseki 人口増加の分析 (An analysis of population increase), Tōkyō, Nihon Hyōronsha, 1944.
A work by a well-known demographer. The first two sections provide a summary of modern views and theories on population. The third part is an analysis of factors explaining the growth of the Japanese population in the present century. Provides much statistical data.

959. Naikaku Tōkeikyoku 内閣統計局 (Cabinet Bureau of Statistics), Meiji gonen ikō waga kuni no jinkō 明治五年以降我國の人口 (Japanese population since 1872), Tōkyō, Tōkyō Tōkei Kyōkai, 1930.
Provides estimates of annual population of Japan beginning with 1872. These estimates were based on such materials as the national population census of 1920, vital statistics of each year, and the population survey of 1872.

960. Nojiri Shigeo 野尻重雄, Nōmin rison no jisshōteki kenkyū 農民離村の實証的研究 (Factual study of the removal of farm population from the village), Tōkyō, Iwanami Shoten, 1942.
A valuable study of the flow of the rural population. There is an introductory review which is followed by attention to such subjects as the relation of size of farm and financial condition to the movement of the farmer, information concerning regions and occupations, reproduction rates in the villages, and the effects of population movement on family labor supply.

961. Okazaki Fuminori 岡崎文規, Nihon jinkō mondai 日本人口問題 (The population problems of Japan), Tōkyō, Meguro Shoten, 1941.
The author is generally regarded as a leading demographer in contemporary Japan.

962. Okazaki Fuminori 岡崎文規, Nihon jinkō no jisshōteki kenkyū 日本人口の實証的研究 (Factual study of Japanese population), Tōkyō, Hokuryūkan, 1950.
A valuable statistical study of population covering the period from 1899 to 1940. The introduction presents a general summary of the population changes since the beginning of World War II, with allowance being made for incomplete and faulty statistical data.

963. Sekiyama Naotarō 関山直太郎, Kinsei Nihon jinkō no kenkyū 近世日本人口の研究 (Study of the population of Japan in the Tokugawa period), Tōkyō, Ryūginsha, 1948.
Chapters on theory are followed by studies of the decrease of agricultural population and the concentration of population in urban areas.

964. Sekiyama Naotarō 関山直太郎, Nihon jinkōshi 日本人口史 (History of Japanese population), Tōkyō, Shikai Shobō, 1942.
Deals with the subject throughout Japanese history, with special attention to population problems during the Tokugawa period. An account of the growth of Japanese population after the Meiji period is included.

965. Sōrichō Tōkeikyoku 総理廳統計局 (Statistics Bureau, Prime Minister's Office), Jōjū jinkō chōsa hōkoku 常住人口調査報告 (Census report of population by permanent residence), Tōkyō, Nihon Hyōronsha, 1949.

966. Tachi Minoru 館稔, Nihon jinkō no shōrai 日本人口の將來 (Future of Japanese population), Tōkyō, Sekai Keizai Chōsakai, 1948.

967. Takahashi Bonsen 高橋梵仙, Nihon jinkōshi no kenkyū 日本人口史の研究 (Studies in the history of Japanese population), Tōkyō, San'yūsha, 1941.

968. Takano Iwasaburō 高野岩三郎, Hompō jinkō no genzai oyobi shōrai 本邦人口の現在及將來 (The present and future of Japanese population), Tōkyō, Tsuzoku Daigakukai, 1916.
The author was a leading figure in the study of statistics. This book presents an analysis of the current population of Japan and an estimate of the future.

969. Watanabe Shin'ichi 渡辺信一, Nihon nōson jinkōron 日本農村人口論 (Japanese rural population), Tōkyō, Nankōsha, 1933.
Deals with the development of hired labor in Japanese agriculture in terms of the development of Japanese capitalism from the Meiji period.

970. Ueda Teijirō 上田貞次郎, Jinkō mondai 人口問題 (The population problem), Tōkyō, Kyōchōkai, 1934-36, 3 v.
The author was a leading figure in the study of Japanese population problems.

971. Ueda Teijirō 上田貞次郎, ed., Nihon jinkō mondai kenkyū 日本人口問題研究 (Studies of the Japanese population problem), Tōkyō, Kyōchōkai, 1933-37, 3 v.
The first volume deals mainly with problems of unemployment and of population growth in Japan; the second with vital statistics and occupational distribution of population; the third with population theory, with industry, and with standards of living.

972. Yanaihara Tadao 矢内原忠雄, Jinkō mondai 人口問題 (The population problem), Tōkyō, Iwanami Shoten, 1928.

Chapter XIII

Labor and Social Problems

Japanese writings in the field which is suggested by the word, labor, may be conveniently classified under three headings: theoretical and general, the development of social policy, and the labor movement.

Works on theory, such as those on the theory of wages, call for no special comment. The labor movement is ordinarily dealt with in historical accounts. This literature has become richer in recent years, that is, since the organization of labor under the policies of the Occupation authorities, but it is to be noted that histories of the labor movement were published before the war.

It is in the field of social policy that the economist and the social scientist have done most effective work. It is quite consistent with Japanese tradition that social policy should have made its appearance at an early date. There was also some relation of German influence among those who took an early interest in social policy. The Shakai Seisaku Gakkai 社會政策學會 (Society for Social Policy), established in 1907, soon made its influence felt by its effective support of the first factory act which became law in 1911. This act and the point of view of those who favored it was that of the protection of labor. If there was socialist backing it was the backing of those who may be called state interventionists. After the early efforts of Marxist socialists to promote and influence the organization of labor, the resistance to their ideas was expressed by such groups as the Kyōchōkai (Reconciliation Association) which worked for harmonious relations between labor and management.

An important contribution in this field of social policy was the advocacy of a solution of labor problems along lines suggested by economic analysis. This so-called economic school of social policy which is still powerful in Japan takes the position that the immediate end of policy is an adequate and efficient labor force which is to help maintain and develop the economic activities of the country. The significant concept is that of proper balance in the return to labor and to capital. Ōkōchi Kazuo and Mori Kōjirō are among the economists who have developed these ideas.

It is desirable to point out once more that important information on labor problems is to be found in the statistical reports and in the journals and magazines listed in the third and fourth chapters.

1. Bibliographies

973. Hosokawa Karoku 細川嘉六, Nihon shakaishugi bunken kaisetsu 日本社會主義文献解説 (Annotated bibliography of Japanese literature relating to socialism) [=v. 4 of Nihon shihonshugi hattatsushi kōza (No. 370)], Tōkyō, Iwanami Shoten, 1932.

974. Ōhara Shakai Mondai Kenkyūsho 大原社會問題研究所 (Ōhara Research Institute for Social Problems), Nihon shakaishugi bunken daiisshū 日本社會主義文献第一輯 (Bibliography of documents on socialism in Japan, first collection), Tōkyō, Dōjinsha Shoten, 1929.
Contains literature on the subject published during the period from 1882 to 1914. Annotated. Provides criticism of or introduction to individual works at the time of publication.

975. Ōhara Shakai Mondai Kenkyūsho 大原社會問題研究所 (Ōhara Research Institute for Social Problems), Nihon rōdō nenkan 日本勞働年鑑 (Japanese yearbook on labor), Tōkyō, Dōjinsha, 1920-41, 1949+, annual.
Various numbers contain lists of books and articles published during the preceding years.

2. General Problems

976. Kambayashi Teijirō 上林貞次郎, Gijutsu oyobi rōdōryoku no riron 技術及び勞働力の理論 (Theories on technology and the labor force), Tōkyō, Itō Shoten, 1947.

977. Kawai Eijirō 河合榮次郎, Rōdō mondai kenkyū 勞働問題研究 (Studies of labor problems), Tōkyō, Iwanami Shoten, 1921.

978. Kawakami Hajime 河上肇, Bimbō monogatari 貧乏物語 (Stories of poverty), Kyōto, Kōbundō, 1917.
An account of social problems for the general reader which first appeared in the daily press.

979. Kawakami Hajime 河上肇, Daini bimbō monogatari 第二貧乏物語 (Stories of poverty, continued), Tōkyō, Kaizōsha, 1930.
A more radical account than the preceding.

980. Kawakami Hajime 河上肇, Shakai mondai kanken 社會問題管見 (Views on social problems), Kyōto, Kōbundō, 1920.
A work by a well-known Marxian economist.

981. Kazehaya Yasoji 風早八十二, Nihon no rōdō saigai 日本の勞働災害 (Labor accidents in Japan), Tōkyō, Itō Shoten, 1948.
One of the few books on this subject. The author is a leading theorist in the Japanese Communist Party. The articles collected here were written during the late 1930s and provide much statistical information.

982. Kita Shūichirō 喜多收一郎, Chika rōdō 地下勞働 (Labor under ground), Umezu Shoten, 1921.

983. Kitazawa Shinjirō 北澤新次郎, Nihon rōdō mondai no seikaku 日本勞働問題の性格 (The nature of Japanese labor problems), Tōkyō, Waseda Daigaku, 1947.

984. Koizumi Shinzō 小泉信三, Shakai mondai kenkyū 社會問題研究 (Studies of social problems), Tōkyō, Iwanami Shoten, 1921.

985. Kubota Shigetaka 久保田重孝, Genka no rōdō hoken mondai 現下の勞働保健問題 (Present problems of labor health), Tōkyō, Rōdō Kagaku Kenkyūsho, 1946.

986. Kushida Tamizō 櫛田民藏, Shakai mondai 社會問題 (Social problems) [=v. 4 of Kushida Tamizō zenshū (Complete works of Kushida Tamizō) (no. 214)], Tōkyō, Kaizōsha, 1949.

987. Kuwata Kumazō 桑田熊藏, Kōjōhō to rōdō hoken 工場法と勞働保險 (Factory legislation and labor insurance), 1909.
A work by a leader in the social reform movement of the time written to promote legislation for the protection of labor.

988. Murayama Shigetada 村山重忠, Rōdō mondai no gaisetsu 勞働問題の概說 (Outline of labor problems), Tōkyō, Chūō Rōdō Gakuen, 1948.

989. Ogawa Gōtarō 小川郷太郎, Shakai mondai to zaisei 社會問題と財政 (Social problems and public finance), Tōkyō, Teikoku Chihō Gyōsei Gakkai, 1921.

990. Ōhara Shakai Mondai Kenkyūsho 大原社會問題研究所 (Ōhara Research Institute for Social Problems), Shūgyō kisoku to shokuba kiritsu 就業規則と職場規律 (Regulations of work and rules at the working place) [=v. 2 of Ōhara Shakai Mondai Kenkyūjo shiriizu (The series of the Ōhara Research Institute for Social Problems), Tōkyō, Daiichi Shuppansha, 1949.

991. Oka Minoru 岡實, Kōjōhōron 工場法論 (On the factory act), Tōkyō, Yūhikaku, 1913.
Provides valuable material and data on the enactment of the Act.

992. Ōkōchi Kazuo 大河内一男, Nihon shakaishugi to rōdō mondai 日本社會主義と勞働問題 (Japanese socialism and labor problems), Tōkyō, Hakujitsu Shoin, 1947.

993. Nishida Nagahisa 西田長壽, Toshi kasō shakai 都市下層社會 (The lower income groups in cities), Tōkyō, Seikatsusha, 1949.

994. Seiji Keizai Kenkyūjo 政治經濟研究所 (Institute for Politics and Economics), Rōdō mondai zensho 勞働問題全書 (Complete series on labor problems), Tōkyō, Takayama Shoten, 1949, 15 v.
Supervised by Suehiro Izutarō, this series covers the whole subject and includes such titles as labor unions, labor disputes, wage problems, relations between union and management, health, legislation, policy and administration, and the current situation.

995. Rōdōshō Tōkei Chōsakyoku 勞働省統計調查局 (Statistics and Research Bureau, Labor Ministry), Rōdō hakusho 勞働白書 (White paper on labor), Tōkyō, Jiji Tsūshinsha, 1949.
Government report on post-war labor conditions.

996. Taiheiyō Mondai Chōsakai 太平洋問題調查會 (Institute of Pacific Relations), Nihon shakai no kihon mondai 日本社會の基本問題 (Basic problems of Japanese society), Tōkyō, Sekai Hyōronsha, 1949.

997. Takahashi Kamekichi 高橋亀吉, Nihon sangyō rōdōron 日本產業勞働論 (A study of Japan's industrial labor), Tōkyō, Chikura Shōbō, 1937,

998. Tsuchiya Takao 土屋喬雄, ed., Shokkō jijō 職工事情 (Conditions of factory workers), Tōkyō, Seikatsusha, 1947-48, 3 v.
An official report on the conditions of labor in the middle of the Meiji period, edited by a well-known economic historian. The original report was published by the Ministry of Agriculture and Commerce in 1903. Highly valuable material on Japanese industrialization in its early stages.

999. Yokoyama Gennosuke 横山源之助, Nihon no kasō shakai 日本の下層社會 (Lower classes in Japan), ed. by Tsuchiya Takao 土屋喬雄, Tōkyō, Chūō Rōdō Gakuen, 1949.
Originally published in 1899. A valuable source of material relating to the labor conditions at that time.

See also entries 253, 307, 955, 956.

3. Policy

1000. Itō Han'ya 井藤半彌 , Shakai seisaku sōron 社會政策総論 (General treatise on social policy), Tōkyō, Shunjūsha, 1949.

1001. Kawai Eijirō 河合榮治郎 , Shakai seisaku genri 社會政策原理 (Principles of social policy), rev. ed., Tōkyō, Nihon Hyōronsha, 1935.
Presents a philosophical approach to the subject. The author is a follower of the British idealism of T. H. Green.

1002. Kawata Shirō 河田嗣郎 , Shakai seisaku genron 社會政策原論 (Principles of social policies), Tōkyō, Yūhikaku, 1934.
Textbook on the subject. Based on the idea of the reconciliation of labor and capital.

1003. Kishimoto Eitarō 岸本英太郎 , Shakai seisakuron no kompon mondai 社會政策論の根本問題 (Basic problems of social policy), Tōkyō, Nihon Hyōronsha, 1950.

1004. Kitaoka Juitsu 北岡壽逸 , Shakai Seisaku gairon 社會政策概論 (Summary of social policy), Tōkyō, Yūhikaku, 1942.
Presents social policy as policy for the reconciliation of classes.

1005. Kondō Bunji 近藤文二 , Shakai seisaku gaisetsu 社會政策概説 (Summary of social policy), Tōkyō, Usui Shoin, 1949.

1006. Mori Kōjirō 森耕二郎 , Shakai seisaku yōron 社會政策要論 (Basic arguments on social policy), Tōkyō, Kōbundō, 1935; repr., Tōkyō, Nihon Hyōronsha, 1950.
The author gives great importance to economics in the field of social policy. He takes the position of opposing an ethical treatment and regards social policy as a government program for curbing the social consequences of the unequal distribution of incomes.

1007. Ōkōchi Kazuo 大河内一男 , Shakai seisaku no kihon mondai 社會政策の基本問題 (Basic problems of social policy), Tōkyō, Nihon Hyōronsha, 1947.
This and the three books that follow are the works of a leader among contemporary students of social policy, who has been a member of the faculty of Tokyo University for some time. He has exercised a profound influence in Japan. His social policy is based on economic policy for the maintenance and distribution of the labor force. He rejects the concept of social policy as protection for the laborer or the reconciliation of social classes. The first section of this work deals with theory and the second with particular topics such as social policy and welfare institutions, human resources and social policy, and social policy and a controlled economy.

1008. Ōkōchi Kazuo 大河内一男 , Shakai seisaku (sōron) 社會政策(總論) (Treatise on social policy: general argument), Tōkyō, Yūhikaku, 1949.

1009. Ōkōchi Kazuo 大河内一男 , Shakai seisaku (kakuron) 社會政策(各論) (Treatise on social policy: specialized arguments), Tōkyō, Yūhikaku, 1950.

1010. Ōkōchi Kazuo 大河内一男 , Shakai seisaku genri 社會政策原理 (Principles of social policy), Tōkyō, Keisō Shobō, 1950.

4. History of Social and Labor Movements

1011. Akamatsu Katsumaro 赤松克麿 , Nihon rōdō undō hattatsushi 日本勞働運動發達史 (Development of the Japanese labor movement), Tōkyō, Bunka Gakkai Shuppambu, 1925.

1012. Akamatsu Katsumaro 赤松克麿 , Nihon shakai undō no rekishi-teki kenkyū 日本社會運動の歴史的研究 (Historical study of Japanese social movements), Tōkyō, Rōmu Gyōsei Kenkyūsho, 1948.

1013. Anzai Kuraji 安齋庫治 and Unno Yukitaka 海野幸隆 , Shūsengo ni okeru waga kuni no rōdō undō 終戦后におけるわが國の勞働運動 (Japanese labor movement after World War II) [= Vol. 5 of Chōryū kōza keizaigaku zenshū 潮流講座經濟學全集 (Chōryū series in economics)], Tōkyō, Chōryūsha, 1949-.
Two of the three volumes planned have been published. The first volume carries the statement that it covers the period from the end of the war to the general strike of Feb. 2, 1947.

1014. Kikuchi Jirō 菊池次郎 , Kinsei Nihon shakai undōshi---shiryōhen 近世日本社會運動史 — 資料篇 (History of social movements in modern Japan: materials), Tōkyō, Hakuyōsha, 1934.
Presents material on Japanese social movements both of the left and of the right.

1015. Kishimoto Eitarō 岸本英太郎 , Nihon rōdō undōshi 日本勞働運動史 (History of the Japanese labor movement), Tōkyō, Kōbundō, 1950.

1016. Kōno Mitsu 河野密 , Nihon rōdō undō shōshi 日本勞働運動小史 (Brief history of the Japanese labor movement), Tōkyō, Nihon Tekkōgyō Keieisha Remmei, 1947.

1017. Kōtsū Rōdō Kenkyūsho 交通勞働研究所 (Research Institute for Transportation Labor), Kokutetsu rōdō undōshi 國鐵勞働運動史 (History of the labor movement in the government-owned railways), Tōkyō, Kōtsū Rōdō Kenkyūsho, 1947.

1018. Komiya Yoshitaka 小宮義孝, Nihon puroretariya hennenshi 日本プロレタリヤ編年史 (Chronological history of the Japanese proletariat), Tōkyō, Dōjinsha, 1931.
Chronological history of the subject from 1867 to 1930.

1019. Kōno Mitsu 河野密 and Akamatsu Katsumaro 赤松克麿, Nihon musan seitōshi 日本無産政党史 (History of proletarian parties in Japan), Tōkyō, Hakuyōsha, 1931.
Consists of the history of the Zenkoku Taishūtō, of the Shakai Minshutō, and of the Rōnōtō. The author belonged to the Rōnōtō Shokikyoku 労農党書記局 or Secretariat of the Labor-Farmer Party.

1020. Kyōchōkai 協調會 (Reconciliation Association), Saikin no shakai undō 最近の社會運動 (Recent labor movements), Tōkyō, Kyōchōkai, 1929, 1421+79 pp.
An extensive description of social and labor movements from 1916 to 1926. The first half of the work which deals with Japan includes the general condition of industry and labor, activities of labor unions, labor disputes, tenants' disputes, farmers' movements, cooperative activities, political movements of proletarian parties, movements of right wing associations, social work, labor and social administration of the government, and legislation relating to this field.

1021. Nishimaki Toshio 西巻敏雄, Nihon kaijō rōdō undōshi 日本海上労働運動史 (History of the Japanese marine laborers' movement), Tōkyō, Nihon Kaiyō Kyōkai, 1949.

1022. Shakai Keizai Rōdō Kenkyūsho 社會經濟労働研究所 (Research Institute for Social Economics and Labor), Katayama Sen-shū: Nihon ni okeru kaikyū tōsō 片山潜集：日本に於ける階級闘争 (Collected works of Katayama Sen: class struggle in Japan), Tōkyō, Itō Shoten, 1948.
The writings of Katayama Sen, the well-known Marxist and initiator of the revolutionary labor movement in Japan.

1023. Tanaka Sōgorō 田中惣五郎, Nihon shakai undōshi 日本社會運動史 (History of Japanese social movements), Tōkyō, Tōzai Shuppansha, 1947, 2 v.
A collection of material relating to the social movements and social problems of Japan during the period 1866-1908.

1024. Taniguchi Zentarō 谷口善太郎, Nihon rōdō kumiai hyōgikai-shi 日本労働組合評議會史 (History of the council of Japanese labor unions), Kyōto, Takagiri Shoin, 1948, 2 v.

5. History of Policy

1025. Azuma Tōsaku 我妻東策, Meiji shakai seisakushi 明治社會政策史 (History of social policies in the Meiji period), Tōkyō, Mikasa Shobō, 1940.
Provision for the unemployed samurai was a serious problem during the first half of the Meiji period. This is an account of the efforts to find a solution.

1026. Azuma Tōsaku 我妻東策, Shizoku jusanshi 士族授産史 (History of the employment problems of the former samurai), Tōkyō, Mikasa Shobō, 1942.
Special account on the subject of the preceding work by the same author. Consists of chapters which deal with the problem at the prefectural level. The situation in Shizuoka, Ōita, Kumamoto, and nineteen other prefectures is examined.

1027. Kazehaya Yasoji 風早八十二, Nihon shakai seisakushi 日本社會政策史 (History of social policies in Japan), Tōkyō, Nihon Hyōronsha, 1937; 1947.

1028. Kishimoto Eitarō 岸本英太郎, Nihon rōdō seisaku shōshi 日本労働政策小史 (Brief history of Japanese labor policies), Tōkyō, Yūhikaku, 1948.

1029. Ōkōchi Kazuo 大河内一男 and Takahashi Seiichirō 高橋誠一郎, Rōdō seisaku to sono haikei 労働政策とその背景 (Labor policy and its background), Tōkyō, Nihon Keizai Shimbunsha, 1949.

1030. Shakai Jigyō Kenkyūsho 社會事業研究所 (Research Institute for Social Work), Nihon shakai jigyō dainempyō 日本社會事業大年表 (Detailed chronological table of Japanese social work), Tōkyō, Tōkō Shoin, 1936.

1031. Shimojō Yasumaro 下條康麿, Nihon shakai seisakuteki shisetsushi 日本社會政策的施設史 (History of institutions relating to Japanese social policy), Tōkyō, Hakubunkan, 1940.

1032. Unno Kōtoku 海野幸徳, Nihon shakai seisaku shiron 日本社會政策史論 (On the history of social policy in Japan), Sekirokaku Shobō, 1931.

1033. Yoshikawa Hidezō 吉川秀造, Shizoku jusan no kenkyū 士族授産の研究 (Study of the employment problem of the former samurai), Tōkyō, Yūhikaku, 1935.
An account of policies to meet a serious social problem of the first half of the Meiji period.

6. Problems of Unemployment

1034. Hijikata Seibi 土方成美, Chō Moriyoshi 長守善, and Iwano Chōjirō 岩野晁次郎, Kanzen koyō no riron to jissai 完全雇傭の理論と實際 (Theory and practice of full employment), Tōkyō, Daiyamondosha, 1947.

1035. Kikuchi Haruo 菊池春雄, Keizai saiken to shitsugyō mondai 經濟再建と失業問題 (Economic reconstruction and the unemployment problem), Tōkyō, Rōdō Bunkasha, 1949.

1036. Kitaoka Juitsu 北岡壽逸, Shitsugyō mondai to sono taisaku 失業問題とその對策 (Unemployment problems and related policy), Tōkyō, Seiji Kyōiku Kyōkai, 1946.

1037. Minoguchi Tokijirō 美濃口時次郎, Koyō to shitsugyō 雇用と失業 (Employment and unemployment), Tōkyō, Chūō Rōdō Gakuen, 1949.

1038. Noda Uichi 野田卯一, Shitsugyō taisaku to kōkyō jigyō 失業對策と公共事業 (Unemployment policy and public works), Tōkyō, Tōyō Keizai Shimpōsha, 1948.

1039. Ōkōchi Kazuo 大河内一男, Rōdō kumiai to shitsugyō mondai 勞働組合と失業問題 (Labor unions and the unemployment problem), Tōkyō, Hakujitsu Shoin, 1947.

1040. Rōdō Daijin Kambō Rōdō Tōkei Chōsabu 勞働大臣官房勞働統計調査部 (Statistics and Research Division, Secretariat of the Minister of Labor), Hikaikosha shotai ni okeru kakei no jittai chōsa 被解雇者世帯における家計の實態調査 (Field survey of the financial situation of discharged workers' households), Tōkyō, 1950.

7. Wages

1041. Andō Masakichi 安藤政吉, Saitei seikatsuhi no kenkyū 最低生活費の研究 (Study of the minimum cost of living), Tōkyō, Kōseikan, 1947.

1042. Fujimoto Takeya 藤本武也, Konnichi no chingin mondai 今日の賃金問題 (Present-day wage problems), Tōkyō, Rōdō Bunkasha, 1948.

1043. Fukuda Tokuzō 福田徳三, Shakai undō to rōgin seido 社會運動と勞銀制度 (Social movements and the wage system), Tōkyō, Kaizōsha, 1922.

1044. Hattori Eitarō 服部英太郎, Chingin seisakuron no shiteki tenkai 賃金政策論の史的展開 (Historical development of the theory of wage policy), Tōkyō, Shinchi Shobō, 1948.

1045. Imai Kazuo 今井一男, Konnichi no kyūyo mondai 今日の給与問題 (Present-day wage problems), Tōkyō, Koyō Mondai Kenkyūkai, 1949.
The emphasis is upon wage policy for government employees.

1046. Inaba Shūzō 稲葉秀三, Chingin wa ika ni shite kimerarete iru ka 賃金はいかにしてきめられてゐるか (How are wages determined?), Tōkyō, Jiji Tsūshinsha, 1948.

1047. Kambayashi Teijirō 上林貞治郎, Chingin riron 賃金理論 (Theory of wages), Tōkyō, Sōgensha, 1949.

1048. Masuchi Yōjirō 増地庸治郎, Chinginron 賃金論 (Treatise on wages), Tōkyō, Chikura Shobō, 1948.

1049. Mori Kōjirō 森耕二郎, Rōchin gakusetsu no shiteki hatten 勞賃學説の史的發展 (Historical development of wage theories), Tōkyō, Rōdō Bunkasha, 1949.

1050. Nagano Junzō 永野順三, Sengo no chingin 戦后の賃金 (Wages in the post-war period), Tōkyō, Itō Shoten, 1949.

1051. Ōhara Shakai Mondai Kenkyūsho 大原社會問題研究所 (Ōhara Research Institute for Social Problems), Chingin tōsei to chingin tosō 賃金統制と賃金鬪爭 (Wage control and wage disputes), Tōkyō, Daiichi Shuppansha, 1948.
Factual study of the subject during the post-war period.

1052. Ōhara Shakai Mondai Kenkyūsho 大原社會問題研究所 (Ōhara Research Institute for Social Problems), Saitei chinginsei no igi 最低賃金制の意義 (Significance of the minimum wage rate system), Tōkyō, Ōhara Shakai Mondai Kenkyūsho, 1949.

1053. Rōdōsha Rōdō Kijunkyoku 勞働省勞働基準局 (Labor Standard Bureau of the Labor Ministry), Genka chingin mondai no honshitsu 現下賃金問題の本質 (The true nature of the present wage problems), Tōkyō, Nihon Rōdō Tsūshinsha, 1950.

1054. Rōdōshō Rōdō Kijunkyoku 勞働省勞働基準局 (Labor Standard Bureau of the Labor Ministry), Shuyō sangyō chingin no sengo no ugoki 主要産業賃金の戦后の動き (Fluctuation of wages in main industries in the post-war period), Tōyō Shokan, 1951.
Covers the period from the end of the war to April, 1951.

1055. Takimoto Tadao 滝本忠男, Chingin kōsei 賃金構成 (Structure of wages), Tōkyō, Rōdō Bunkasha, 1949.

8. Labor Unions

1056. Gotō Kiyoshi 後島清 , Rōdō kyōyaku rironshi 勞働協約理論史 (History of theories concerning labor agreements), Tōkyō, Yūhikaku, 1946.

1057. Horie Kiichi 堀江歸一 , Rōdō kumiairon 勞働組合論 (On labor unions), Kokubundō, 1921.

1058. Morito Tatsuo 森戸辰男 , Rōdō kumiai no kadai 勞働組合の課題 (Tasks of labor unions), Tōkyō, Kimijima Shobō, 1947.

1059. Rōdōshō Rōseikyoku 勞働省勞政局 (Labor Administration Bureau of the Ministry of Labor), Rōdō kumiai chōsa hōkoku 勞働組合調査報告 (Report of the labor union survey), Tōkyō, Rōdōshō Rōseikyoku, 1949.

1060. Seiji Keizai Kenkyūsho 政治經濟研究所 (Research Institute for Politics and Economics), Sangyō shakaika to rōdō kumiai no keiei sanka 產業社會化と勞働組合の經營参加 (Socialization of industry and participation of labor unions in management) [=vol. 5 of Seiji Keizai Kenkyūsho, Rōdō mondai zensho (no. 994)], Tōkyō, Takayama Shoten, 1949.

1061. Tōkyō Daigaku Shakai Kagaku Kenkyūsho 東京大學社會科學研究所 (Research Institute of Social Science of Tōkyō University), Sengo rōdō kumiai no jittai 戰後勞働組合の實態 (The actual condition of labor unions in the post-war period), Tōkyō, Nihon Hyōronsha, 1950.

1062. Yamanaka Tokutarō 山中篤太郎 , Rōdō kumiai to shakaiseisaku 勞働組合と社會政策 (Labor unions and social policy), Tōkyō, Keiei Hyōronsha, 1948.

1063. Suehiro Izutarō 末弘嚴太郎 , Rōdō kumiaihō kaisetsu 勞働組合法解說 (Commentary on the Trade Union Act), Tōkyō, Nihon Hyōronsha, 1948.
Work of the leading lawyer in the field of labor legislation.

1064. Suehiro Izutarō 末弘嚴太郎 , Rōdō kankei chōseihō kaisetsu 勞働関係調整法解說 (Commentary on the act regulating labor relations), Tōkyō, Nihon Hyōronsha, 1947.

Chapter XIV

National Income

The employment of the concepts and methods of national income study is recent in Japan as it is elsewhere in the world. Among scholars the method is now widely accepted but the effective workers in this field are still comparatively few. As their number increases they will influence economic science in Japan but it is too early to estimate that influence. The study of national income could not have been carried forward without the provision of statistical information by a large number of the agencies of the Japanese government. The government has, in fact, provided leadership in the actual carrying out of studies. Work in this field is likely to be important in the development of economic policy. The debate over rearmament policy offers an illustration. Since materials for the study of the national income of Japan are much sought after, they have been listed separately from the theoretical studies.

1. Theoretical Works

1065. Fukuda Tokuzō 福田德三 , Kōsei keizai kenkyū 厚生經濟研究 (Study of welfare economics), Tōkyō, Tōkō Shoin, 1930.

1066. Hijikata Sêibi 土方成美 , Kokumin shotoku no kōsei 國民所得の構成 (Structure of national income), Tōkyō, Nihon Hyōronsha, 1933.
A study of the business cycle, as it has appeared in Japan, by means of an analysis of the national income structure. The author is recognized as one of the early students of the Japanese national income.

1067. Morita Yūzō 森田優三 , Kokumin shotoku no hyōka to bunseki 國民所得の評價と分析 (Evaluation and analysis of national income), Tōkyō, Tōyō Keizaisha, 1949.
The author is a well-known statistician in contemporary Japan. The book, based on his lectures, deals with the problems of the statistical measurement of national income.

1068. Nakagawa Tomonaga 中川友長 , Kokufu oyobi kokumin shotoku 國富及國民所得 (National wealth and national income), Tōkyō, Tōyō Shuppansha, 1935.
Appendix V presents a list of references on the estimating of national wealth and income.

1069. Nihon Tōkei Gakkai 日本統計學會 (Japan Statistical Society), Nihon Tōkei Gakkai nempō (Shōwa jūshichi nen)---kokumin shotoku no tōkeiteki kenkyū 日本統計學會年報（昭和十七年）—國民所得の統計的研究 (Annual report of the Japan Statistical Society - 1942: statistical study of national income), Tōkyō, Nihon Tōkei Gakkai, 1942.
The results of the collaboration of five members of the Society, Sudō, Morita, Tamura, Hayakawa, and Shiyomi, on this subject.

1070. Nihon Tōkei Gakkai 日本統計學會 (Japan Statistical Society), Kokumin shotoku to sono bumpu 國民所得とその分布 (National income and its distribution), Tōkyō, Nihon Tōkei Gakkai, 1943.
Revised edition of the preceding work.

1071. Shiomi Saburō 汐見三郎, ed., Kokumin shotoku no bumpai 國民所得の分配 (Distribution of national income), Tōkyō, Yūhikaku, 1933; rev. 1941.
Among the six chapters are "A method of study of the distribution of national income" and "Study of the distribution of national income through income tax legislation."

1072. Takahashi Kamekichi 高橋亀吉, Sensō to Nihon keizairyoku 戦争と日本經濟力 (War and Japanese economic power), Tōkyō, Chikura Shobō, 1937.
An estimate of the war burden supportable by the Japanese economy.

1073. Takahashi Taizō 高橋泰藏, Kokumin shotoku no kihon mondai 國民所得の基本問題 (Fundamental problems of national income), Tōkyō, Tōyō Keizai Shimpōsha, 1947.

1074. Tōyō Keizai Shimpōsha 東洋經濟新報社 (Oriental Economist), Kokumin shotoku no kenkyū 國民所得の研究 (Study of national income), Tōkyō, Tōyō Keizai Shimpōsha, 1948.
A collection of articles written by three leading economists in this field, Takahashi Chōtarō, Yamada Yūzō, and Morita Yūzō.

1075. Toyozaki Minoru 豊崎稔, Keizaigaku no kokuminteki shutai 經濟學の國民的主体 (The nation as the central subject of economics), Tōkyō, Kōbundō Shoten, 1943.
Chapter three of the book is devoted to national income study.

1076. Yamada Yūzō 山田雄三, ed., Kokumin shotoku no bunseki 國民所得の分析 (Analysis of national income), Tōkyō, Nihon Hyōronsha, 1947.
A collection of factual studies.

1077. Yamada Yūzō 山田雄三, Kokumin shotoku no keikaku riron 國民所得の計画理論 (The theory of national income planning), Tōkyō, Iwanami Shoten, 1949.
The author is a leading student of national income in Japan. First, the relation between macro-economics and micro-economics is discussed. In this way the author tries to approach the problem of so-called social accounting which, as he sees it, provides the theoretical basis of national economic planning. A valuable synthesis of previous work.

1078. Yamaguchi Shigeru 山口茂, ed., Kokka shiryoku no mondai 國家資力の問題 (Problems of the economic power of the nation), Tōkyō, Risōsha, 1944.
A collection of articles by authoritative writers in the field.

1079. Yamaguchi Shigeru 山口茂, ed., Keizai keikaku to kokumin shotoku 經濟計画と國民所得 (Economic planning and national income), Tōkyō, Jitsugyō no Nihonsha, 1950, 2 v.

See also entry 363.

2. Materials

1080. Kokuseiin Daiichibu 國勢院第一部 (First Division of the Board of National Power), Senzen sengo ni okeru kokufu tōkei 戦前戦後における國富統計 (National wealth statistics in the pre-war and post-war periods), Tōkyō, 1921.

1081. Naikaku Tōkeikyoku 内閣統計局 (Statistics Bureau of the Cabinet), Kokufu suikei 國富推計 (The estimating of national wealth), Tōkei Kyōkai, 1928.

1082. Naikaku Tōkeikyoku 内閣統計局 (Statistics Bureau of the Cabinet), Kokufu chōsa hōkoku Shōwa gonen 國富調査報告(昭和五年) (National wealth statistics in 1930), Tōkyō, Naikaku Tōkeikyoku, 1933.

1083. Naikaku Tōkeikyoku 内閣統計局 (Statistics Bureau of the Cabinet), Shōwa gonen kokumin shotoku chōsa hōkoku 昭和五年國民所得調査報告 (Report of the estimate of national income in 1930), Tōkyō, Tōkei Kyōkai, 1934.

1084. Ōkurashō Rezaikyoku 大蔵省理財局 (Finance Bureau, Ministry of Finance), Shōwa jūgonen yori Shōwa jūkunen ni itaru kokumin shotoku suikei 昭和十五年より昭和十九年に至る國民所得推計 (Estimates of national income from 1940 to 1944), Tōkyō, Ōkurashō, 1947.

1085. Sōrifu Tōkeikyoku 総理府統計局 (Statistics Bureau of the Prime Minister's Office), Shōwa jūnen ni okeru waga kokufu oyobi kokumin shotokugaku 昭和十年における我が國富及び國民所得額 (Japanese national wealth and national income in 1935), Tōkyō, Sōrifu Tōkeikyoku, 1948.

1086. Sawa Raitarō 澤來太郎, Teikoku kokuyū zaisan sōran 帝國國有財産総覧 (Complete list of the national property of the Japanese empire), Tōkyō, Sawa Seimu Chōsajo, 1917, 216+1502+78 pp.

1087. Shiomi Saburō 汐見三郎, Kakkoku no kokumin shotoku 各國の國民所得 (National income of various countries), Tōkyō, Yūhikaku, 1947.

1088. Yamada Yūzō 山田雄三 , Sekai kakkoku ni okeru kokumin shotoku no hikaku 世界各國における國民所得の比較 (International comparison of national incomes), Tōkyō, Akagi Shobō, 1947.

1089. Yamada Yūzō 山田雄三 , ed., Nihon kokumin shotoku suikei shiryō 日本國民所得推計資料 (Materials for the estimating of Japanese national income), Tōkyō, Tōyō Keizai Shimpōsha, 1951.

A valuable collection of estimates of the national income of Japan. There is some explanation and criticism of method.

Chapter XV

The Corporation and the Zaibatsu

Literature on the zaibatsu was extensive before the Second World War and it has been notably increased as the result of Occupation policy which was expressed in the so-called anti-trust act and in the act to curb the excessive concentration of economic power. The term zaibatsu carries two meanings. The first meaning is general and carries in some measure that which is attached in the United States to the two phrases, big business and Wall Street, but in Japan the reference is to the powerful and wealthy business families. Each of these families controlled a number, sometimes a large number, of corporations. The second meaning is a specific one and the Japanese refer to the Mitsui or Sumitomo zaibatsu. In addition to accounts of the zaibatsu the list below includes works on general aspects of the corporation and a number of histories of individual companies and firms. Many such histories have appeared in Japan and they are a valuable source of information which must, however, be used with care. The histories of the larger banks are of special importance.

1. Zaibatsu in General

1090. Hasegawa Kōtarō 長谷川光太郎 , Nihon zaikai no genseiryoku 日本財界の現勢力 (The current power in Japanese business), Tōkyō, Chikura Shobō, 1935.

1091. Higuchi Hiroshi 樋口弘 , Nihon zaibatsuron 日本財閥論 (On the Japanese zaibatsu), Tōkyō, Mitō Shooku, 1940, 2 v.

1092. Masuchi Yōjirō 増地庸治郎 , Waga kuni kabushikikaisha ni okeru kabushiki bunsan to shihai 我國株式會社における株式分散と支配 (Distribution of and control over the stocks in Japanese corporations), Tōkyō, Dōbunkan, 1936.

1093. Minobe Ryōkichi 美濃部亮吉 , Karuteru torasuto, kontserun (Nihon no bu) カルテル・トラスト・コンツェルン (日本の部) (Cartels, trusts, and konzerns: Japan) [=v. 47, part 2 of Keizaigaku zenshū 經濟學全集 (Anthology on economics)], Tōkyō, Kaizōsha, 1931.

A work by a specialist in the field. There are separate chapters on the development of the cartel in Japan, on cartels in various industrial fields, and on Japanese imperialism and the cartel.

1094. Nihon kontserun zensho 日本コンツェルン全書 (Complete series of the konzern in Japan), Tōkyō, Shunjūsha, 1937, 19 v.

This series of nineteen volumes begins with a general work on the Japanese zaibatsu by Takahashi and Aoyama. This is followed by separate volumes on the various zaibatsu by journalists and writers on economics. The whole series provides a useful factual account.

1095. Suzuki Mosaburō 鈴木茂三郎 , Nihon zaibatsuron 日本財閥論 (On the Japanese zaibatsu), Tōkyō, Kaizōsha, 1934.

A valuable work which shows the network of control over the Japanese economy by the zaibatsu. In his first chapters the author deals with government capital and the zaibatsu and with the position of zaibatsu in military industries.

1096. Takahashi Kamekichi 高橋亀吉 , Nihon zaibatsu no kaibō 日本財閥の解剖 (Dissection of the Japanese zaibatsu), Tōkyō, Chūō Kōronsha, 1930.

General and individual surveys. Deals with Mitsui, Mitsubishi, Sumitomo, Yasuda, Asano, Ōkura, Furukawa, Kawasaki, and Ōkawa.

2. Development of Zaibatsu

a. Origin of Zaibatsu

1097. Iwai Ryōtarō 岩井良太郎 , Mitsui Mitsubishi monogatari 三井三菱物語 (The stories of the Mitsui and the Mitsubishi), Tōkyō, Chikura Shobō, 1934.

1098. Morooka Kuni 師岡國 , ed., Mitsubishi Kaisha uchimaku hibunroku 三菱會社内幕秘聞錄 (Collection of inside facts concerning the Mitsubishi Company), in Sumida, ed., Kaiji shiryō sōsho (No. 1189).

b. Zaibatsu during the Meiji and Taishō Periods

1099. Kanno Watarō 菅野和太郎, Nihon kaishakigyō hasseishi no kenkyū 日本會社企業發生史の研究 (Study of the history of the beginning of Japanese corporate enterprises), Tōkyō, Iwanami Shoten, 1931.
An account of the establishment and development of the corporation from the later Tokugawa period to the early Meiji period.

1100. Nishino Kiyosaku 西野喜與作, Hanseiki zaikai sokumenshi 半世紀財界側面史 (A half century's side-lights on the history of Japanese business), Tōkyō, Tōyō Keizai Shimpōsha, 1932.

1101. Shirayanagi Shūko 白柳秀湖, Gendai zaibatsu zaiakushi 現代財閥罪惡史 (History of the crimes of the zaibatsu), Tōkyō, Chikura Shobō, 1932.

1102. Shirayanagi Shūko 白柳秀湖, Sumitomo monogatari 住友物語 (The story of the Sumitomos), Tōkyō, Chikura Shobō, 1931.

c. Zaibatsu and Economic Crises

1103. Inomata Tsunao 猪俣津南雄, Kyōkō-ka Nihon shihonshugi 恐慌下の日本資本主義 (Japanese capitalism during the crisis), Tōkyō, Kaizōsha, 1931.

1104. Inomata Tsunao 猪俣津南雄, Nihon no dokusen shihonshugi---kin'yū shihon no kyōkō taisaku 日本の獨占資本主義—金融資本の恐慌對策 (Japanese monopolistic capitalism---financial capitalists' counter-measures against crisis), Tōkyō, Namboku Shoin, 1932.

1105. Kojima Seiichi 小島精一, Kyōkō to dokusen 恐慌と獨占 (Crisis and monopoly), Tōkyō, Nihon Hyōronsha, 1928.

1106. Kojima Seiichi 小島精一, Nihon kin'yū shihonron 日本金融資本論 (On Japanese financial capital), Tōkyō, Chikura Shobō, 1929.

1107. Tōkyō Shōkō Kaigisho Chōsaka 東京商工會議所調査課 (Research Section, Tōkyō Chamber of Commerce), Mitsuike Mitsubishike chokuei oyobi kankei ginkō narabi ni jigyō gaisha 三井家三菱家直營及び關係銀行竝事業會社 (Banks and corporations under the direct or indirect control of the Mitsui and Mitsubishi families), Tōkyō, Shōkō Kaigisho, 1928.

1108. Takahashi Kamekichi 高橋龜吉, Nihon shihonshugi no gōrika 日本資本主義の合理化 (The rationalization of Japanese capitalism), Tōkyō, Shun'yōdō, 1930.

d. Zaibatsu during the Periods of Quasi-war and War Economy

1109. Asahi Shimbun Keizaibu 朝日新聞經濟部 (Economic Section of the Asahi Press), Shōwa zaikaishi 昭和財界史 (History of business during the Shōwa period), Tōkyō, Asahi Shimbunsha, 1936.

1110. Chūgai Sangyō Chōsakai 中外産業調査會 (Chūgai Research Association for Industry), Zaibatsu Mitsui no shinkenkyū 財閥三菱の新研究 (A new study of the Mitsui zaibatsu), Tōkyō, Chūgai Sangyō Chōsakai, 1936.

1111. Chūgai Sangyō Chōsakai 中外産業調査會 (Chūgai Research Association for Industry), Zaibatsu Mitsubishi no shinkenkyū 財閥三菱の新研究 (A new study of the Mitsubishi zaibatsu), Tōkyō, Chūgai Sangyō Chōsakai, 1937.

1112. Chūgai Sangyō Chōsakai 中外産業調査會 (Chūgai Research Association for Industry), Zaibatsu Sumitomo no shinkenkyū 財閥住友の新研究 (A new study of the Sumitomo zaibatsu), Tōkyō, Chūgai Sangyō Chōsakai, 1937.

1113. Iwai Ryōtarō 岩井良太郎, Sensō to zaibatsu 戰爭と財閥 (War and the zaibatsu), Tōkyō, Chikura Shobō, 1938.

1114. Shizuta Hitoshi 静田均, Karuteru to keizai dantai カルテルと經濟團体 (Cartels and associations of economic bodies), Tōkyō, Nihon Hyōronsha, 1943.

1115. Suzuki Mosaburō 鈴木茂三郎, Tenkanki o yuku Nihon zaibatsu no kaibō 轉換期を行く日本財閥の解剖 (Analysis of Japanese zaibatsu during a period of transition), Tōkyō, Konnichi no Mondaisha, 1936.

e. Colonial Expansion of Zaibatsu

1116. Chōsen Ginkō 朝鮮銀行 (Bank of Chōsen), Chōsen ni okeru naichi shihon no ryūshutsunyū ni tsuite 朝鮮に於ける内地資本の流出入について (On the inflow and outflow of Japanese capital to and from Korea), Chōsen Ginkō Chōsaka, 1933.

1117. Higuchi Hiroshi 樋口弘, Nihon no taishi tōshi kenkyū 日本の對支投資研究 (Study of Japanese investment in China), Tōkyō, Seikatsusha, 1935.

1118. Mitsui Kōzan Kabushiki Kaisha 三井鑛山株式會社 (Mitsui Mining Company), ed., Nampō kankei tōsha jigyō gaiyō 南方關係當社事業概要 (Outline of the company's undertakings relating to the South Sea Islands area), Mitsui Kōzan Kabushiki Kaisha, 1942.

1119. Shōkōshō Shōmukyoku Bōekika 商工省商務局貿易課 (Foreign Trade Section, Bureau of Commercial Affairs, Ministry of Commerce and Industry), Kaigai ni okeru shuyō hompō shōsha no tōshijigyō 海外における主要本邦商社の投資事業 (Overseas investment of important Japanese corporations), Tōkyō, Shōkōshō, 1929.

See also entries 631, 633, 636, 637, 638, 640, 641.

3. Liquidation of Zaibatsu

1120. Hashimoto Ryūgo 橋本龍伍, Dokusen kinshihō to waga kokumin keizai 獨占禁止法と我が國民經濟 (The anti-trust act and our national economy), Tōkyō, Nihon Keizai Shimbunsha, 1947.

1121. Ishii Ryōzō 石井良三, Dokusen kinshihō 獨占禁止法 (Anti-trust act), Tōkyō, Umiguchi Shoten, 1948.
This work and the following one are commentaries on the Japanese anti-trust act. This work is a legal exposition and the following is a comment from the viewpoint of economics.

1122. Mochikabukaisha Seiri Iinkai 持株會社整理委員會 (Holding Company Liquidation Committee), ed., Kado keizairyoku shūchū haijohō no kaisetsu 過度經濟力集中排除法の解說 (Commentary on the act to eliminate the excessive concentration of economic power), Tōkyō, Jiji Tsūshinsha, 1948.
Explanation of the act worked out by the official agency which took charge of the liquidation of zaibatsu.

1123. Mochikabukaisha Seiri Iinkai 持株會社整理委員會 (Holding Company Liquidation Committee), Nihon zaibatsu to sono kaitai 日本財閥とその解体 (Japanese zaibatsu and their liquidation), Tōkyō, Mochikabukaisha Seiri Iinkai, 1950, 2 v.
Vol. 1 covers the general development of zaibatsu, the details of liquidation and materials concerned with the control of zaibatsu over important industries. Vol. 2 contains detailed and valuable materials relating to the liquidation of zaibatsu such as the amount of stocks, public bonds, and investment trust shares held by each zaibatsu, the list of names of companies under the control of each zaibatsu, and so on. Includes a valuable bibliography.

1124. Ōsumi Ken'ichirō 大隅健一郎, Zaibatsu no kikō to sono kaitai 財閥の機構とその解体 (Organization of zaibatsu and their liquidation), Tōkyō, Yūhikaku, 1946.

1125. Toda Shintarō 戸田慎太郎, Zaibatsu kaitai-go ni okeru dokusen shihon 財閥解体後に於ける獨占資本 (Monopolistic capital after the liquidation of the zaibatsu), Tōkyō, Chōryūsha, 1949.

1126. Wagatsuma Sakae 我妻榮, Keizai saiken to tōsei rippō 經濟再建と統制立法 (Economic reconstruction and control legislation), Tōkyō, Yūhikaku, 1948.

See also entry 474.

4. Histories of the Individual Companies

1127. Abe Ichisuke 阿部市助, ed., Kawasaki zōsenjo yonjūnenshi 川崎造船所四十年史 (Forty-year history of the Kawasaki Shipbuilding Company), Kawasaki, Kawasaki Zōsenjo, 1936.

1128. Arai Gensui 新井源水, Tōkyō Ishikawajima zōsenjo gojūnenshi 東京石川島造船所五十年史 (Fifty-year history of the Tōkyō Ishikawajima Ship-building Company), Tōkyō, Ishikawajima Zōsenjo, 1930.

1129. Daiichi Ginkō 第一銀行 (Daiichi Bank), Daiichi ginkō gojūnenshi 第一銀行五十年史 (Fifty-year history of the Daiichi Bank), Tōkyō, Daiichi Ginkō, 1926, 148+12 pp.

1130. Daiwa Ginkō 大和銀行 (Daiwa Bank), Nomura ginkō sanjūnenshi 野村銀行三十年史 (Thirty-year history of the Nomura bank), Daiwa Ginkō, 1948.

1131. Hitachi Seisakusho 日立製作所 (Hitachi Manufacturing Company), Hitachi Seisakusho-shi 日立製作所史 (History of the Hitachi Manufacturing Company), Tōkyō, Hitachi Seisakusho, 1948.

1132. Hokkaidō Tankō Kisen Kabushiki Kaisha 北海道炭鑛汽船株式會社 (Hokkaidō Coal Shipping Company), Hokkaidō Tankō Kisen Kabushiki Kaisha gojūnenshi 北海道炭鑛汽船株式會社五十年史 (Fifty-year history of the Hokkaidō Coal Shipping Company), Hokkaidō Tankō Kisen Kabushiki Kaisha, 1939.

1133. Kabushiki Kaisha Kōbe Seikōsho 株式會社神戸製鋼所 (Kōbe Steel Company), ed., Shinkō sanjūnenshi 神鋼三十年史 (Thirty-year history of the Kōbe Steel Company), Kōbe Seikōsho, 1938.

1134. Kokusai Tsūun Kabushiki Kaisha 國際通運株式會社 (Kokusai Shipping Company), Kokusai Tsūun Kabushiki Kaisha-shi 國際通運株式會社史 (History of Kokusai Shipping Company), Kokusai Tsūun Kabushiki Kaisha, 1938.

1135. Mitsubishi Zōsen Kabushiki Kaisha Nagasaki Zōsenjo 三菱造船株式會社長崎造船所 (Nagasaki Dockyard of the Mitsubishi Ship-building Company), Mitsubishi Nagasaki Zōsenjo-shi 三菱長崎造船所史 (History of the Mitsubishi Nagasaki dockyard), Mitsubishi Zōsen Kabushiki Kaisha, 1928.
Presents three periods: late Tokugawa, period of governmental management, and period of Mitsubishi management. Convenient materials to review the whole history of Japanese ship-building.

1136. Mitsui Ginkō 三井銀行 (Mitsui Bank), Mitsui Ginkō gojūnenshi 三井銀行五十年史 (Fifty-year history of the Mitsui Bank), Mitsui Ginkō, 1926.

1137. Nihon Kangyō Ginkō Chōsaka 日本勧業銀行調査課 (Research Section, Japan Hypothec Bank), Nihon Kangyō Ginkō yonjūnenshi 日本勧業銀行四十年志 (Forty-year history of the Japan Hypothec Bank), Tōkyō, Nihon Kangyō Ginkō, 1938.

1138. Nihon Kōgyō Ginkō 日本興業銀行 (Japan Industrial Bank), Nihon Kōgyō Ginkō shōshi 日本興業銀行小史 (A brief history of the Japan Industrial Bank), Tōkyō, Nihon Kōgyō Ginkō, 1946.

1139. Nihon Kōkan Kabushiki Kaisha 日本鋼管株式會社 (Japan Steel Tube Company), ed., Nihon Kōkan Kabushiki Kaisha sōgyō sanjūnenshi 日本鋼管株式會社創業三十年史 (Thirty-year history of the Japan Steel Tube Company in retrospect), Kawasaki, Nihon Kōkan Kabushiki Kaisha, 1942.

1140. Nihon Sekiyu Kabushiki Kaisha 日本石油株式會社 (Japan Petroleum Company), Nisseki gojūnen 日石五十年 (Fifty-year history of the Japan Petroleum Company), Tōkyō, Nihon Sekiyu Kabushiki Kaisha, 1937.

1141. Nihon Yūsen Kabushiki Kaisha 日本郵船株式會社 (Japan Mail Steamship Company), Nihon Yūsen Kabushiki Kaisha gojūnenshi 日本郵船株式會社五十年史 (Fifty-year history of the Japan Mail Steamship Company), Tōkyō, Nihon Yūsen Kabushiki Kaisha, 1935.

1142. Ōsaka Kabushiki Torihikijo 大阪株式取引所 (Ōsaka Stock Exchange), Daikabu gojūnen shōshi 大株五十年小史 (Brief fifty-year history of the Ōsaka Stock Exchange), Ōsaka Kabushiki Torihikijo, 1928.

1143. Ōsaka Shōsen Kabushiki Kaisha 大阪商船株式會社 (Ōsaka Shōsen Company), Ōsaka Shōsen Kabushiki Kaisha gojūnenshi 大阪商船株式會社五十年史 (Fifty-year history of the Ōsaka Commercial Steamship Company), Ōsaka, Ōsaka Shōsen Kabushiki Kaisha, 1934, 880+72 pp.

1144. Shibaura Seisakusho 芝浦製作所 (Shibaura Manufacturing Company), Shibaura Seisakusho rokujūgonenshi 芝浦製作所六十五年史 (Sixty-five year history of the Shibaura Manufacturing Company), Shibaura Seisakusho, 1940.

1145. Sumitomo Ginkō 住友銀行 (Sumitomo Bank), Sumitomo Ginkō sanjūnenshi 住友銀行三十年史 (Thirty-year history of the Sumitomo Bank), Ōsaka, Sumitomo Ginkō, 1926.

1146. Sumitomo Honsha 住友本社 (Main Office of Sumitomo), Besshi kaikō nihyakugojūnenshi 別子開坑二五〇年史 (Two hundred fifty year history of the Besshi mine), Ōsaka, Sumitomo Honsha, 1941.

1147. Tama Zōsenjo 玉造船所 (Tama Dockyard), Mitsui Bussan Kabushiki Kaisha Zōsembu nijūnenshi 三井物產株式會社造船部二十年史 (Twenty-year history of the Ship-building Division of the Mitsui Trading Company), Mitsui Bussan Kabushiki Kaisha, 1938.

1148. Tōkyō Kabushiki Torihikijo 東京株式取引所 (Tōkyō Stock Exchange), Tōkyō Kabushiki Torihikijo gojūnenshi 東京株式取引所五十年史 (Fifty-year history of the Tōkyō Stock Exchange), Tōkyō, Tōkyō Kabushiki Torihikijo, 1928.

1149. Tōkyō Kabushiki Torihikijo 東京株式取引所 (Tōkyō Stock Exchange), Tōkyō Kabushiki Torihikijo-shi 東京株式取引所史 (History of the Tōkyō Stock Exchange), Tōkyō, Tōkyō Kabushiki Torihikijo, 1933; 1938, 2 v.

1150. Yasuda Ginkō 安田銀行 (Yasuda Bank), Yasuda Ginkō rokujūnenshi 安田銀行六十年史 (Sixty-year history of the Yasuda Bank), Tōkyō, Yasuda Ginkō, 1940, 490+40 pp.

See also entries 488-495, 505.

Chapter XVI

Cooperative Activities

The cooperative movement in Japan is relatively new but it has some roots that run far back into Japanese social and economic organization in the past. There has been an interest in the subject among economists and other social scientists since the early years of Meiji. This interest has been stimulated by the increased reliance upon cooperatives, especially rural cooperatives, during the post-war years. While the cooperative movement has been of great importance in agriculture, it is to be observed that it has played a part in small-scale industry as well.

1. Bibliographies

1151. Hon'iden Akio 本位田祥男 , "Shōhi kumiai bunken 消費組合文献 (Literature relating to consumers' cooperatives)," in Shōhi kumiai undō (Consumers' cooperative movement), Tōkyō, Nihon Hyōronsha, 1931.

1152. Sangyō Kumiai Chūōkai 產業組合中央會 (Central Body of Industrial Cooperatives), Sangyō kumiai bunken mokuroku 產業組合文献目錄 (Catalogue of literature relating to cooperative bodies), 1926.
List of works published during the period from 1891 to 1926. Contains both separate works and articles in journals.

1153. Sangyō Kumiai Chūōkai 産業組合中央會 (Central Body of Industrial Cooperatives), Sangyō kumiai nenkan 産業組合年鑑 (Yearbook on industrial cooperatives) (no. 100), "Sangyō kumiai bunken 産業組合文献 (Literature relating to industrial cooperatives)."

2. General Accounts and History

1154. Hon'iden Akio 本位田祥男, Shōhi kumiai undō 消費組合運動 (The consumers' cooperative movement), Tōkyō, Nihon Hyōronsha, 1931.
Approaches the subject through the historical analysis of the development of cooperatives in various countries.

1155. Hon'iden Akio 本位田祥男, Kyōdō kumiai kenkyū 協同組合研究 (Study of cooperatives), Tōkyō, Kōyō Shoin, 1936.
A collection of the author's articles concerned with cooperatives which includes one on the theory of the cooperative movement.

1156. Hon'iden Akio 本位田祥男, Shōkō kyōdō kumiai 商工協同組合 (Commercial and industrial cooperatives), Tōkyō, Nihon Hyōronsha, 1949.

1157. Inomata Tsunao 猪俣津南雄, Nihon ni okeru nōgyō kyōkō to sangyō kumiai 日本に於ける農業恐慌と産業組合 (Agricultural crisis and industrial cooperatives in Japan), Tōkyō, Gakugeisha, 1935.

1158. Inoue Harumaru 井上晴丸, Nihon kyōdō kumiairon 日本協同組合論 (On Japanese cooperatives), Tōkyō, Kenshinsha, 1949.
A new edition of the author's Nihon sangyō kumiairon (On Japanese industrial cooperatives) published in 1937. This work, strongly influenced by Marxist thought, deals with the rationale of the cooperative movement, the relation between Japanese capitalist organization and cooperatives, and the inherent contradictions in Japanese cooperatives.

1159. Kaji Masao 梶正雄, ed., Zenkōren jūgonenshi 全購聯十五年史 (Fifteen-year history of the National Association of Purchasing Cooperatives), Tōkyō, Zenkoku Kōbai Kumiai Rengōkai, 1938.

1160. Kondō Yasuo 近藤康男, Kyōdō kumiai genron 協同組合原論 (Principles of cooperatives), Tōkyō, Kōyō Shoin, 1934.
A theoretical work by a leading agricultural economist.

1161. Kyōchōkai 協調會 (Reconciliation Association), Hompō kōgyō rōdōsha no shōhi kumiai undō 本邦工業勞働者の消費組合運動 (The consumers' cooperative movement among Japanese laborers in the manufacturing industry), Tōkyō, Kyōchōkai, 1928.

1162. Minoguchi Tokijirō 美濃口時次郎, Shōhi kumiai hattatsushiron 消費組合發達史論 (On the history of the development of consumers' cooperatives), Tōkyō, Iwanami Shoten, 1920.

1163. Nōrinshō 農林省 (Agriculture and Forestry Ministry), Nihon nōgyō dantai nempyō 日本農業團体年表 (Chronological history of Japanese agricultural associations), Tōkyō, Nōrinshō, 1947.

1164. Nōrinshō Nōseikyoku Nōseika 農林省農政局農政課 (Agricultural Administration Section, Agricultural Administration Bureau, Agriculture and Forestry Ministry), Nōgyō kyōdō kumiaihō no kaisetsu 農業協同組合法の解説 (Commentary on the act concerning agricultural cooperatives), Tōkyō, Nōrinshō Nōseikyoku Nōseika, 1948.

1165. Okutani Matsuji 奥谷松治, Nihon shōhi kumiai nempyō 日本消費組合年表 (Chronological account of Japanese consumers' cooperatives), Tōkyō, Kyōdō Kumiai Kenkyūjo, 1934.

1166. Okutani Matsuji 奥谷松治, Nihon shōhi kumiaishi 日本消費組合史 (History of Japanese consumers' cooperatives), Tōkyō, Kōyō Shoin, 1935.
Deals with their development from the Meiji period.

1167. Okutani Matsuji 奥谷松治, Nihon kyōdō kumiaishi 日本協同組合史 (History of Japanese cooperatives), Tōkyō, Nōgyō Kyōdō Kumiai Kenkyūkai, 1947.
Revised edition of the author's earlier work which deals with the origin and development of cooperatives, cooperatives during the world depression, and cooperatives during the war period.

1168. Sangyō Kumiai Chūōkai 産業組合中央會 (Central Body of Industrial Cooperatives), Nihon sangyō kumiaishi 日本産業組合史 (History of Japanese industrial cooperatives), 1926.
Appendices provide laws, ordinances, and statistics relating to the subject.

1169. Sangyō Kumiai Chūōkai 産業組合中央會 (Central Body of Industrial Cooperatives), Hompō sangyō kumiai kan narabi ni shokiteishū 本邦産業組合款並諸規程集 (Collection of regulations and rules of Japanese industrial cooperatives), Tōkyō, Sangyō Kumiai Chūōkai, 1932.

1170. Sangyō Kumiai Chūō Kinko 産業組合中央金庫 (Central Depository of Industrial Cooperatives), Sangyō Kumiai Chūō Kinko jūnenshi 産業組合中央金庫十年誌 (Ten years history of the Central Depository of Industrial Cooperatives), Tōkyō, Sangyō Kumiai Chūō Kinko, 1934.

1171. Satō Kanji 佐藤寛次, *Shin'yō kumiairon* 信用組合論 (On the credit cooperatives), Tōkyō, Nishigahara Kankōkai, 1930.
Deals with historical development, functions, and organization.

1172. Tōhata Seiichi 東畑精一, *Kyōdō kumiai to nōgyō mondai* 協同組合と農業問題 (Cooperatives and agricultural problems), Tōkyō, Kaizōsha, 1947.
This is a work by a leading agricultural economist dealing with the particular significance of cooperative activities in Japanese agriculture.

1173. Tōura Shōji 東浦荘治, *Nihon sangyō kumiaishi* 日本産業組合史 (Development of Japanese industrial cooperatives), Tōkyō, Kōyō Shoin, 1935.
An analysis of the development of Japanese cooperatives in connection with changes in agricultural policies.

1174. Tsuji Makoto 辻誠, *Nihon sangyō kumiai shikō* 日本産業組合史講 (Lectures on the development of Japanese cooperative bodies), Tōkyō, Kōyō Shoin, 1937.
Contains two chapters which deal with the general history of Japanese cooperatives and cooperative activities after World War I.

See also entry 427.

Chapter XVII

Transportation

Transportation takes its place in general economics, in economic history, and in the history of economic development in accordance with the principle that division of labor is limited by the extent of the market. The subject should, therefore, be pursued in general treatises and historical works as well as in the special publications which are listed here.

1175. Aoe Shū 青江秀, ed., *Dainihon kōtsūshi* 大日本交通史 (History of transportation in Japan), Tōkyō, Chōyōkai, 1928, 152+115+598 pp.
A reprint of *Dainihon teikoku ekiteishikō* 大日本帝國驛遞史考 (Thoughts on the history of Japanese postal and transportation service), edited by Aoe in 1882. Deals with the development of transportation from ancient times to the beginning of the Meiji period. Provides useful historical material relating to the subject.

1176. Furuta Ryōichi 古田良一, *Edo jidai no kōtsu* 江戸時代の交通 (Transportation in the Tokugawa period), Tōkyō, Iwanami Shoten, 1934.

1177. Furuta Ryōichi 古田良一, *Nihon kaiunshi kōyō* 日本海運史綱要 (Outline of the history of Japanese maritime transportation), Tōkyō, Keizai Tosho Kabushiki Kaisha, 1944.

1178. Honjō Eijirō 本荘栄治郎, ed., *Nihon kōtsūshi no kenkyū* 日本交通史の研究 (Research on the history of transportation in Japan), Tōkyō, Kaizōsha, 1929.
A collection of articles written by Honjō Eijirō, Ōyama Shikitarō, Kuroha Hyōjirō, and Kokushō Iwao. All articles are concerned with transportation during the Tokugawa period.

1179. Kuroha Hyōjirō 黒羽兵治郎, *Kinsei kōtsūshi kenkyū* 近世交通史研究 (Studies in the history of transportation in the modern age), Tōkyō, Nihon Hyōronsha, 1943.

1180. Miyamoto Gennosuke 宮本源之助, ed., *Meiji un'yushi* 明治運輸史 (History of transportation in the Meiji period), Tōkyō, Un'yu Nipponsha, 1921.
There are chapters on land transportation, maritime transportation, and shipping. Covers the period from the Meiji Restoration.

1181. Nihon Rekishi Chiri Gakkai 日本歴史地理學會 (The Japan Historical Geography Society), *Nihon kōtsūshi no kenkyū* 日本交通史の研究 (Study of Japanese transportation history), Nakososha, 1931.
A special volume of the periodical *Rekishi chiri* (Historical geography) containing articles on the history of transportation in Japan before the Meiji period.

1182. Noguchi Masao 野口雅雄, *Nihon unsōshi* 日本運送史 (History of shipping in Japan), Tōkyō, Kōtsū Jihōsha, 1929.
Covers the period from ancient times to the present.

1183. Ōshima Nobujirō 大島延次郎, *Nihon kōtsūshi ronsō* 日本交通史論叢 (A collection of articles on the Japanese transportation history), Tōkyō, Kokusai Kōtsū Bunka Kyōkai, 1939.

1184. Ōshima Nobujirō 大島延次郎, *Nihon kōtsūshi* 日本交通史 (History of Japanese transportation), Tōkyō, Shikai Shobō, 1942.

1185. Ōshima Tōtarō 大島藤太郎, *Kokuyū tetsudō no shiteki hatten* 國有鐵道の史的發展 (Historical development of government-owned railways), Tōkyō, Itō Shoten, 1949.

1186. Ōta Kōhei 太田康平, Nihon kaiun no genjō oyobi shōrai 日本海運の現狀及將來 (The present and future of Japanese marine transportation), Tōkyō, Sangensha, 1948.

1187. Ozasa Kiyone 小篠清根, ed., Kaiun shiryō 海運史料 (Historical data on marine transportation), Tōkyō, Hakubundō, 1886.

A collection of materials relating to marine transportation during the early Meiji period.

1188. Sumida Shōichi 住田正一, Kaijō unsō shiron 海上運送史論 (On the history of marine shipping), Tōkyō, Ganshōdō, 1925.

A collection of articles on maritime transportation throughout Japanese history. Among the subjects are maritime transportation during various periods, the origin of words relating to ships, and maritime legislation at various times.

1189. Sumida Shōichi 住田正一, ed., Kaiji shiryō sōsho 海事史料叢書 (Collection of materials relating to maritime affairs), Tōkyō, Ganshōdō, 1929-31, 20 v.

A collection of legislation, documents, and other materials relating to maritime affairs during the Toyotomi, Tokugawa, and early Meiji periods.

1190. Sumida Shōichi 住田正一, Kaisen shikimoku no kenkyū 廻船式目の研究 (Study of regulations pertaining to maritime transportation), 1944.

A study of the regulation of maritime transportation in the Tokugawa period.

1191. Tetsudōshō 鐵道省 (Railway Ministry), Nihon tetsudōshi 日本鐵道史 (History of railways in Japan), Tōkyō, Tetsudōshō, 1921.

Detailed history of Japanese railways from the early Meiji period to the establishment of the Railways Ministry in 1920.

See also entry 564.

APPENDIX

List of Publishers

A

Achikku Myūjiamu アチックミユージアム	Tōkyō
Ajia Shobō アジア書房	Tōkyō
Akagi Shobō 赤城書房	Tōkyō
Akatsuki Shoin 暁書院	Tōkyō
Aoki Shoten 青木書店	Tōkyō
Aoyama Shoten 青山書店	Tōkyō
Asahi Shimbunsha 朝日新聞社 (The Asahi Newspaper Company)	Ōsaka
Asahi Shimbunsha Keizaibu 朝日新聞社經濟部 (Economic Department, The Asahi Newspaper Company)	Tōkyō
Asano Shoten 淺野書店	Tōkyō

B

Baifūkan 培風館	Tōkyō
Bungadō 文雅堂	Tōkyō
Bungei Shunjūsha 文芸春秋社	Tōkyō
Bunka Gakkai Shuppambu 文化學會出版部	Tōkyō
Bukka Chōsakai 物價調査會 (Institute of Price Survey)	Tōkyō
Bunseisha 文精社	Tōkyō
Bun'yōsha 文養社	Tōkyō

C

Chihō Jichichō Zaiseibu 地方自治廳財政部 (Finance Division, Local Autonomy Agency)	
Chijin Shokan 地人書館	Tōkyō
Chikura Shobō 千倉書房	Tōkyō
Chōryūsha 潮流社	Tōkyō
Chōsa Shiryō Kyōkai 調査資料協會	Tōkyō
Chōsen Ginkō Chōsakyoku 朝鮮銀行調査局 (Research Bureau, The Bank of Korea)	Keijō
Chōsen Shokusan Ginkō Chōsaka 朝鮮殖産銀行調査課 (Research Section, the Industrial Bank of Korea)	Keijō
Chōsen Sōtokufu Zaimukyoku 朝鮮総督府財務局 (Bureau of Finance, Governor's Office of Korea)	Keijō
Chōyōkai 朝陽會	Tōkyō
Chūbunkan Shoten 中文館書店	Tōkyō
Chūgai Sangyō Chōsakai 中外産業調査會	Tōkyō
Chūgai Shōgyō Shimpōsha 中外商業新報社 (The Chūgai Commercial Press)	Tōkyō
Chūgoku Kenkyūjo 中國研究所 (Institute of Chinese Research)	Tōkyō
Chūō Kōronsha 中央公論社	Tōkyō
Chūō Kyōka Dantai Rengōkai 中央教化團体連合會 (Central Federation of Educational Associations)	Tōkyō
Chūō Rōdō Gakuen 中央勞働學園 (Central Labor School)	Tōkyō
Chūō Rōdō Iinkai Jimukyoku 中央勞働委員會事務局 (Executive Bureau, Central Labor Relations Committee)	Tōkyō
Chūō Shakaijigyō Kyōkai 中央社會事業協會 (Central Association of Social Work)	Tōkyō
Chūshō Kigyōchō 中小企業廳 (Medium and Small Enterprises Agency)	Tōkyō
Chūwa Shoin 中和書院	Tōkyō

D

Daidō Shoin 大同書院	Tōkyō
Daiichi Ginkō 第一銀行 (Daiichi Bank)	Tōkyō
Daiichi Shuppansha 第一出版社	Tōkyō
Dai-Nihon Bōseki Rengōkai 大日本紡績連合會 (Japan Federation of Cotton Spinners)	Ōsaka
Dai-Nihon Sankai 大日本蠶會 (Japanese Association of Sericulture)	Tōkyō
Dai-Nihon Sanrinkai 大日本山林會 (Japan Forestry Association)	Tōkyō
Dai-Nihon Seitō Kabushiki Kaisha 大日本製糖株式會社 (Japan Sugar Refining Co., Ltd.)	
Daiwa Ginkō 大和銀行 (Daiwa Bank)	Ōsaka
Daiyamondosha ダイヤモンド社	Tōkyō
Daiyūkaku 大雄閣	Tōkyō
Dōbunkan 同文館	Tōkyō
Dōjinsha Shoten 同人社書店	Tōkyō
Dōmei Tsūshinsha 同盟通信社	Tōkyō
Dōshisha Kōshō Shōgyō Kenkyūkai 同志社高商商業研究會 (Research Seminar for Commerce, the Dōshisha Higher Commercial College)	Kyōto
Dōyūsha 同友社	Tōkyō

F

Fuji Shuppansha 富士出版社 Tōkyō
Fukuda Shobō 福田書房 Tōkyō
Fumin Kyōkai 富民協會 Tōkyō
Futami Shobō 二見書房 Tōkyō
Fuzambō 富山房 Tōkyō

G

Gaimushō Tsūshōkyoku 外務省通商局 (International Trade Bureau, Ministry of Foreign Affairs) Tōkyō
Gakusei Shobō 學生書房 Tōkyō
Gakushi Shoin 學而書院 Tōkyō
Gakugeisha 學芸社 Tōkyō
Gakujutsu Tosho Shuppansha 學術圖書出版社 Tōkyō
Gakuyō Shobō 學陽書房 Tōkyō
Ganshōdō 巖松堂 Tōkyō
Ganzansha Shoten 丸山舎書店 Tōkyō
Genrin Shobō 玄林書房 .... Kyōto
Getsuyō Shobō 月曜書房 Tōkyō
Ginkō Mondai Kenkyūkai 銀行問題研究會 (Research Society on Banking Problems) Tōkyō
Ginza Shuppansha 銀座出版社 Tōkyō

H

Hakubunkan 博文館 Tōkyō
Hakugei Shobō .... Ōsaka
Hakujitsu Shoin 白日書院 Tōkyō
Hakuhōsha 白鳳社 Tōkyō
Hakutōsha 白東社 Tōkyō
Hakuyōsha 白揚社 Tōkyō
Heibonsha 平凡社 Tōkyō
Heiwa Shobō 平和書房 Tōkyō
Hibonkaku 非凡閣 Tōkyō
Hihansha 批判社 Tōkyō
Hiroshima-ken Jichi Kyōkai 廣島縣自治協會 (Association for Hiroshima Prefectural Autonomy) .... Hiroshima
Hitachi Seisakusho 日立製作所
Hitotsubashi Gakkai 一橋學會 Tōkyō
Hōbunkan 寶文館 .... Ōsaka
Hōchi Shimbunsha 報知新聞社 (Hōchi Newspaper Company) Tōkyō
Hodaka Shobō 保高書房 Tōkyō
Hōjō Shoten 北條書店 Tōkyō
Hoken Ginkō Shintaku Jihōsha 保険銀行信託時報社 Tōkyō
Hokkaidō Tankō Kisen Kabushiki Kaisha 北海道炭鑛汽船株式會社
Hokkaidō Takushoku Ginkō 北海道拓殖銀行 .... Sapporo
Hokubunkan 北文館 Tōkyō
Hokuryūkan 北隆館 Tōkyō
Hori Shoten 堀書店 .... Ōsaka
Hōritsu Bunkasha 法律文化社 .... Kyōto
Hoshino Shoten 星野書店 Tōkyō
Hyōgensha 表現社 Tōkyō

I

Ichigensha 一元社 Tōkyō
Ikkōsha Zasshibu 一光社雑誌部 Tōkyō
Ikuseisha 育生社 Tōkyō
Imin Mondai Kenkyūkai 移民問題研究會 (Research Institute on Emigration Problems) Tōkyō
Inoue Ronsō Hensankai 井上論叢編纂會 Tōkyō
Inukai Tsuyoshi Kankōkai 犬養毅刊行會 Tōkyō
Isobe Kōyōdō 磯部甲陽堂 Tōkyō
Itagaki Shoten 板垣書店 Tōkyō
Itō Shoten 伊藤書店 Tōkyō
Iwanami Shoten 岩波書店 Tōkyō

J

Jichikan 自治館 Tōkyō
Jichōsha 時潮社 Tōkyō
Jiji Tsūshinsha 時事通信社 Tōkyō
Jinkō Mondai Kenkyūjo 人口問題研究所 (Research Institute on Population Problems) Tōkyō
Jitsugyō Kyōkasho Kabushiki Kaisha 實業教科書株式會社 Tōkyō

Name	Location
Jitsugyō no Nihonsha 實業之日本社	Tōkyō
Jitsugyō no Sekaisha 實業之世界社	Tōkyō
Jiyū Shobō 自由書房	Tōkyō
Junshindō	Tōkyō

K

Name	Location
Kabushiki Kaisha Kōbe Seikōsho 株式會社神戸製鋼所	
Kahei Seido Chōsakai 貨幣制度調査會 (Society for Investigation into Monetary Systems)	Tōkyō
Kaihōsha 解放社	
Kaikoku Gojūnenshi Hakkōjo 開國五十年史發行所 (Office for Publication of a Fifty-year History after	Tōkyō
the Opening of Japan)	Tōkyō
Kaizōsha 改造社	Tōkyō
Kamakura Bunko 鎌倉文庫	Tōkyō
Kan'i Hokenkyoku 簡易保険局 (Postal Insurance Bureau)	
Kansai Keieisha Remmei Jimukyoku 関西經營者連盟事務局 (Executive Bureau of Kansai Employers' Associations)	Ōsaka
Kantō Gakuin Shōgakkai 関東學院商學會 (Society of Commerce of Kantō Gakuin College)	Yokohama
Kantōchō Bunshoka 関東廳文書課 (Document Section of the Kwantung District Office)	
Kantōsha 酣燈社	Tōkyō
Kawade Shobō 河出書房	Tōkyō
Kawasaki Zōsenjo 川崎造船所	
Keibundō 敬文堂	Tōkyō
Keibunsha 啓文社	Tōkyō
Keidanren Nissankyō Jimukyoku 經團連日産協事務局 (Executive Office of the Federation of the Association of Economic Bodies and Japan Industrial Association)	Tōkyō
Keiei Hyōronsha 經營評論社	Tōkyō
Keijisha	Tōkyō
Keiki Kenkyūjo 景氣研究所 (Research Institute on Business Conditions)	Tōkyō
Keimeisha 啓明社	Tōkyō
Keiō Gijuku Press 慶應義塾プレス	Tōkyō
Keiō Shuppansha 慶應出版社	Tōkyō
Keisō Shobō 勁草書房	Tōkyō
Keizai Antei Hombu 經濟安定本部 (Economic Stabilization Board)	Tōkyō
Keizai Chishikisha 經濟知識社	Tōkyō
Keizai Dantai Rengōkai 經濟團体連合會 (Federation of Associations of Economic Bodies)	Tōkyō
Keizai Jōhōsha 經濟情報社	Tōkyō
Keizai Ōraisha 經濟往來社	Tōkyō
Keizai Shingichō 經濟審議廳 (Economic Council Board)	Tōkyō
Keizai Shimpōsha 經濟新報社	Tōkyō
Keizai Taimususha 經濟タイムス社	Tōkyō
Keizai Zasshisha 經濟雜誌社	
Kenshinsha 研進社	Tōkyō
Ken'yoku Chōseikai 乾浴長生會	Tōkyō
Kibōkaku 希望閣	Tōkyō
Kimijima Shobō 君島書房	Tōkyō
Kimura Shobō 木村書房	Tōkyō
Kinkōdō 金港堂	Tōkyō
Kinrō Jihōsha 勤労時報社	Tōkyō
Kinsei Chihō Keizai Shiryō Kankōkai 近世地方經濟史料刊行會	
Kinseidō 金星堂	Tōkyō
Kirinkaku 麒麟閣	
Kisetsusha 季節社	Tōkyō
Kōa Bunka Kyōkai 興亞文化協會	Tōkyō
Kōbundō 弘文堂	Tōkyō
Kōbundō Shoten 弘文堂書店	Tōkyō and Kyōto
Kōbundō Shoten 甲文堂書店	Ōsaka
Kōbunkan 晃文館	
Kōbunsha 光文社	Tōkyō
Kōdosha 黄土社	Tōkyō
Kōgakusha 好學社	Tōkyō
Kōgyō Shimbunsha 工業新聞社	Tōkyō
Kōgyō Shiryō Kankōkai 工業史料刊行會 (Publishing Association of Historical Materials on Industries)	Tōkyō
Koishikawa Shobō 小石川書房	Tōkyō
Kōjinsha 巧人社	Ōsaka
Kōjō Konwakai 工場懇話會	Tōkyō
Kokubundō 國文堂	
Kokumin Bunka Kenkyūkai 國民文化研究會	Tōkyō
Kokumin Kyōikusha 國民教育社	Tōkyō
Kokuritsu Kokkai Toshokan 國立國會圖書館 (National Diet Library)	Tōkyō
Kokusai Bunka Kyōdōsha 國際文化協同社	Tōkyō
Kokusai Kōtsū Bunka Kyōkai 國際交通文化協會	Tōkyō
Kokusai Tsūun Kakushiki Kaisha 國際通運株式會社	
Kokuseiin Daiichibu 國勢院第一部 (First Division, Board of National Power)	
Kokuseisha 國勢社	Tōkyō

Kokushi Kōshūkai 國史講習會 Tōkyō
Kokusho Kankōkai 國書刊行會 Tōkyō
Kokutai Kagakusha 國体科學社
Kondō Shoten 近藤書店 Tōkyō
Kōsan Keizai Chōsakai 鑛産經濟調査會 (Economic Research Association of the Mining Industries) Tōkyō
Kōsei Torihiki Iinkai Chōsabu 公正取引委員會調査部 (Research Division of the Fair Trade Commission) Tōkyō
Kōseikan 厚生館 Tōkyō
Kōseishō Hokenkyoku 厚生省保險局 (Insurance Bureau, Ministry of Welfare) Tōkyō
Kōseishō Kambō Chōsa Tōkeibu 厚生省官房調査統計部 (Research and Statistics Division, Minister's Secretariat, Ministry of Welfare) Tōkyō
Kōseishō Rōdōkyoku 厚生省勞働局 (Labor Bureau, Ministry of Welfare) Tōkyō
Kōtsū Jihōsha 交通時報社
Kōtsū Keizaisha 交通經濟社 Tōkyō
Kōtsū Rōdō Kenkyūjo 交通勞働研究所 (Research Institute on Transportation Labor) Tōkyō
Koyō Mondai Kenkyūkai 雇用問題研究會 (Research Circle on Employment Problems) Tōkyō
Kōyō Shoin 高陽書院 Tōkyō
Kōzan Konwakai 鑛山懇話會 Tōkyō
Kunimoto Shobō 國本書房 Tōkyō
Kunitachi Shoin 國立書院 Tōkyō
Kureha Shoten Tōkyō
Kuriyama Yasuhei Shoten 栗山安平書店
Kyōbunkan 教文館 Tōkyō
Kyōchōkai 協調會 Tōkyō
Kyōdō Kumiai Kenkyūjo 協同組合研究所 (Research Institute on Cooperative Associations) Tōkyō
Kyōdō Shuppansha 共同出版社 Tōkyō
Kyōdōsha 共働社
Kyōritsusna 共立社 Tōkyō
Kyōritsu Shuppan Kabushiki Kaisha 共立出版株式會社 Tōkyō
Kyōseikaku 共生閣 Tōkyō

M

Mado Shoin 窗書院 Tōkyō
Mainichi Shimbunsha Jinkō Mondai Chōsakai 毎日新聞社人口問題調査會 (Mainichi Newspaper Company, Research Association on Population Problems) Tōkyō
Maki Shobō 牧書房 Tōkyō
Manchōhōsha 萬朝報社 Tōkyō
Mankōsha Tōkyō
Mantetsu Honsha Chōsabu 満鉄本社調査部 (Research Division, South Manchurian Railway Company)...... Dairen
Mantetsu Shachōshitsu Chōsaka 満鉄社長室調査課 (Research Section, President's Office, South Manchurian Railway Company)
Mantetsu Tōa Keizai Chōsakyoku 満鉄東亜經濟調査局 (Research Bureau for Eastern Asian Economics, South Manchurain Railway Company) Tōkyō
Marukusu Shobō マルクス書房 Tōkyō
Maruyama Shoten 丸山書店 Tōkyō
Maruzen Shoten 丸善書店 Tōkyō
Masu Shobō 鱒書房 Tōkyō
Meguro Shoten 目黒書店 Tōkyō
Meibundō 明文堂 Tōkyō
Meiji Seitō Kabushiki Kaisha 明治製糖株式會社 Tōkyō
Meiji Shoin 明治書院 Tōkyō
Mengyōsha 綿業社 .... Ōsaka
Meirinkaku 明倫閣 Tōkyō
Meizensha 明善社 Tōkyō
Mibu Shoin 壬生書院 Tōkyō
Mikasa Shobō 三笠書院 Tōkyō
Minshu Hyōronsha 民主評論社 Tōkyō
Min'yūsha 民友社 Tōkyō
Mita Shigakkai 三田史學會 (Mita History Society) Tōkyō
Mita Shobō 三田書房 Tōkyō
Mitsubishi Keizai Kenkyūjo 三菱經濟研究所 (Mitsubishi Institute of Economic Research) Tōkyō
Mitsubishi Zōsen Kabushiki Kaisha Nagasaki Zōsenjo 三菱造船株式會社長崎造船所
Mitsui Kōzan Kabushiki Kaisha 三井鑛山株式會社
Mitsui Ginkō 三井銀行 (Mitsui Bank)
Mochikabu Kaisha Seiri Iinkai 持株會社整理委員會 (The Holding Company Liquidation Committee)
Mōkyō Ginkō Chōsaka 蒙疆銀行調査課 (Research Section, Mongolian Bank)............................ Mōkyō
Momiyama Shoten 籾山書店 Tōkyō
Moriyama Shoten 森山書店 Tōkyō
Murakami Kōeidō .... Ōsaka
Myōjō Shoin 明星書院 Tōkyō

N

Nagasaki Kōshō Kenkyūkan 長崎高商研究館 (Research Institute of Nagasaki Higher Commercial College) Nagasaki

Naigai Shuppan Kabushiki Kaisha 内外出版株式會社 .... Tōkyō and Kyōto

Naikaku Insatsukyoku 内閣印刷局 (Printing Bureau of the Cabinet) Tōkyō

Naikaku Kirokukyoku 内閣記錄局 (Recording Bureau of the Cabinet) Tōkyō

Naikaku Tōkeikyoku 内閣統計局 (The Statistics Bureau of the Cabinet) Tōkyō

Naimushō Chihōkyoku 内務省地方局 (Prefectural Affairs Bureau of the Home Affairs Ministry) Tōkyō

Naimushō Fukkōkyoku 内務省復興局 (Reconstruction Bureau of the Home Affairs Ministry) Tōkyō

Naimushō Shakaikyoku 内務省社會局 (Social Affairs Bureau of the Home Affairs Ministry) Tōkyō

Nakososha 勿來社

Namboku Shoin 南北書院 Tōkyō

Nankōdō 南江堂 Tōkyō

Nankōsha 南晃社 Tōkyō

Nankōsha 南郊社 Tōkyō

Nan'yōchō Tōkyō Jimusho 南洋廳東京事務所 (Tokyo Office, South Sea Islands Government Office) Tōkyō

Natsume Shoten 夏目書店 Tōkyō

Naukasha ナウカ社 Tōkyō

Nihon Beikoku Kyōkai 日本米穀協會 (Japan Rice Association) Tōkyō

Nihon Bōeki Kyōkai 日本貿易協會 (Japan Foreign Trade Association) Tōkyō

Nihon Bōseki Kyōkai 日本紡績協會 (Japan Cotton Spinning Association) .... Ōsaka

Nihon Bōseki Kyōkai Chōsabu 日本紡績協會調査部 (Research Division, Japan Cotton Spinning Association) Tōkyō

Nihon Chisso Hiryō Kabushiki Kaisha 日本窒素肥料株式會社

Nihon Daigaku Shōgakkai 日本大學商學會 (Society of Commercial Studies, Nihon University) Tōkyō

Nihon Gakujutsu Fukyūkai 日本學術普及會 (Society of Science Promotion) Tōkyō

Nihon Ginkō Chōsakyoku 日本銀行調査局 (Research Bureau, Bank of Japan) Tōkyō

Nihon Ginkō Tōkeikyoku 日本銀行統計局 (Statistics Bureau, Bank of Japan) Tōkyō

Nihon Horitsu Kenkyūkai 日本法律研究會 (Japan Institute of Judicial Research) Tōkyō

Nihon Hyōronsha 日本評論社 Tōkyō

Nihon Jinzō Kinuorimono Kōgyō Kumiai Rengōkai 日本人造絹織物工業組合連合會 (The Federation of Associations of Japanese Artificial Silk Weaving Companies) Tōkyō

Nihon Kaiin Shūkaijo 日本海員集會所 (Seamen's Club of Japan) .... Kōbe

Nihon Kaiyō Kyōkai 日本海洋協會 (Japanese Oceanic Association) Tōkyō

Nihon Kangyō Ginkō 日本勸業銀行 (Japan Hypothec Bank) Tōkyō

Nihon Keieisha Dantai Remmei 日本經営者團体連盟 (Japan Federation of Employers' Associations) Tōkyō

Nihon Keizai Fukkō Kyōkai 日本經濟復興協會 (Japan Economic Rehabilitation Association) Tōkyō

Nihon Keizai Shimbunsha 日本經濟新聞社 Tōkyō

Nihon Keizai Shimpōsha 日本經濟新報社 Tōkyō

Nihon Keizai Sōsho Kankōkai 日本經濟叢書刊行會 (Society for the Publication of a Series on Japanese Economy)

Nihon Keizai Zenshi Hakkōjo 日本經濟全史發行所 (Publisher of the Complete Economic History of Japan)

Nihon Keizaishi Hensankai 日本經濟史編纂會 (Society for the Editing of Japanese Economic History) Tōkyō

Nihon Keizaishi Kankōjo 日本經濟史刊行所 (Society for the Publication of Japanese Economic History) .... Kyōto

Nihon Kōgyōkai 日本鑛業會 (Japan Mining Association) Tōkyō

Nihon Kōgyō Kurabu 日本工業倶樂部 Tōkyō

Nihon Kōkan Kabushiki Kaisha 日本鋼管株式會社

Nihon Kokuyū Tetsudō Kōsha 日本國有鉄道公社 (Public Corporation of the Japanese National Railways)

Nihon Kōgyō Ginkō 日本興業銀行 (Japan Industrial Bank)

Nihon Kyōdō Kumiai Dōmei 日本協同組合同盟 (Japan Federation of Cooperatives) Tōkyō

Nihon Mengyō Kurabu 日本綿業倶樂部 (Japanese Cotton Industry Club) .... Ōsaka

Nihon Nōmin Kumiai 日本農民組合 (Japan Farmers' Association) Tōkyō

Nihon Nōritsu Kyōkai 日本能率協會 (Japanese Institute of Efficiency) Tōkyō

Nihon Nōson Shinkōkai 日本農村振興會 Tōkyō

Nihon Rekishi Chiri Gakkai 日本歴史地理學會 (Japan Society of History and Geography) Tōkyō

Nihon Rōdō Tsūshinsha 日本勞働通信社 Tōkyō

Nihon Sangyō Kyōkai 日本産業協會 (Japanese Industry Association) Tōkyō

Nihon Seishi Rengōkai 日本製紙連合會 (Japanese Paper Manufacturing Association) Tōkyō

Nihon Sekiyu Kabushiki Kaisha 日本石油株式會社 Tōkyō

Nihon Shakai Jigyō Kyōkai 日本社會事業協會 (Japan Social Service Association) Tōkyō

Nihon Shōkō Kaigisho 日本商工會議所 (Chamber of Commerce and Industry of Japan) Tōkyō

Nihon Sozei Gakkai 日本租税學會 (Japan Taxation Society)

Nihon Tekkōgyō Keieisha Remmei 日本鉄鋼業經営者連盟 (Japan Federation of Employers in the Iron and Steel Industry) Tōkyō

Nihon Tōkei Gakkai 日本統計學會 (Japan Statistics Society) Tōkyō

Nihon Tōkei Kyōkai 日本統計協會 (Japanese Statistical Association) Tōkyō

Nihon Tosho Kaisha 日本圖書會社 Tōkyō

Nihon Yōgyō Kyōkai 日本窯業協會 (Japan Ceramic Industries Association)

Nihon Yūsen Kabushiki Kaisha 日本郵船株式會社

Nihon Zaimu Kyōkai 日本財務協會 (Japan Financial Affairs Association) Tōkyō

Nikkō Shoin 日光書院 Tōkyō

Nishigahara Kankōkai 西ヶ原刊行會 Tōkyō

Nishōdō Shoten 二松堂書店 Tōkyō

Nittōsha 日登社

Nichirinsha 日輪社 .... Niigata
Nōgyō Gijutsu Kyōkai 農業技術協會 (Association of Agricultural Techniques) Tōkyō
Nōgyō Kyōdō Kumiai Kenkyūkai 農業協同組合研究會 (Research Society of Agricultural Cooperatives) Tōkyō
Nōgyō Kumiai Kyōkai 農業組合協會 (Association of Agricultural Cooperatives) Tōkyō
Nōgyō to Suisansha 農業と水產社 Tōkyō
Nomura Shoten 野村書店 Tōkyō
Nōrin Tōkei Kyōkai 農林統計協會 (Agriculture and Forestry Statistics Association) Tōkyō
Nōrinshō Beikokubu 農林省米穀部 (Rice Department, Agriculture and Forestry Ministry) Tōkyō
Nōrinshō Nōgyō Sōgō Kenkyūjo 農林省農業總合研究所 (Agricultural Research Institute, Agriculture and Forestry Ministry) Tōkyō
Nōrinshō Nōmukyoku 農林省農務局 (Bureau of Agricultural Affairs, Agriculture and Forestry Ministry) Tōkyō
Nōrinshō Nōseikyoku Nōseika 農林省農政局農政課 (Agricultural Administration Section, Agricultural Administration Bureau, Ministry of Agriculture and Forestry) Tōkyō
Nōrinshō Sanrinkyoku 農林省山林局 (Forestry Bureau, Ministry of Agriculture and Forestry) Tōkyō
Nōrinshō Shokuryōchō 農林省食糧廳 (Food Agency, Ministry of Agriculture and Forestry) Tōkyō
Nōrinshō Suisankyoku 農林省水產局 (Fisheries Bureau, Ministry of Agriculture and Forestry) Tōkyō
Nōsei Chōsakai 農政調査會 (Research Circle on Agricultural Administration) Tōkyō
Nōshōmushō 農商務省 (Ministry of Agriculture and Commerce) Tōkyō
Nōshōmushō Kōzankyoku 農商務省鑛山局 (Mining Bureau, Ministry of Agriculture and Forestry) Tōkyō

O

Ōhata Shoten 大畑書店 Tōkyō
Ōhara Shakai Mondai Kenkyūjo 大原社會問題研究所 (Ōhara Research Institute for Social Problems) Tōkyō
Ōji Seishi Kabushiki Kaisha 王子製紙株式會社
Ōita Kōshō Shōgyō Kenkyūkai 大分高商商業研究會 (Society of Commerce of Ōita Commercial College)..... Ōita
Ōkurashō Rizaikyoku 大藏省理財局 (Financial Bureau, Ministry of Finance) Tōkyō
Ōkurashō Shuzeikyoku 大藏省主税局 (Taxation Bureau, Ministry of Finance) Tōkyō
Ōkurashō Zeikambu 大藏省税關部 (Division of Customs, Ministry of Finance)
Ōkura Zaimu Kyōkai 大藏財務協會 Tōkyō
Ōokayama Shoten 大岡山書店 Tōkyō
Ōsaka Hōbunkaku 大阪寶文閣 .... Ōsaka
Ōsaka Keiri Kenkyūjo 大阪經理研究所 Ōsaka
Ōsaka Ryōgaeshō Kumiai 大阪兩替商組合 (Ōsaka Exchange Merchants Association) Ōsaka
Ōsaka Shiminkyoku 大阪市民局 (Civilian Affairs Bureau, Ōsaka Municipal Office) Ōsaka
Ōsaka Shiritsu Daigaku Keizai Kenkyūjo 大阪市立大學經濟研究所 (Research Institute in Economics, Ōsaka Municipal University) Ōsaka
Ōsaka Shiyakusho 大阪市役所 (Ōsaka Municipal Office) Ōsaka
Ōsaka Shōka Daigaku Keizai Kenkyūjo 大阪商科大學經濟研究所 (Research Institute in Economics, Ōsaka Commercial College) Ōsaka
Ōsaka Shōsen Kabushiki Kaisha 大阪商船株式會社
Ōsaka Kabushiki Torihikijo 大阪株式取引所 (Ōsaka Securities Exchange) Ōsaka
Ōsaka Zaimu Kyōkai 大阪財務協會 Ōsaka
Ōsakashi Shakaibu 大阪市社會部 (Social Affairs Division, Ōsaka Municipal Office) Ōsaka
Otaru Kōshō Kenkyūshitsu 小樽高商研究室 (Research Seminar, Otaru Commercial College).............. Otaru
Ōyashimasha 大八洲社 Tōkyō

R

Reimei Shobō 黎明書房 .... Nagoya
Rikkyō Daigaku Keizaigakubu Kenkyūshitsu 立教大學經濟學部研究室 (Research Seminar of the Economics Department of Rikkyō University) Tōkyō
Rironsha 理論社 Tōkyō
Risōsha 理想社 Tōkyō
Rōdō Bunkasha 勞働文化社 Tōkyō
Rōdō Daijin Kambō Rōdō Tōkei Chōsabu 勞働大臣官房勞働統計調査部 (Labor Statistics and Research Division, Labor Minister's Secretariat) Tōkyō
Rōdō Kagaku Kenkyūkai 勞働科學研究會 (Research Society for Labor Science) Tōkyō
Rōdō Kagaku Kenkyūjo 勞働科學研究所 (Research Institute for Labor Science) Tōkyō
Rōdō Shuppambu 勞働出版社 Tōkyō
Rōdōshō Rōdō Kijunkyoku 勞働省勞働基準局 (Labor Standards Bureau, Labor Ministry) Tōkyō
Rōdōshō Rōdōkyōikuka 勞働省勞働教育課 (Labor Education Section, Labor Ministry) Tōkyō
Rōdōshō Rōseikyoku 勞働省勞政局 (Labor Administration Bureau, Labor Ministry) Tōkyō
Rōdōshō Shokugyō Anteikyoku 勞働省職業安定局 (Employment Bureau, Labor Ministry) Tōkyō
Rōdōshō Tōkei Chōsakyoku 勞働省統計調査局 (Labor Statistics and Research Bureau, Labor Ministry) Tōkyō
Rōmu Gyōsei Kenkyūjo 勞務行政研究所 (Research Institute for Labor Administration) Tōkyō
Rōmusha Engo Zaidan Shuppambu 勞務者援護財團出版部 Tōkyō
Ryōsho Fukyūkai 良書普及會 Tōkyō
Ryōyukai 糧輔會 Tōkyō
Ryūbunkan 隆文館 Tōkyō
Ryūginsha 龍吟社 Tōkyō

S

Name	Location
Saiken Kyōkai 債券協會	
Sambō Hombu 參謀本部 (General Staff Office)	Tōkyō
Sangensha 三元社	Tōkyō
Sangyō Keizai Shimbunsha 產業經濟新聞社	Ōsaka
Sangyō Kumiai Chūōkai 產業組合中央會 (Central Association of Industrial Cooperatives)	Tōkyō
Sangyō Kumiai Chūō Kinko 產業組合中央金庫 (Central Treasury of Industrial Cooperatives)	Tōkyō
Sangyō Rōdō Chōsajo 產業勞働調査所 (Research Institute for Industrial Labor)	Tōkyō
Sangyō Tosho 產業圖書	Tōkyō
San'ichi Shobō 三一書房	Kyōto
Sanseidō 三省堂	Tōkyō
Sanshigyō Dōgyō Kumiai Chūōkai Seisan Jimusho 蠶絲業同業組合中央會清算事務所 (Liquidation Office of the Central Association of Sericultural Cooperatives)	
Sara Shobō 沙羅書房	Tōkyō
Sawa Seimu Chōsajo 澤政務調査所	Tōkyō
Seibidō 成美堂	Tōkyō
Seibundō 誠文堂	Tōkyō
Seibunkan 精文館	Tōkyō
Seiji Keizai Hyōronsha 政治經濟評論社	Tōkyō
Seiji Kyōiku Kyōkai 政治教育協會 (Association for Political Education)	Tōkyō
Seikatsusha 生活社	Tōkyō
Seitōdō 西東堂	
Seiunkaku 青雲閣	Tōkyō
Seiya Shoten 青也書店	Tōkyō
Seiwa Shoten 清和書店	Tōkyō
Sekai Hyōronsha 世界評論社	Tōkyō
Sekai Keizai Chōsakai 世界經濟調査會 (Research Institute for World Economy)	Tōkyō
Sekai Shoin 世界書院	Tōkyō
Sekirokaku Shobō 赤爐閣書房	Tōkyō
Seki Shobō 關書房	Kyōto
Seki Shoin 關書院	Tōkyō
Sekiyu Keizai Kenkyūkai 石油經濟研究會 (Research Institute for Petroleum Economy)	Tōkyō
Sembaikyoku 專賣局 (Monopoly Bureau)	Tōkyō
Senshinsha 先進社	Tōkyō
Sen'yūkai 泉友會	Ōsaka
Shakai Hoken Hōki Kenkyūkai 社會保險法規研究會 (Society for Social Insurance Legislation)	Tōkyō
Shakai Hyōronsha 社會評論社	Yokohama
Shakai Keizaishi Gakkai 社會經濟史學會 (Society for Social Economic History)	Tōkyō
Shakai Shisō Kenkyūjo 社會思想研究所 (Research Institute for Social Thought)	Tōkyō
Shakai Shobō 社會書房	Tōkyō
Shibaura Seisakusho 芝浦製作所	
Shibun Shoin 斯文書院	Tōkyō
Shichō Shorin 思潮書林	Tōkyō
Shigenchō Kambō Tōkeika 資源廳官房統計課 (Statistics Section, Resources Board)	Tōkyō
Shigenkyoku Shiryōshitsu 資源局資料室 (Materials Room, Resources Bureau)	
Shikai Shobō 四海書房	Tōkyō
Shinchi Shobō 新地書房	Tōkyō
Shinchisha 新知社	Tōkyō
Shinchōsha 新潮社	Tōkyō
Shin-Keizaisha 新經濟社	Tōkyō
Shin-Kigensha 新紀元社	Tōkyō
Shinkō Shuppansha 新興出版社	Tōkyō
Shinsho Shuppansha 新書出版社	Tōkyō
Shinzenbisha 真善美社	Tōkyō
Shiritsusha 而立社	Tōkyō
Shisei Chōsakai 市政調査會 (Research Institute for Municipal Administration)	Tōkyō
Shōbundō 昭文堂	Tōkyō
Shōkasha 章華社	Tōkyō
Shōkō Gyōseisha 商工行政社	Tōkyō
Shōkō Shoin 彰考書院	Tōkyō
Shōkōshō Chōsa Tōkeikyoku 商工省調査統計局 (Research and Statistics Bureau, Commerce and Industry Ministry)	Tōkyō
Shōkōshō Shōmukyoku Boekika 商工省商務局貿易課 (Trade Section, Commercial Affairs Bureau, Ministry of Commerce and Industry)	Tōkyō
Shokuryōchō 食糧廳 (Food Agency)	Tōkyō
Shosekishō Kumiai 書籍商組合 (Association of Book Sellers)	Tōkyō
Shōwa Keizai Kurabu 昭和經濟クラブ	Tōkyō
Shimizu Shoten 清水書店	Tōkyō
Shūbunkaku 秀文閣	Tōkyō
Shūgiin Jimukyoku 衆議院事務局 (Secretariat of the House of Representatives)	Tōkyō
Shūhōkaku 聚芳閣	Tōkyō

Shūkan Kyōiku Shimbunsha 週刊教育新聞社 Tōkyō

Shunjūsha 春秋社 Tōkyō

Shun'yōdō 春陽堂 Tōkyō

Shuppan Nyūsusha 出版ニュース社 Tōkyō

Sōbunkaku 叢文閣 Tōkyō

Sōgensha 創元社 Tōkyō

Sōrifu Tōkeikyoku 総理府統計局 (Statistics Bureau, Prime Minister's Office) Tōkyō

Sugamo Kōshō Kenkyūshitsu 巣鴨高商研究室 (Research Seminar of the Sugamo Commercial College) Tōkyō

Sumitomo Honsha 住友本社 (Sumitomo Main Office) .... Ōsaka

T

Taguchi Ukichi Zenshū Kankōkai 田口卯吉全集刊行會 (Publication Society for the Complete Works of Taguchi Ukichi) Tōkyō

Taibunsha 泰文社 Tōkyō

Taiheisha 太平社 Tōkyō

Taihōkaku Shobō 大寶閣書房 Tōkyō

Taiseisha 大成社 Tōkyō

Taitōkaku 大鐙閣 Tōkyō

Taiwan Ginkō 台灣銀行 (Bank of Formosa) .... Taihoku

Taiwan Jihō Hakkōjo 台灣時報發行所 Taihoku

Taiwan Nōyūkai 台灣農友會 Taihoku

Taiwan Shuppan Bunka Kabushiki Kaisha 台灣出版文化株式會社 Taihoku

Taiwan Sōtokufu 台灣總督府 (Governor's Office of Formosa) Taihoku

Taiwan Tsūshinsha Shuppambu 台灣通信社出版部 Taihoku

Takagiri Shoin 高桐書院 .... Tōkyō

Takahashi Keizai Kenkyūjo 高橋經濟研究部 (Takahashi Institute for Economic Research) Tōkyō

Takase Shobō 高瀨書房 Tōkyō

Takayama Shoten 高山書店 Tōkyō

Takushoku Daigaku Gakujutsu Kenkyūkai 拓殖大學學術研究會 (Research Institute of Science, Colonial University) Tōkyō

Tama Zōsenjo 玉造船所

Teikoku Chihō Gyòsei Gakkai 帝國地方行政學會 (Imperial Society for Local Administration) Tōkyō

Teikoku Kōshinsho 帝國興信所 Tōkyō

Teikoku Nōkai 帝國農會 (Imperial Agricultural Association) Tōkyō

Teikoku Tetsudō Kyōkai 帝國鉄道協會 (Imperial Railway Association) Tōkyō

Teikoku Toshokan 帝國圖書館 (Imperial Library) Tōkyō

Teishinshō Denkikyoku 遞信省電氣局 (Telegraph and Telephone Bureau, Ministry of Communications) Tōkyō

Teishinshō Kansenkyoku 遞信省管船局 (Ship Control Bureau, Ministry of Communications) Tōkyō

Tetsudō Daijin Kambō Bunshoka 鉄道大臣官房文書課 (Document Section, Minister's Secretariat, Ministry of Railways) Tōkyō

Tetsudōin 鉄道院 (Railway Board) Tōkyō

Tetsudōshō 鉄道省 (Ministry of Railways) Tōkyō

Tetsudōshō Keirikyoku 鉄道省經理局 (Accounting Bureau, Ministry of Railways) Tōkyō

Tettō Shoin 鉄塔書院 Tōkyō

Tōa Dōbunkai 東亞同文會 Tōkyō

Tōa Jisshinsha 東亞實進社

Tōa Keizai Chōsakyoku 東亞經濟調查局 (Research Bureau for Eastern Asia Economy) Tōkyō

Tōa Keizai Kenkyūjo 東亞經濟研究所 (Research Institute for Eastern Asia Economy) .... Kyōto

Tōgyō Hattatsushi Hensan Jimusho 糖業發達史編纂事務所 (Editorial Office for a History of Sugar Refining)

Tōhōsha 東邦社 Tōkyō

Tōhō Shobō 東峰書房 Tōkyō

Tōkakai Shuppambu 十日會出版部

Tōkei Kyōkai 統計協會 (Statistics Institute) Tōkyō

Tōkō Shoin 東光書院 Tōkyō

Tōkō Shoin 刀江書院 Tōkyō

Tōkyō Daigaku Fuzoku Toshokan 東京大學附屬圖書館 (Tōkyō University Library) Tōkyō

Tōkyō Daigaku Keizaigakkai 東京大學經濟學會 (Society of Economics, Tōkyō University) Tōkyō

Tōkyō Daigaku Kyōdō Kumiai Shuppambu 東京大學協同組合出版部 Tōkyō

Tōkyō Daigaku Shakai Kagaku Kenkyūjo 東京大學社會科學研究所 (Research Institute for Social Science, Tōkyō University) Tōkyō

Tōkyō Gasu Kabushiki Kaisha 東京ガス株式會社 Tōkyō

Tōkyō Ginkō Shūkaijo 東京銀行集會所 (Tōkyō Bankers' Club) Tōkyō

Tōkyō Ishikawajima Zōsenjo 東京石川島造船所 Tōkyō

Tōkyō Kabushiki Torihikijo 東京株式取引所 (Tōkyō Securities Exchange) Tōkyō

Tōkyō Kaimai Shijō 東京廻米市場 (Tōkyō Rice Market) Tōkyō

Tōkyō Kōzan Kantokukyoku 東京鑛山監督局 (Tōkyō Mine Inspection Bureau) Tōkyō

Tōkyō Shisei Chōsakai 東京市政調查會 (Research Institute for Tōkyō Municipal Administration) Tōkyō

Tōkyō Shōkō Kaigisho 東京商工會議所 (Chamber of Commerce and Industry of Tōkyō) Tōkyō

Tōkyō Zaimu Nikakai 東京財務二課會 Tōkyō

Tōkyōdō 東京堂 Tōkyō

Tōkyōsha 東京社 Tōkyō

Tōyō Keizaisha 東洋經濟社 Tōkyō

Tōyō Shoin 東洋書院 Tōkyō

Tōyō Keizai Shimpōsha 東洋經濟新報社 Tōkyō

Tōyō Shokan 東洋書館 Tōkyō

Tōyō Shuppansha 東洋出版社 Tōkyō

Tōzai Shuppansha 東西出版社 Tōkyō

Tsūshō Sangyōshō 通商産業省 (Ministry of International Trade and Industry) Tōkyō

Tsūshō Sangyōshō Daijin Kambō Chōsa Tōkeibu 通商産業省大臣官房調査統計部 (Research and Statistics Division, Minister's Secretariat, Ministry of International Trade and Industry) Tōkyō

Tsūzoku Daigakkai 通俗大學會 Tōkyō

U

Uijinsha Tōkyō

Unebi Shobō 畝傍書房 Tōkyō

Un'yu Daijin Kambō Kikakuka 運輸大臣官房企画課 (Planning Section, Minister's Secretariat, Ministry of Transportation) Tōkyō

Un'yu Chōsakyoku 運輸調査局 (Research Bureau for Transportation) Tōkyō

Un'yu Nippōsha 運輸日報社 Tōkyō

Un'yushō Kambō 運輸省官房 (Minister's Secretariat, Ministry of Transportation) Tōkyō

Usui Shoin 碓氷書院 Tōkyō

W

Waseda Shōgaku Dōkōkai 早稲田商學同好會 (Group of Students of Commerce, Waseda University) Tōkyō

Watanabe Shōbō 渡辺書房 Tōkyō

Y

Yakumo Shoten 八雲書店 Tōkyō

Yamaguchi Kōshō Shōgakkai 山口高商商學會 (Society for Commerce Study, Yamaguchi Commercial College) .... Yamaguchi

Yamakawa Shoten 山川書店 Tōkyō

Yasuda Ginkō 安田銀行 (The Yasuda Bank) Tōkyō

Yokohama Bōeki Shimpōsha 横濱貿易新報社 .... Yokohama

Yoshikawa Kōbundō 吉川弘文堂 Tōkyō

Yūfūkan Shobō 雄風館書房 Tōkyō

Yūfūkaku 雄風閣 Tōkyō

Yūhikaku 有斐閣 Tōkyō

Yuibutsuron Kenkyūjo 唯物論研究所 (Research Institute on Materialism) Tōkyō

Yūkōsha 有光社 Tōkyō

Yushutsu Sen'i Kyōkai 輸出纖維協會 (Textile Export Association) .... Ōsaka

Yūzankaku 雄山閣 Tōkyō

Z

Zaimu Konwakai 財務懇話會 Tōkyō

Zaisei Keizai Gakkai 財政經濟學會 (Society for Financial Economics) Tōkyō

Zaisei Keizai Jihōsha 財政經濟時報社 Tōkyō

Zen-Nihon Kinzoku Rōdō Kumiai 全日本金屬勞働組合 (All-Japan Metal Industries Labor Union) Tōkyō

Zenkoku Ginkō Kyōkai Rengōkai 全國銀行協會連合會 (National Federation of Associations of Banks) Tōkyō

Zenkoku Keizai Chōsa Kikan Rengōkai 全國經濟調査機關連合會 (National Federation of Economic Research Organizations) Tōkyō

Zenkoku Kōbai Kumiai Rengōkai 全國購買組合連合會 (National Federation of Purchasers' Coopèratives) Tōkyō

Zenkoku Nōkō Ginkō Hattatsushi Hakkōjo 全國農工銀行發達史發行所 (Office of Publication of the History of the Development of Agricultural and Industrial Banks) Tōkyō

Zenkoku Nōgyōkai Chōsabu 全國農業會調査部 (Research Division, National Federation of Agricultural Associations) Tōkyō

Zenkoku Toshi Mondai Kaigi Jimukyoku 全國都市問題會議事務所 (Executive Office of the National Conference of Metropolitan Problems) Tōkyō

Zenkoku Torihikijo Dōmei Rengōkai 全國取引所同盟連合會 (National Federation of Associations of Securities Exchanges)

Zōheikyoku 造幣局 (Mint) .... Ōsaka

Zōheikyoku-nai Sen'yūkai 造幣局内泉友會 Ōsaka

Zōsen Kyōkai 造船協會 (Shipbuilding Association) .... Tōkyō

Zōshindō 増進堂 Tōkyō

www.ingramcontent.com/pod-product-compliance
Lightning Source LLC
LaVergne TN
LVHW062149200926
848484LV00007B/1893